Asian Feminisms and Transnational Activism

EGEP BOOK SERIES

Asian Feminisms and Transnational Activism

Edited by CHANG Pilwha, LEE Myoung Sun and ROH Jieun

Asian Center for Women's Studies

Ewha Womans University Press

Contents

Preface

This book was conceived by the Asian Center for Women's Studies (ACWS) as part of the textbook publication project launched at the opening of the Ewha Global Empowerment Program (EGEP) in 2012. To foster the next generation of women leaders who will lead changes for women's rights and gender equality, EGEP is a two-week residential educational program that takes place twice a year at Ewha Womans University. Substantially, EGEP is created as a new platform for international women's education based on Ewha Womans University's 131 years of teaching women and 40 years of institutionalizing women's studies.

During the EGEP, participants and lecturers from all across the world gather together and share their experiences as feminists, activists, and scholars in order to produce new feminist knowledge and develop their potential to grow as agents of change in transnational feminist movements, which enable solidarity beyond national boundaries and areas of focus. As of 2017, a total of 215 women activists from 42 Asian and African countries completed the program with the participation of approximately 30 lecturers and gender experts. Based on the EGEP principles of feminist pedagogy, participatory learning, and reciprocal learning, this book is special in that it is a visible outcome of the knowledge production and practices made possible through the EGEP.

The title of this book, *Asian Feminisms and Transnational Activism*, is an important epistemic value and core theme that flows throughout the EGEP. Eight of the twelve chapters in this book were selected from the lectures and open forum at the EGEP. The other four chapters were originally published in the *Asian Journal of Women's Studies* owned by ACWS.

Although this book started from the need for a textbook for the EGEP participants, we hope that this book will be valuable to everyone, including women activists, feminist scholars, gender experts, and women's policy experts. I would like to thank all co-authors for meaningfully putting together papers based on their lecture, and enduring through the challenges of publishing this book. I also want to express gratitude to the researchers of ACWS for their cooperation, Ewha Womans University for their support, and last but not least, the Ewha Womans University Press.

Kim Eun-Shil
Director, Asian Center for Women's Studies
Ewha Womans University

Introduction

Raising Asian Women's Studies:

Asian Feminist Knowledge Production and Exchange

CHANG Pilwha,
LEE Myoung Sun,
ROH Jieun

This book represents a collaborative endeavor by Asian feminist scholars on the theme of "Asian Feminisms and Transnational Activism." For the past 20 years, the Asian Center for Women's Studies (ACWS) has been an active producer and practitioner of Asian feminist knowledges, expanding Asian feminisms and institutionalizing Asian Women's Studies through diverse joint research, publishing and academic projects with Asian women scholars. The present book was born from the perceived need for a reader in Asian feminisms designed for the growing number of feminist scholars and activists interested in the topic.

Just what is 'Asian feminisms'? To answer very simply, 'Asian feminisms' is feminisms based on the experiences and perspectives of Asian women in Asian contexts. But that definition, while succinct, fails to answer the question clearly and ultimately raises even more complex questions. For example, what is meant by 'Asian contexts'? Do they denote geographical or spatial contexts, or epistemological ones? What are the 'experiences and perspectives of Asian women'? Do Asian women share certain commonalities or attributes that justify their analysis as a single category or point of view? Does such an amalgamation not threaten to erase the abundant diversity and differentiation existing among them? And if that is the case, does this not constitute yet another form of Othering, of generalizing? And so on. When we first began to speak of 'Asian feminisms,' many such questions were raised, not only by feminists in Korea, but also by Western researchers. Some of these questions continue to be posed at present.

As implied by the use of the plural, 'Asian feminisms' is not a single fixed theory or concept. Rather, it is an array of feminist discourses constructed within processes of knowledge production and the practices of Asian women scholars. A concrete approach to Asian feminisms may therefore necessitate an understanding of why, by whom, and how 'Asian feminisms' has developed as a feminist theory; which communities have participated in its knowledge production and practices; how women's issues are understood and theorized through it; and the practices of agency it is implementing for social change.

In this context, we hope that readers can better understand the ongoing construction of 'Asian feminisms' discourses through a history of Asian Women's Studies as it has been practiced and produced by Asian women scholars who have participated in the projects of the Asian Center for Women's Studies at Ewha Womans University.

A Journey from 'Women's Studies in Asia' to 'Asian Women's Studies'

The myriad stories of 'Asian feminisms' being recounted today have their origin in projects for knowledge production and practices first undertaken by the Asian Center for Women's Studies (ACWS) at Ewha Womans University in Seoul, Korea. Created in 1995, Professor Jang Sang, then chair of the steering committee for the Center's construction, explains the founding philosophy of the Center as follows: "Asian women's issues must be addressed from the standpoint of feminism based in Asian women's experiences. For that goal, Asian women need a communal space where they can form alliances for knowing, understanding, encouraging and empowering one another."[1] From 1996, it began instituting organization projects and knowledge production between Asia women scholars, most notably at its first international conference, "The Rise of Feminist Consciousness Against the Asian Patriarchy." The conference warned against Confucian revivalist and capitalist discourses purporting to reassert 'Asian values,' while debating important issues such as how feminism can intervene in the realities of Asian women and whether or not alliances could be forged between feminists.[2] It was also at this conference that Chang Pilwha, who was the Center's director, raised the question 'What does it mean to do Women's Studies in Asia?'[3] and she sharply criticized the tendency within Korean society and academe to view feminism negatively as an "importation of Western academia." Prof. Chang explained, "Such has resulted from a lack of understanding of the history of Korean feminism as a resistance to Korean patriarchy and as something that evolved in that context … a prejudice emerging from ultra-nationalist thought which imposes national borders around feminism and derides it as merely an "importation of Western theory." Chang further reflected, "Through scholarly works by Westerners, Asians have perceived themselves through the gaze of the Other. For a long time, knowledge, academic theories, and information have been imported unilaterally into Asia from the West, during which time the knowledge which Asians possess about Westerners has become incomparably broader and more varied than the obverse, while on the other hand, we have gained little knowledge and information about our Asian neighbors." She also emphasized, "When we think about Asian Women's Studies, we must also expose and evaluate

1 Chang Sang (1995), "The Role of the Asian Center for Women's Studies," Conference proceedings on *The 1st International Conference on Feminism in Asia*, Seoul: Korean Women's Institute, Ewha Womans University, unpublished.

2 Cho, Haejeong (1997), "Feminist Intervention in the Rise of 'Asian' Discourse," *Asian Journal of Women's Studies*, Seoul: Ewha Womans University Press, 3(3): 127-156.

3 Chang, Pilwha (1996), "The Rise of Women's Education Against the Korean Patriarchy," Conference proceedings on *The Rise of Feminist Consciousness Against the Asian Patriarchy*, Seoul: ACWS, Ewha Womans University, unpublished.

Western-centrism within Asia. A consciousness of the inequality between Western and Eastern knowledge has become an important issue striking a sympathetic chord among women scholars in Asia with respect to the initiation and development of future Women's Studies projects. Based in such sympathy and reflection, Asian Women's Studies can grow as an alternative feminist theory and discourse through reciprocal exchanges of knowledge."

The 1996 conference resulted in a flourishing of Asian feminist networks and knowledge exchanges evidenced in several important researches and publishing projects. An early project of great significance was "Women's Studies in Asia: Knowledge Exchange, Theory and Practice" (henceforth "WSA project"), a 3-year project (1997-2000), designed by Ewha to develop a Women's Studies curriculum and theorize Asian feminisms in different regional contexts in Asia. Sponsored by the United Board for Christian Higher Education in Asia, the project embarked on the goal of promoting the development of "Women's Studies in Asia" by enabling cross-comparison of Women's Studies histories in eight Asian countries (Korea, China, India, Indonesia, Japan, the Philippines, Taiwan, and Thailand), each contributing a volume providing an overview of their country's history over the preceding 20-30 years. The number of scholars participating in the project as "co-ordinators" was 18 in totals, with 350 scholars from 220 universities joining in the researches and exchanges over the course of three years (Kim and Kang, 2001:107).[4]

An important outcome of the knowledge exchanges was the discovery of theretofore unknown aspects of Women's Studies, women's lives, and women's movements in various regions of Asia. One participant from Southeast Asia told of her surprise upon hearing that Women's Studies was a full-fledged discipline in East Asia. Also, diverse opinions and perspectives came to light in the basic premises and epistemologies of the

4 Kim, Hyun Mee and Kang, Sun-Mi (2001), "Achievements and Challenges of an Asian Women's Studies Project," *Asian Journal of Women's Studies*, 7(4): 106-121.

women scholars with respect to feminism, patriarchy, and relations with the state. Regarding the impacts of Women's Studies and academic autonomy, too, huge differences emerged according to region and state, as well as in what each saw as authentic resistance and critique.[5] On the other hand, the inaugural workshop initiated a process of reiterating and reasserting the concepts and goals of "feminist" ideals through an understanding of the history of Women's Studies as an arduous struggle to carry out the research necessary for women's needs and lives. The participants came to appreciate the various strategies employed in efforts to institutionalize Women's Studies in each country with close ties to women's movements for gender equality and the empowerment of women. Moreover, as feminist researchers charged with the task of creating Women's Studies theory and teaching through Women's Studies programs, participants formed mutually supportive bonds in appreciation of the difficulties inherent in developing a creative theoretical model for understanding and analyzing the diverse life conditions in which Asian women are situated. This was the problem commonly being faced as feminists located in peripheral 'Asia' where modern neo-liberal hegemony operates not only within the academy but also in gender relations amid the historical whirlwind of 'coloniality,' 'modernity' and 'globalization' in tandem with the advance of Western/white/male-centristic capitalism.

One of the keen early debates arising in the course of cooperation among the Asian feminist scholars was whether a Women's Studies based on Asian women's lives and experiences and constructed within an Asian context indicated a 'Women's Studies in Asia' emphasizing Asian regionality, or an 'Asian Women's Studies,' a brand new academic discipline coined by ACWS. From the project's beginning in 1995, uncertainties existed about how Women's Studies in Asia would proceed and what sort of

5 Miske, Shirley, Chang Pilwha and Lee Sang Wha (1998), "Expanding the Network: Building Women's Studies in Asia, Workshop I," Asian Journal of Women's Studies, 4(3): 164-180; Kim, Hyun Mee and Kang Sun-Mi (2001), "Achievements and Challenges of an Asian Women's Studies Project," *Asian Journal of Women's Studies*, 7(4): 106-121.

feminist scholars and researchers existed in Asia, so the WSA project had little choice but to proceed from a 'Women's Studies in Asia.' In fact, at the beginning, this concept served as a satisfactory framework for comprehending one another's commonalities and differences, but later, amid continuous discussions and debates about the 3-year project, the theorization of an 'Asian Women's Studies' was undertaken, transforming 'Women's Studies in Asia' into a new research area for Women's Studies, a vision for the future.

The term 'Asian Women's Studies' appeared officially for the first time in 2000 at an international conference titled "Women's Studies in Asia 2000" held on Jeju Island, Korea"[6] which was organized for the purpose of synthesizing the WSA project. Kim, Hyun Mee, she was a coordinator of the WSA project, pointed out that "to conceptualize Asian Women's Studies is to comprehend the complicated political mechanism connected with such 'naming'" (Kim, 2000: 6) and she anticipated 'Asian Women's Studies' as "an independent body of knowledge" is an emerging discipline of feminism which is based on collective and communal work among Women's Studies scholars to make Asian women active agent of historical processes (Kim, 2000: 10).[7]

The process of raising and answering the question 'What is Asian Women's Studies?' moved Asian women scholars beyond the existing practice of relying on the knowledge production of Western Women's Studies and install a paradigm in which they created and constructed new feminist learning. This process entailed, firstly, pride and reflection regarding the development of a 'regional Women's Studies' nurtured in the scholars' native milieus; secondly, the desires and limitations of seeking to develop a 'Women's Studies in Asia' by comparing Women's Studies

6 See Kim, Hyun Mee (2000), "Asian Women's Studies: Concept and Practice," *Women's Studies in Asia 2000 I*; Sobritchea, Carolyn (2000), "Imaging the Future of Asian Women's Studies and Feminist Scholarship"; Chun-koh, Hesung (2000), "Asian Women's Studies Information Exchange," *Women's Studies in Asia 2000 II*, ACWS, Ewha Womans University.

7 Kim, Hyun Mee (2000), "Asian Women's Studies: Concept and Practice," *Women's Studies in Asia 2000 I*, 3-12, ACWS, Ewha Womans University.

among countries, and finally, sharing the promise of an 'Asian Women's Studies.' Such is a process not only of training in feminist criticism in which the individual scholar realizes the limitations of her present self-awareness, but also one of experimentally seeking new horizons for pursuing scholarly exchanges as a form of group knowledge.[8]

At the 9th International Interdisciplinary Congress on Women (IICW Women's Worlds 2005), the concept of "Asian Women's Studies" became a subject of worldwide interest. A tri-annual event, the Congress was held for the first time in Asia in 2005, hosted by Ewha Womans University and the Korean Association of Women's Studies and coordinated by the ACWS. The Congress, a global forum for feminist scholarship, took place on the Ewha campus and was attended by over 3000 participants including scholars, activists, students, journalists, policy makers, and volunteers from 79 countries worldwide, with noticeably two-third participants were from Asian region. This surprising achievement was an important turning point that changed the course of Women's Studies in Asia which from the 1970s had been led by the West, and one that heightened global feminist interest in Asian Women's Studies.

Two years later, in 2007, the Asian Association of Women's Studies

8 As part of the project for conceptualizing and theorizing Asian Women's Studies, KWI has carried out its task as a priority research institute in three stages over a 9-year period from 2005-2014. KWI has received support from the National Research Foundation of Korea to research Asian Women's Studies as an alternative knowledge proceeding from the construction of academic categories, the production of experience-based knowledge, and comprehensive practice. Stage 1, themed "Global Cultural Changes and Post-Colonial Experiences of Asian Women: Asian Women's Studies as a Discipline," enacted a multi-level research on genealogical/epistemological explorations of "things Asian" and "Asian women," cultural changes in the global era, and the experiences of migrant women. Stage 2, "Feminist Knowledge Production and the Building of 'Asian Women's Studies,'" reviewed and resignified indigenous Asian knowledge excluded within the existing academic system, centered on the two axes of "alternative knowledge production for Asian women" and "the quality of Asian women's lives and fair globalization," while also carrying out critical regional studies for transforming structures and systems of inequality ushered in by present-day globalism. Stage 3, under the theme of "The Systematic Establishment and Integrated Practices of 'Asian Women's Studies': Women's Studies, Women's Movements, Women's Policies," conducted joint researches with the objective of establishing a system of Asian Women's Studies enabling the integrated practice of theories, movements, and policies.

(AAWS) was founded as an academic community of Asian feminist scholars. It is now an international association with 614 individual members and 23 member institutions from 41 countries. The Association embraced a vision for creating better communities through education and research, communities for sharing feminist values despite differences in language, culture, society, history and religion, and for the goal of creating an institutional foundation for Asian feminist education and research in league with various local scholars, activists and research institutions. Since its inaugural conference in Ewha Womans University, Seoul in 2007, AAWS has hosted an academic congress thrice yearly. At the 2nd general assembly and conference held in Penang, Malaysia in December 2010 under the theme of "Debating Gender Justice in Asia." Professor Rashidah Shuib praised the joint participation of the three organizations AAWS, KANITA of Universiti Sains Malaysia, and SAMA (Southeast Asian Women's Studies Association) as highly significant, as well as the broad participation by Women's Studies researchers, activists, and students from nearby Southeast Asian regions in what was Malaysia's first Women's Studies conference. In December 2013, the 3rd AAWS general assembly and conference titled "Women's Studies in the Information Age" was held at University of the Philippines, Diliman, hosted by AAWS and the Women's Studies Association of the Philippines. In her keynote speech, Professor Grace J. Alfonso discussed changes in information technology and its growing potentials and risks, the lives of women in Asian regions, and their opportunities for education. Since 2012, AAWS has also been developing an Korea-ASEAN Cooperation Project on "Education and Exchange Program for Young Scholars in Women's Studies" to nurture and expand networks for next-generation Women's Studies scholars.

In the two decades since ACWS opened its doors in 1995, leading to the birth of Asian Women's Studies networking and projects for knowledge production, the field has continued to develop through the establishment of the AAWS. The history of this knowledge exchange and practice is not so much the product of special theories and studies by a few special feminists, as it is a process, a site of practices, constructed through partnerships and joint projects by members of the Asian Women's Studies community.

Transnational Feminisms and Women's Activism

One of ACWS's recent projects is a feminist training program called the Ewha Global Empowerment Program (EGEP) for Asian young women activists launched in January 2012 under the theme of "Asian Feminisms and Transnational Activism." EGEP, a two-week residential education program on feminist theories and practices organized by ACWS at Ewha Womans University. Fully funded by the University, the program is offered bi-annually as a vehicle for empowering women activists and experts working in non-governmental public sectors, and for fostering young women leaders who will spearhead the changes for women's rights and gender equality in the future. EGEP is now in its 8th batch and has hosted a total of 169 women activists from 40 Asian and African countries. Some of EGEP's graduates participated in AAWS conferences in specially-organized sessions called "Voices from Asian Feminist Activism," presenting on the theme of regional women's movements in Asia. The AAWS conference proved to be a new, experimental arena of expanding significance as a site of knowledge production not only for scholars but also for women activists. A laboratory for feminist education, EGEP incorporates principles from feminist pedagogy like 'participatory education' and 'reciprocal learning,' encouraging the program's faculty and participants to share and discuss their experiences as feminists, as women activists, and as women scholars, as they engage in feminist knowledge production and practice.[9] Additionally aimed at strengthening capabilities between Asian and African women activists, EGEP nurtures transnational women's alliances that

9 Lee, Myoung Sun (2014), "Asian Feminist Pedagogy and Women's Empowerment: A Preliminary Analysis of EGEP," *Asian Journal of Women's Studies*, 20(2): 7-33.

move past differences in country, culture, and religion. Both epistemologically and genealogically, the EGEP exists within a process and history of Asian feminist knowledge production and practice, and as the main theme of the first EGEP "Asian Feminisms and Transnational Activism" shows, the publication of this book is part of an effort to share and enrich that process and those achievements.

The feminist perspective/epistemology known today as 'Asian feminisms' has been constructed by a community of Asian feminists over the course of two decades. Based in feminist knowledge production and research exchanges, it is not a regional/local feminism in opposition to so-called global feminism, but espouses alternative discourses and values critical of the hierarchical Western-centrism of existing feminism. 'Asian feminisms' is a feminist political arena and locus of practice for Asian women subjects who make their experiences and voices heard in response to their marginalization by the Western gaze. The Asian feminist scholars concerned, however, are not 'victims' as portrayed by patriarchal society or Western feminists, nor are they objects of patriarchal oppression, but subjects who create change and produce feminist knowledge and practice, in which capacity they assert their agency and subjectivity. Rather than a feminism based in a particular regionality, 'Asian feminisms' is a feminist perspective and theory which enjoins the agency of female subjects that have been 'Othered' and relativized.

As a feminist theory and practice, 'Asian feminisms' does not seek or presume a regional, cultural, or historically essential or universal base or commonality between women, but on the contrary, values diversities and differences between women appearing in the varied, concrete contexts of their life. In this sense, the concept of 'Asian feminisms' promotes the potential for alliances with transnational feminisms. The problems faced by women in different regions take many forms, but in nearly all societies women experience victimization through violence and discrimination. Social problems like migration, the environment, peace, human rights, labor and poverty exist in close correlation with so-called 'women's issues' like discrimination and violence against women, human trafficking, and socio-economic gender inequality. Amidst rapidly advancing globalization, in particular, women's problems surpass the realm of 'the local' and are becoming intertwined with 'the global.' Transnational alliances between women are built upon recognition of one another's differences, mutual understanding, empathy and the formation of cross-border feminist communities among nations based in constructive international and interpersonal relations.

Against the above background, this book aims to address contemporary women's issues, activisms, and Asian feminisms as transnational practices in the context of glocal politics within Asia. Part I of this book addresses the history of Women's Studies in Asia and feminist research practices for creating Asian feminist knowledge. Part II reflects inter-relations among glocal women's issues, activism, solidarity and gender policy from transnational feminist perspectives. Part I, "Asian Women's Studies and Transnational Research Practices," presents writings allowing comparison of the categories and concepts used to define Asian Women's Studies, and the experience of its institutionalization in Korea, Japan, and China. The section includes six essays embodying key theoretical, historical and experiential perspectives from the field's leading scholars. Each essay, addressing one or several focal points or problemata, is intended both as an independent treatise but also as a part of the larger spectrum of ideas and testimonies forming Asian Women's Studies discourse at the present historical juncture.

Chapters 1, 2, and 3, published previously in AJWS, are judged by the compilers to be appropriate introductory texts for inclusion in the present volume. What is the meaning of 'Asia,' of 'Asian-ness,' and of 'Asian woman?' and how may these be developed as strategic categories for feminist politics? In Chapter 2, Lee Sang Wha describes these as ideas in the process of being created in accordance with changing historical contexts, a process she calls "the ontology of becoming." As a philosophical basis for theorizing Asian Women's Studies, she equates her ontology with "our future task to develop a methodology to accommodate the politics of difference and politics of identity into a politics of solidarity by studying the analytical category of 'Asian women' in a more concrete locational context, and to theoretically expand exploration areas to Western feminism." In Chapter 3, Kim Eun-Shil charts the emergence of discourse on Asian Women's Studies amidst changes in the landscape of feminism and Women's Studies in Korean society. What factors conditioned the emergence of Asian Women's Studies, and what is its global significance? Pointing to the historical and political embeddedness of the concept of 'Asia,' Kim's essay describes the journey of Korean/Asian Women's Studies as one of "swaying back and forth between universality and particularity," between the global and the local. However, with the "rise of Asia" and the "discovery of Asia" as a global context/reference in past decades, a new space was "opened up for reinterpreting the framework of universality and particularity newly organizing and subverting it from the position of Korean/Asian Women's Studies," thus enabling a new category for criticizing Western knowledge systems and theoretical frameworks formerly considered universal. Chapter 1 asks, "How can Asian Women's Studies histories be re-conceptualized in the global era?" Using Ewha Womans University as a model case to foreground women's agency and leadership, Chang Pilwha points out that early educational institutions exclusively for women were not "simply an outcome of ... external constraints" like Confucian patriarchal structures, but that of "significant commitment and reflection" on the necessity of gender equality in society. Such a conceptualization foregrounds the leadership of women committed to and reflecting on "feminist values that hold all women in esteem." Thus viewed, Chang says, the establishment of the Korean Women's Institute in 1977 represents a continuation of that early feminist "pioneering spirit," with commitment to mainstreaming women's knowledges through new paradigms. Presented at a symposium in 2014 commemorating the 30th anniversary of the founding of the Korean Association of Women's Studies, Chang's chapter discusses the institutionalization of Korean Women's Studies by borrowing cases from the historical experience of "Ewha Women's Studies." A comparison of the writings from Korean Women's Studies, Women's Studies at Ewha, and Asian Women's Studies reveals the close alliance and the common knowledge production and practices they share.

Chapters 4 and 5 are developed versions of papers presented at the EGEP Open Forum held at Ewha Womans University on January 6th and 7th, 2012. They show the historical experience and contexts of Women's Studies in Japan and China. They have been included with Part I for their investigation of how, especially since the UN World Conference on Women, alliances with feminist researchers have impacted regional Women's Studies researches and women's movements. Adopting a "global origins" perspective, Hara Hiroko's historicization of Japanese feminism in Chapter 4 notes the importance on the UN First World Conference on Women (1975) as a touchstone for Japanese attendees who subsequently began describing Japanese feminist movements as embodiments of "solidarity among Asian women," leading to the pioneering of institutions like the Asia-Japan Women's Resource Center (1994). Hara introduces statistical data to map the changes in women's/gender studies in Japan both within universities like Ochanomizu, and non-university institutions. The UN First World Conference also served as a turning point for the All China Women's Federation (1949). In Chapter 5, Du Fangqin notes a new commitment to "feminist participatory action research" as the Federation's central form of knowledge production, while synthesizing it with the CPC Central Committee's policy for "gender mainstreaming." Another turning point in ACWF was the year 2000 when it began its outreach to feminist researchers, activists, and government specialists for assistance in creating change within legal and policy-making institutions. ACWF's endeavors have impacted reforms at the village level, resulting in changes to village rules and regulations hand-in-hand with the advocacy of "new marriage," signifying the organization's commitment to "action" in the real world.

Chapter 6 is a preliminary analysis of the Ewha Global Empowerment Program (EGEP). In this chapter, Lee Myoung Sun argues that the capacity of Women's Studies to bring about individual and social change is not only because of feminist ideology, but also due to the praxis of 'feminist pedagogy.' She, based on the case of EGEP as a field of 'Asian Feminist Pedagogy,' looks at the concrete makeup of the program and analyzes the experiences of the Asian Women activists who participated in EGEP to show how it empowers women and produces 'Asian women subjectivity.'

Part II, "Transnational Feminist Issues and Asian Women's Activism," is an assemblage of discussions casting fresh light on Asian Women's Studies in the dimension of transnational feminism. Chapters 7, 8, and 9 were taken from discussions at the EGEP Open Forum. Chapters 10, 11, and 12 include, by theme, discussions presented at EGEP lecture seminars. These show how regional feminist movements by Asian women activists can be linked to transnational feminist activism through case studies of glocal feminist practices.

Are histories always what they seem? Chapter 7 addresses the hidden politics/histories waiting to be uncovered by Asian feminist activist scholarship. Saskia E. Wieringa calls for an exposure of "the deeply gendered and sexual processes" embedded in the ongoing process of modernity and nation formation, in particular, the aspect of sexual politics in relation to nation building. Such deeply gendered and sexual connotations within state-building projects, she says, have far-ranging effects on people's lives, disempowering women and sexual minorities. "Gender and sexual subordination should ultimately not be reproduced," she says, "but resolved in the utopian process that a nation formation is." Moving to a focus on concrete sexual policies and practices, Jyotsna Agnihotri Gupta in Chapter 8 discusses reproductive ethics and women's bodies in the Indian context, analyzing some of the developments in the application of reproductive technologies, especially those for sex (pre-)selection and their effects on society and women. She fears that the proliferation of sex-selection technologies, now a "big business" in India, will operate as a tool for perpetuating cultural gender bias against females, replicating or exacerbating existing inequalities, and creating new forms of disparity. Offering another "view from below," Chapter 9 focuses on alternatives to top-down models of feminist movements. Mala Khullar highlights the vital importance of civil society participation in women's movements as viewed through the lens of modern Indian history. Civil society's role in bringing largely urban feminist movements to the rural areas provides one example of that importance. Bogged down by their multiple agendas, states and governments require the support and intervention of social groups such as feminist publishers. Still, she notes, both the local and the transnational must be considered in configuring women's movements; and indeed the 'globa' (or pan-Asian) may be germane to the overcoming of Western Othering.

Chapter 10 continues with the idea that feminist NGOs can play an important intermediary role between 'above' and 'below.' Lee Mikyoung focuses on NGO responses to the anti-sexual violence movement in Korea, suggesting less concern should be given to legislating new laws and more given to actively implementing existing laws and institutions and to evaluating their efficacy. She stresses the importance of viewing sexual violence not as a "personal problem" but as a "human rights abuse," and also one that is not unique to women. Such realizations within Korean society, she says, can lead to "change in the daily lives of the general public" rather than simply in laws and institutions. Similarly, in her account of 'femocrats' in Australia and Korea, Kyungja Jung in Chapter 11 looks at the alienation of women's policy machinery from the women's movement that inspired it. Originally driven by women's studies graduates and feminist scholars, the 'femocracy' has "markedly lost its policy gains and energy." Jung wishes to bring attention to the women's movements as the origin of the women's policy machinery in seeking to bring appreciation to the transformative nature of those movements. Rather than being controlled by a handful of prominent individuals at the top, the impact and effectiveness of women's movements to achieve social, political and cultural change lie in its "collectivity based on mass mobilization and membership." Academic research should thus return to the feelings and thoughts of the activists on the ground, because "the role of activists … is an essential component of the reconceptualization of feminist practices in both internal and external environments." Challenging top-down forms of cooperation between developed and developing countries is the theme in Yonson Ahn's essay in Chapter 12, who describes her personal experience with transnational solidarity and cross-border activism by South Korean and Japanese civil groups in support of the comfort women redress movement. In particular, she points to the Women's International War Crimes Tribunal in Tokyo (2000), organized by women's NGOs across Asia on behalf of comfort women, and the "Wednesday demonstration" rallies in Seoul, as examples of grass-roots initiatives fostering an expansion of support and awareness for the cause. These actions represent "inclusive, participatory and horizontally-configured" alternatives that "contribute to a resistance against patriarchal nationalisms and multiple and overlapping indigenous oppressions against women."

In this context, this book includes various themes, theories, and field expereinces which has produced and grown through the journey of Asian feminisms. We would like to express our deep gratitude to the feminist community of Asian feminist scholars, who have supported and inspired to us on this journey with the Asian Center for Women's Studies.

Part I

Asian Women's Studies and Transnational Research Practices

Chapter 1

Feminist Consciousness and Women's Education:

The Case of Women's Studies, Ewha Womans University[1]

CHANG Pilwha

1. Introduction

Amongst the many rapid social changes South Korean society has undergone during the last thirty years or so, changes in gender relationships can be regarded as most interesting. In 2007, the Korean Women's Institute of Ewha Womans University celebrated its 30th anniversary, while witnessing a panorama of dynamic scenes of change. In early 2008, the conservative party came into power after ten years of progressive government. During the transition process the plan of the new government to eliminate the Ministry of Gender and Family Affairs and transfer some of its functions to a bureau of the Ministry of Health and Welfare was stalled by a high level of opposition by women's organizations and scholars. The transition committee relented and finally decided to divide the Ministry into two parts: the Ministry of Gender and a new Bureau of Child Care as part of the Ministry of Health and Welfare. During the two months while

1 This paper was originally published in the *Asian Journal of Women's Studies*, Vol. 14 No. 2, 7-29, 2008, Seoul: Ewha Womans University Press.

this process was underway, strong resentful voices were heard regarding what feminists have achieved in the previous decades.

In the midst of this great turn of events, it is worthwhile to historically review the beginnings of women's studies. This paper reviews and reflects on the evolution of women's studies in Korea, focusing on the experience of Ewha Womans University. Feminist consciousness starts from the awareness of societally determined unequal gender relationships. The history of this awareness is surely as old as the beginning of subordination of women as a group and thus not necessarily and exclusively fostered through formal education. Nevertheless, it brings into focus the importance of institution-building, which needs to be given due recognition and for which we need a more solid basis or sustainable institution in order to develop "the autonomous definition by women of their goals and strategies for changing their condition, and to develop an alternative vision of the future" (Lerner, 1993: 274).

More recently, the significance of education for women was very clearly demonstrated by Mukhtar Mai, the Pakistani woman who has become an internationally renowned activist. During the traumatic time after being gang raped, she said, "It was educated people who helped me when I considered killing myself, and it was uneducated people who tried to stop me from suing the men who raped me. That was when I first came to think about the importance of education." Having won the court trial, she realized that "Education is the key to putting an end to the infringement of human rights, which I hear about and witness every day. That's why I founded my school." Mukhtar is determined to change Pakistani women's way of thinking through education. As she went on to note, "Illiterate Pakistani women are totally economically dependent on men and they consider their husbands to be their owners. As a result, they see the world through their husbands. I want to change that." At least children who attend her school will become different, she hopes (Mukhtar Mai, 2006). Her hopes are shared by billions of women and girls on this planet and this paper starts with the historical juncture when no education was provided for women in Korea.

This paper is Part 1 of a larger study of Ewha experiences of women's education, women's studies and institution-building. It initially covers the background of the early years of Ewha School for Girls, founded in 1886, followed by a review of the process of the founding of KWI and the development of women's studies. Some points still relevant in today's struggle for promoting education for women surface in the review, such as women's only institutions, women's movements, women's policy, leaders, and leadership questions. These points will be taken up in a later report along with comparative analyses with other countries (Satha-Anand, 2004; Sobritchea, 2004; Chang and Kim, 2005; Du and Zheng, 2005; Lin and Hsieh, 2005; Powerwandari, 2005; Juyal, 2005; Khullar, 2005).

2. Early Struggles for Women's Education and Feminist Consciousness against Patriarchy

Ewha as the first school for women in this country, started not only women's education but also stimulated the women's movement. Ewha has survived over 122 years in a patriarchal society as a women-only institution, without losing its original objectives. It has become one of the world's largest women's universities, aspiring to serve the wider community of women across the world, rather than its limited number of alumnae and students.

2.1 The Beginning of Korean Women's Education

When Mrs. Scranton came to Korea in 1885, there was no school for women. A full year had to be spent before the first student could be enrolled and the opened. The first permanent pupil was brought by a woman who could not support her daughter any longer. The number of students increased to 28 in 1890 and 76 in 1901 (Kim, 1976: 219). These students practiced as pupil teachers and after graduation became teachers at Ewha and other Ewha day schools that spread around Seoul and other provincial cities from the early 1890s onwards.

Until the first public school for girls was established in 1909, more than 20 years later, Ewha graduates were the only human resources who worked as teachers and professionals (Kim, 1976). Their pioneering work paved the road for the beginning of the first women's movement. Their work showed that women could work as well as men and created the first conditions for realizing the possibility of women's human rights, gender equality, and the autonomy of people as citizens. The fact that the first demand of the women's movement in Korea was for women's education needs to be understood in this context. As rational bases for the demand for women's education, it was often mentioned that there were schools for women in other countries.

2.2 The Beginning of the Women's Movement: Demand for Women's Education

The Korean women's movement started with the demand for women's education. This utilized the then current discourses of modernization such as the dominant assertion that women and men were not different but equal in terms of their rights. This was a direct challenge to the predominant ideology of the Confucian hierarchy between men and women. Then, validity was sought in examples of women's schools in other countries, where education ensured that women gained freedom and equality with men; and lastly, the imperative of 'saving the nation,' which was to be achieved by educating women who comprised half the population. The need for education was stressed to build a new civilization and to ensure that the nation becomes equal with other nations.[2]

2 According to the first statement issued by some widows from the Yang-ban (noble) class in Pukchon in Seoul in September of 1898. They were the first women's group ever to mobilize themselves for a cause in the history of the women's movement, and the first cause they took

> Without a school, intelligent girls would find no place to learn … We appeal that girls' schools can be established so that young girls can take academic lessons. Through this our country can become a civilized country and be treated as equally as other nations (*Tongnip Sinmun*, 13 October, 1989).

The royal court did not respond to the appeal promptly and the first public school for girls took another 11 years to be established. On the other hand, "Chan-yang-hoe" (The Promotion Society for Sunsong School) members themselves established a school for girls in the same year, which was closed down within two years due to lack of resources (Choi, 1986).

The publication of a periodical and monographs began to serve as opinion leaders. The first women's magazine *Yeo-ja-ji-nam* (Women's Compass) was published a year before the girls' public school was opened. Many of the contributors were young girl students and the common themes included in the magazine, for example, were on "the liberating nature of women's education" and that "women's contribution to the society cannot be different from that of men."[3]

2.3 Women's Movement as "Save the Nation" and "Independence" Movement

The end of the Joseon dynasty coincided with the crisis of losing sovereignty. In this context, women's demand for education was directly con-

---

up was that of women's education. The group called themselves members of 'chan-yang-hoe' and went on to submit an appeal to Emperor Kojong on Oct. 13 in 1898 (Choi, 1986: 108-115).

3 Lee Ryong-ja, a 13 year old girl student, was one of the most articulate writers in the magazine. She wrote: "[…] it is because of the fact that men can have knowledge that there are many great men in history, but many women were without knowledge … women and men have the same potential but women lost their equal status (due to the lack of education) […]" In her appreciation of the educational opportunity finally given to women, she recommended to everyone they read the magazine, *Women's Compass*, which was to direct the future path for women *(Yeo-ja-ji-nam,* 1908*)*.

nected with national concerns and interests. In the process of persuading both men and women about the need to be rid of restrictions which hitherto confined women to their homes, the sameness of women and men was emphasized again. However, further reasons were added such as that women should participate in saving the nation by using their education and that they should achieve liberation by participating in campaigns and getting rid of confining sex roles. "Save the Nation" campaigns, conducted by women, took many forms such as jewelry donation and collecting rice from each household in order to repay the debt to Japan, which was used as a rationale for the annexation of Korea. We find many examples of the logic women presented regarding why they should be involved in the movement in the 1907 statement of Taegu Association of Ring Donation. This read as follows:

> God created human beings, and men and women are the same human beings. As Korean women we could not pursue learning but got busy with weaving and cooking, so we do not know our duty as human beings … When we repay the debt, we not only recover the sovereignty of our nation but demonstrate our power in the world and also secure equal rights between women and men … When we take off our rings, we will get rid of the bondage on our finger which has existed for thousands of years [...] (*Jeaguk Sinmun*, 23 April, 1907).

2.4 Critique of Male-Centered Sexual Morality

With education women became critical of the world around them and equipped themselves with the skills of arguing and presenting their criticisms logically. We find many examples of debates between men and women in newspaper articles and magazines of the time. One of the most powerful arguments made was on the issue of double standards in sexual morality (Lee, 2003).

Some courageous women voiced their criticisms openly and clearly regarding the norm of chastity imposed only on women. Na Hye-suk was one of the most famous 'new-women,' who did not hesitate to reveal her feelings of injustice and injury through her private life. She wrote, "Korean men's psychology is strange … They do not have the sense of chastity, but demand it from women and furthermore attempt to rob woman of hers […]" She concludes with a radical statement: "our liberation is the liberation from chastity" (Na, 1932).

3. Feminist Education and Women's Studies

The educational aim of fostering 'women leaders,' as sought by Ewha, characterized the institution as a women's organization or a women-only institution. The concept of 'woman leader' itself was an alien concept for patriarchy and so also was the notion of a women's institution. The definition of 'woman leader' was different, depending on the time, situation and values of the society in which the concept was defined.

The growth of a women's institution, however, became possible within the limits permitted by the oppressive patriarchal society. Predictably, resistance to it was inevitable, especially when the women's institution sought to cross certain limits. In the following pages we seek an overview of the history of Ewha as a women's institution and appraise the background within which women's studies as a subject was developed.

3.1 Fostering Korean Women Leaders

The goal of education in the earliest days of Ewha was to "make Koreans better Koreans, who have pride in Korean characteristics … under the teachings of Jesus" (The Committee for Historiography on 100 Years of Ewha, 1994: 78). The emphasis on education for Koreans, on the one hand, was stressed to overcome the peoples' sense of mistrust regarding the missionaries.

On the other hand, the core aim was to surpass the poverty, ignorance and bad aspects of traditional culture which needed to be challenged. It may be argued that the seeming contradiction between the two aims of 'education for Koreans' and 'challenging Korean customs' could be rendered compatible only through the fostering of Korean women leaders. When Korean women sought to pioneer new ways of contributing to society and launch social reform, the two aims converged. In this sense, the goal of fostering women leaders was most essential. In concrete terms, this goal started as a means of fostering teachers who, as mentioned earlier, helped the emergence of the women's movement in Korea.

The educational aims were resisted by culturally given impediments and political changes that came into existence under Japanese rule. When college education started in 1910, the total number of schooling years was extended to 18. Public opinion was negative about the fact that women over 20 years still went to school and were horrified by the prospect of having highly educated women at home and in society. Even more serious obstacles were placed by the Japanese colonial government, which imposed administrative controls in order to pursue their policy of assimilating Korean education within their Japanese rule. Given the historical context, this was a trying time, during the darkest period of history under Japanese rule at the end of the war, when the first Korean woman President of Ewha, Dr. Helen Kim, was appointed in 1939 (The Committee for Historiography on 100 Years of Ewha, 1994: 263-266).

"The cry of Korean women"[4] was a symbol which guided Helen Kim's devotion to analyze the cause of women's oppression and to search for ways to liberate them. With a sense of calling, she chose the subject of

4 Dr. Helen Kim wrote in her autobiography of the most important moment in her life at the age of 14 as follows; "I heard the sermon of a preacher who said 'Confess your sins, and seek for the love of God.' I felt, 'I haven't sinned enough to confess,' so I was feeling rebellious about the sermon. I made up my mind that either I give up my faith or learn the true meaning of faith, so I prayed for days and nights. One day, I heard the voice saying, 'Don't you hear that cry? That is the cry of Korean women. How can you sit here calmly and comfortably hearing that cry?'" (Kim, 1976: 221).

"Problems and Enlightenment of Rural Communities" for her Ph.D. thesis. Until the mid-sixties, she tried to continue her commitment to improving rural communities, where the majority of the population still resided. This personal sketch is crucial for understanding her belief that "Ewha does not exist for Ewha but for all Korean women." I think this was how she understood what is meant by 'women leaders' and tried to persuade the students of Ewha to respond to this message and adopt their calling. As she put it: "Every one of you is representing 200,000 Korean women. You are here in this higher educational institute in their place" (Chang, 1993: 164).

3.2 The Need for a Women's Institution

At the end of the last century it was impossible for women to go outdoors freely, let alone both sexes being allowed to sit together in school. Co-education was not allowed. However, all-women's educational institutions were not simply an outcome of such external constraints. In the case of Ewha, the decision to maintain it as a women-only institution was due to a significant commitment and reflection. This was the commitment based on the judgment that women's universities are of necessity to achieve gender equality in this land and until then Ewha had to stay a women's institution.

Under US Military rule, after the liberation from Japan, it became fashionable to think that co-education was more desirable. In a sense, this was a symbol of modernization and direction that the liberated Korea should be heading towards. In particular, the missionary support organizations started to pressurize Ewha to go co-ed. Helen Kim called a meeting of the entire faculty and students and declared:

> We are under a strong pressure to amalgamate with other colleges. I want to say to you very clearly that I will never give in to this pressure. Until we realize gender equality in this country, I declare that I will make

Ewha develop as a women's university (Chang, 1993: 196).

The question, "Why does Ewha stay a Women's university?" had often been raised then. Sometimes, Helen Kim answered, "When women occupy half the National Assembly, it may be alright to go co-ed" (Chang, 1993). This example is especially poignant in hindsight; the number of women candidates elected as Representatives of the National Assembly decreased rather than increased compared with the 1950s, until the beginning of the 2000s. Her judgment on this must have been based on hardships related to managing a women-only institution, which in turn convinced her of the necessity to maintain it as a women's institution, so as to support women and to make them autonomous. One of the most telling examples of the disadvantages of being a women's institution was experienced when applying for university status after the end of the Second World War, which also brought the Japanese occupation to an end.

Despite the confusion and turmoil of the period immediately after liberation, Helen Kim continued with her efforts to develop and improve the institution and Ewha was the first college to apply for the status of University. A major obstacle encountered in the process was the bureaucrats who thought it improper for a women's university to register as the first university in Korea. This was yet another manifestation of the deep-rooted patriarchal culture that upheld male superiority. These experiences of injustice, however, strengthened rather than weakened feminist consciousness and confirmed the need to foster women leaders and the empowerment of women. Furthermore, Helen Kim went on to say that "Ewha's struggle is more than a struggle for women's education. It is for women's liberation" (Chang, 1993: 157).

Dr. Helen Kim's feminist consciousness started with the belief in the equal rights of women and men as human beings and gradually developed into the need to define women's differences. Her critique of masculine culture and an alternative vision of women is evident in the following phrase: "Men's brains and strong power drove the tools of civilization into the state of wars. Human history was led by women and women will continue to lead it with more distinct power in the future" (Chang, 1993: 157). This new position, combined with her sense of calling for women leaders, produced her proposal of 'superwoman' as an ideal of womanhood in the 1960s, which needs to be discussed further at a later stage. In any case, under her leadership as president of the university, some important publications and educational activities addressed themes like, "women's power," "women's movement," and the contribution of women in many areas. One good example was the Introduction to Korean Women's Culture, published in 1958. This collection of papers may be considered Korea's first multi-disciplinary women's studies publication. To sum up, Ewha fostered a group of women and men who could utilize an historical moment such as the International Women's Year as an opportunity and turning point for change.

4. Women's Studies/Feminist Studies: Systematization of Knowledge Production

4.1 The United Nations' "International Women's Year" and Growth of Feminism

Any number of approaches may be used to discuss the background to the establishment of the Korean Women's Institute in 1977, but the UN's designation of 1975 as International Women's Year certainly played a major role. Many programs emerged from the Women's Year, but we may broadly identify two in connection with the Institute: One was the Korea Christian Academy led by Pastor Kang Won-yong, which took advantage of the historical occasion and became a pivotal moment for undertaking several years of program planning. It also became a contact point for university professors, leaders of women's groups, activists, press people, and so on.

The other was the establishment of the Women's Studies Research Committee at Ewha Womans University. Also, in commemorating the 5th memorial anniversary of Dr. Helen Kim, two important conferences were organized by the university in the same year. These may be viewed as landmark attempts that sought to systematize women's issues through academic theorization at a time when such issues were viewed only in connection with social movements.

4.2 The 1975 Academic Conferences: "Women's Power"

The academic conference, held in memory of Dr. Helen Kim's 5th death anniversary, brought together papers from a range of disciplines, all of which focused on women as their primary subject matter.[5] Apart from the presenters, these academic conferences were the site of heated debates among many prominent and progressive attendees. The fact that the theme of the first conference was "women's power" is noteworthy. The papers brimmed with earnestness and passion, which was evident in the manner in which the presenters approached and handled the themes. Each presenter showed her own distinct understanding of perspective and emphases; they had their own interpretations of "power" and assessments of causes and results. The reports of the academic conferences also included summaries of the debates following each presentation. In the discussion session following the second conference ("Women in Future Society"), we find discussants moved beyond discussion on the papers and engaged in communal efforts in the attempt to arrive at general directions and strategies for the future.

5 A list of the papers and the authors who presented these at the conference is as follows:
Conference 1: Traditional Society and Women's Power
- Lee Nam-Duk, Modern Society and Women's Power
- Lee Tae-Young, Guest lecture
Conference 2: Women in Future Society
- Hyeon Young-Hak, The concept of "power"
- Lee Hyo-Chei, Trends in International Women's Consciousness
- Yoon Sun-Duk (Yoon Hoo-Jung), Direction for the Korean Women's Problem

In the second conference, held in the autumn, more analytical and systematic papers were presented, presumably because participants had benefited from the diverse critiques and discussions held in the spring session. In the autumn discussions, the opinions of the variety of debaters were collected and recorded and published in the proceedings. Agendas such as economic independence, family law reform, freeing feminism from its middle-class orientation, ideology of motherhood, the feminist and labor movements, and concepts of yin-yang etc. were among the subjects that were covered. These themes, which continue to be controversial today, took place in a very comprehensive manner. Of particular interest was the fact that in the final part of the discussions, summaries of the concrete suggestions made by the discussants were included in the proceedings. I include partial excerpts:

> 1. Guarantees from the social system must exist if women are to exhibit the power of their existence. To attain this, they require organizational power. 2. Family law must be reformed. The establishment of a pan-Korea Association for the Reform of Family Laws was suggested. 3. Pregnancy and delivery should receive the protection of the state's social welfare system in the same manner as male military service is protected. 4. There is an urgent need for education to foster 'women's consciousness.' Preliminary studies should be made about how to carry this out. 5. The women's movement should not be tied to the middle-class. If the women's movement is to be a human rights movement, family-centered values must be dispensed with. 6. We must investigate cases of women at the bottom rungs of the social ladder, develop the consciousness of the leader class and middle class, especially so that they can be spokespersons for lower class women. [...] 15. We propose that a third gathering be held for the purpose of holding investigations regarding the content of women's education (Hyun, 1976).

The Helen Kim Memorial Project Association, hoping for more concrete contributions, proposed a third meeting. In so doing, they opened the path for the birth of "women's studies" in Korea.

4.3 The Birth of "Women's Studies"

The Korean Women's Institute played a major role in developing educational programs for women's studies, conducting the programs and assuming leadership for promoting new educational methods. It was thought that having each student debate individually was the most appropriate method to finding out how the new perspectives and theoretical analyses offered by courses in "women's studies" had been understood and realized by each student. Teaching assistants (TAs) were assigned to lead discussion sessions, while Saturdays were devoted to women's studies debates. The justifiability, the propriety and the demand for undergraduate education in women's studies, led to the establishment of a graduate program in the field. The Korean Women's Institute developed and operated the course program until the Department of Women's Studies was established in 1982 (Korean Women's Institute, 2007).

4.4 Creating New Space for a Feminist "Knowledge Community"

The Korean Women's Institute opened a new space. As an institution of learning for women, Ewha Womans University already existed as a symbol of women's space. But it was only indirectly so in the past, while the Institute, which gave birth to women's studies, has more directly and positively offered a feminist space. From the outset, this has been a lively space, bustling and noisy with the comings and goings of students taking women's studies courses, and since the founding of the women's studies department, has also been used as an office space. Projects for the city's low-income families and rural women, and programs for farmers, laborers and the press make the center bustle with activity. Many groups have been formed with the support of the Institute; many were organized in preparation of the setting up of the Korean Association of Women's Studies. Likewise, the Institute was also an important 'agitating point' for discussions, communications and preparations for the founding members of the Korea Sexual Violence Relief Center, which was established by professors, alumnae and students of the Women's Studies department. In addition, more and more professors and student organization leaders are now trying to establish women's studies programs at universities all over the country. The Institute responds to all their enquiries, providing a service that often requires the time and commitment of a full-time advisory institution. Such examples of "unseen" labor have helped to produce a "domino effect" in the setting up of women's studies courses all over the country. The Institute offered space for those who created a new base for social activism as a result of sharing physical and human resources.

4.5 Expansion of the Meaning of "Academic work" through Women's Studies

As seen above, the process of building women's studies came from multi-disciplinary approaches and academic institutional researches, which the Korean Women's Institute has supported through varied means. Studies in women's history have occupied an important area from the very beginnings of the Institute. Another research area was Legal Women's Studies. A research project entitled, "Investigations of Changes in Adjacent Fields in the Wake of the Development of Women's Studies," which centered on home economics, theology, and sociology, has analyzed the advances in women's studies researches emerging in existing academic fields (Chang, 1993; Moon, 1993).

A subsequent project, "The Reception of Feminism and Subsequent Changes in the Academic System," showed that women's studies had become a methodology for the purposes of literature and criticism, by providing a basic framework for sublimating women's experience into literature (Kim, 2000). Also, in the case of media studies, which began to be influenced by feminism, as of the 1980s, women's studies provided a platform for the raising questions about the real structure of gender-based prejudices in the media (Choi, 2000). In accordance with these studies, each academic field established its own women's studies association.

4.6 Mainstreaming and the Paradigm Shift

Women's education and women's studies are based on feminist values that hold all women in esteem. Freedom, liberation, equality, peace, life, and care all are values which guide feminism. In this sense, feminism is motivated not so much by value neutrality, as it is by the pursuit of realizing values. Those who share in these values form a community with passion and the belief that the community can bring about desirable changes by becoming a force for realizing values. New changes are to be brought about not only by the brain, but must also be accompanied by the heart.

Feminist values demand new standards not shared by the value standards of patriarchal society. Here, a new standard of sensibility occupies an important place. Sensibility re-evaluates the marginalized, the outcast, and the despised. This leads to new perspectives, giving new definitions to speed, efficiency and productivity. The members of the feminist studies community, to a degree, share in this common sensibility. The will to critique and to attempt to alter existing hierarchical dualities between the sexes, between public and private spheres, as well as between culture/nature, and reason/emotion, produces a new sensibility. In order for feminist values to have an impact on society, as alternative values to patriarchal norms, an "empowering" of the "intellectual community" of women's research is necessary (Agarwal, 1995; Cho, 2005; Lee, 2005). Here, discussions of leadership develop. Our interest is in seeking new forms of leadership, in which feminism and leadership are combined. Our values are not those of the conqueror; rather, we see the necessity of "values for the ecological age in which we all must live," and traditionally, such values have been realized in the lives of a majority of women (Chung, 2005).

5. Conclusion

This paper started with a review of the early days of opening a women's school in the early decades of Ewha's history, followed by the process whereby the Korean Women's Institute was born and developed over the last thirty years. In this investigation we can see that feminist knowledge production is not an easy task, requiring as its challenges for the future, a dynamic matching of two seemingly opposed strategic methods: mainstreaming (intervention) and the framing (construction) of new paradigms. With these highly complex processes as its objectives, efforts to mainstream, carried out by feminist theory and practice, have accumulated and produced many outcomes. The many changes in the legal system and value system are proof of the fact that the social bodies effecting changes in the paradigms of politics, society, knowledge production, scholarship and education have become empowered and a strong basis has been laid so that social change may be generated.

There can be no doubt that the UN's declaration of the "International Women's Year" and the "Proclamation of a Decade of Women's Development" were international trends, which strengthened the women's movement in Korea. Also, the process of the introduction and intellectual reception into Korea of western studies, theories and hypotheses played a large role in enriching women's studies theory. But the inaccuracy in the views that "women's studies" and "feminist studies" are mere "imports from the West" becomes clear from the examination of the historical process of women's studies as seen above. The recognition that we must find problems in Korean history and culture and seek alternatives has clearly existed since the first stirrings of women's studies in Korea. The Korean Women's Institute has, on the one hand, attempted to diagnose and resolve women's problems rooted in tradition through the study of women's history. On the other hand, it has striven not to miss the connections with the real locus of Korean society, and for a long time has given significance to consciousness-raising programs, facilitating on-site studies, and helping farming women, women laborers, and low-income urban women in leading independent lives. Research on diverse aspects such as on-site studies, theories, political implications etc. is a task to be carried out in the future.

Ewha Womans University leaders were committed to the task of theorizing on women's issues as their concrete goal and they have since systematized women's education and continued women's studies as a means to realizing that goal. We can evaluate the past 30-year history as a response to an important social demand that existed in Korean society, but that for a long time did not come to the surface. The emergence of women's studies has brought great changes to Korean society, and of course these did not result from the Korean Women's Institute's efforts alone. Rather, much strength and support came from thriving knowledge production activities of institutions that were created with the Institute playing an important role. The Korean Women's Institute has contributed to this process by carrying out tasks in the way of invisible groundwork and has served as an incubator for the women's studies department in the Ewha Graduate School, through its contributions towards the preparation and first contributions by the Korean Women's Association, and by the great and small energies it has poured into institutions like the Asian Center for Women's Studies and the Center for Women's Leadership Development. In the process, several researchers from many schools and diverse countries have responded positively to the Institute's invitation to pool in their assistance and energies. These contributions to Korean society have been a communal project, the concerted efforts of many people. The provision of space for cooperative projects is not only a physical space, but is also connected with new cultural production.

Over the past 30 years, women's studies has in some respects surpassed our expectations in terms of rapid and quantitative growth. Some view it as an academic area which will disappear once the oppression of women ceases to exist, an academic field which seeks its own extinction. While there seem to be superficial signs that the oppression of women is disappearing, we are not there yet.

The goal of research is to challenge boundaries of knowledge while allowing us to comprehend a variety of values, to think creatively, to reason critically and to dialogue effectively. We must carry out "good research" to avoid losing our souls to scientific technology. In that way, the knowledge produced will be knowledge for the future, and can save the future. To that end, we must have strength. We must pursue mainstreaming tactics. But that is only the tip of the iceberg. We require sincerity of purpose to pool together our ideal, physical, and emotional strengths; sympathize with those who suffer and unite our energies to find workable solutions. The forthcoming report will include discussions on the role of the university as well as feminist oriented activists in the government and other social organizations to springboard comparative studies with experiences in some countries in Asia and other parts of the globe.

References

Agarwal, Bina (1995), "Gender, Property and Land Rights: Bridging a Critical Gap in Economic Analysis and Policy," *Out of the Margin: Feminist Perspectives on Economics*, Edith Kuiper and Jolanda Sap (eds.), New York: Routledge: 264-295.

Chang, Pilwha and Kim Eun-Shil (eds.) (2005), *Women's Experiences and Feminist Practices in South Korea*, Seoul: Asian Center for Women's Studies and Ewha Womans University Press.

Chang, Sang (1993), "The Reception of Feminism and Its Impact on Theology (Yeoseonghak-i Sinhak-e Michin Yeonghyang)," *Korea Women's Review (Yeoseonghak nongip)*, 9(2): 55-83.

Cho, Hyung (ed.) (2005), *Feminist Values and Maternal Leadership (Yeoseongjuui Gachi-wa Moseongjeok Rideosip)*, Seoul: Ewha Womans University Press.

Choi, Sook-kyung (1986), "Formation of Women's Movement in Korea,"

Challenges for Women: Women's Studies in Korea, Chung Sei-wha (ed.), Seoul: Ewha Womans University Press: 103-126.

Choi, Sun Yul (2000), "The Reception of Feminism and Subsequent Changes in the Academic System: The Feminist Impact on Mass Communication (Feminijeum-ui Suyong-gwa Geue Tttareun Hakmoon Chegye-ui Byeonhwa: Feminijeum-i Eollonhak-e Kkichin Yeonghyang)," *Korea Women's Review (Yeoseonghak nongip)*, 17(1): 115-165.

Chung, Daihyun (2005), "Feminist Value of the Leadership (Seonggiseong-Mul: Rideosip-ui Yeoseongjuijeok Gaachi)," *Feminist Values and Maternal Leadership (Yeoseongjuui Gachi-wa Moseongjeok Rideosip)*, Cho Hyung (ed.), Seoul: Ewha Womans University Press: 15-62.

Du, Fangqin and Xinrong Zheng (eds.) (2005), *Women's Studies in China: Mapping the Social, Economic and Policy Changes in Chinese Women's Lives*, Seoul: Asian Center for Women's Studies and Ewha Womans University Press.

Hyun, Young Hak (1976), "The Concept of 'Power'(Him-ui gaenyeom)," *The Past and Future of Korean Women (Hankuk Yeoseong-ui Eoje-wa Naeil)*, Dr. Helen Kim Commemoration Committee (Kim Wwalan baksa 5-jugi Ginyeom Hankuk Yeoseongyeonguheopuihoe), Seoul: Ewha Womans University Press: 135-148.

Jeaguk Sinmun (1907), 23 April (Newspaper).

Juyal, Pooja (ed.) (2005), *Some Contemporary Contours: Women's Studies in India*, Seoul: Asian Center for Women's Studies and Ewha Womans University Press.

Khullar, Mala (ed.) (2005), *Writing the Women's Movement: A Reader*, New Delhi and Seoul: Zubaan, Asian Center for Women's Studies and Ewha Womans University Press.

Kim, Hyun Sook (2000), "The Reception of Feminism and Subsequent Changes in the Academic System: The Feminist Impact to Korea Women's Literature (Feminijeum-ui Suyong-gwa Geue Tttareun Hakmoon Chegye-ui Byeonhwa: Feminijeum-i Hankuk Heoseong Munhak-e Kkichin Yeonghyang)," *Korea Women's Review (Yeoseonghak nongip)*, 17(2): 3-26.

Kim, Yung-Chung (1976), *Women of Korea: A History from Ancient Times to 1945*, Seoul: Ewha Womans University Press.

Korean Women's Institute (ed.) (2007), "The 30 years History of the Institute of Korea Women's Studies: 1977-2007," Unpublished.

Lee, Myoung Sun (2003), "A Study on the Emergence of 'New Woman' during Modern Times in Korea: With a Focus on Gender and Sexuality (Sikminji Geumdae 'Sinyeoseong' Juche Hyeongseong-e Gwanhan Yeongu)," Unpublished Ph.D. Thesis, Seoul: Ewha Womans University.

Lee, Sang Wha (2005), "Feminist Reconstruction of Leadership and Power (Rideosip-gwa Geollyeok-e Daehan Yeoseongjuuijeok Jaegaenyeomhwa)," *Korea Women's Review (Yeoseonghak nongip)*, 22(1): 3-22.

Lerner, Gerda (1993), *The Creation of Feminist Consciousness: From the Middle Ages to Eighteen-Seventy*, Oxford: Oxford University Press.

Lin, Wei-hung and Hsiao-chin Hsieh (eds.) (2005), *Gender Culture and Society: Women's Studies in Taiwan*, Seoul: Asian Center for Women's Studies and Ewha Womans University Press.

Moon, Sook-jae (1992), "The Reception of Feminism and Its Impact on Home Economics (Yeoseonghak-ui Doip-e Ttareun Injeop Hakmun-ui Byeonhwa-e Daehan Gochal: Gajeonghak-eul Jungsim-euro)," *Korea Women's Review (Yeoseonghak nongip)*, 9(1): 15-53.

Mukhtar, Mai (2006), *In the Name of Honor: A Memior* (Kindle Edition), Arita Books.

Na, Hye-suk (1932), "A Confession of My Divorce (Ihon Gobaeksoe)," *Journal Samchulri*.

Poerwandari, Kristi (ed.) (2005), *Indonesian Women in Changing Society*, Seoul: Asian Center for Women's Studies and Ewha Womans University Press.

Satha-Anand, Suwanna (ed.) (2004), *Women's Studies in Thailand: Power, Knowledge and Justice*, Seoul: Asian Center for Women's Studies and Ewha Womans University Press.

Sobritchea, Carolyn (ed.) (2004), *Gender, Culture and Society: Selected Readings in Women's Studies in the Philippines*, Seoul: Asian Center for

Women's Studies and Ewha Womans University Press.
The Committee for Historiography on 100 years of Ewha (ed.) (1994), *The 100 Year History of Ewha (Ewha Byaeknyeonsa)*, Seoul: Ewha Womans University Press.
Tongnip Sinmun (1989), 13 October (Newspaper).
Yeo-ja-ji-nam (Women's Compass) (1908).

Chapter 2

Conceptualizing 'the Asian' and Asian Women's Studies[1]

LEE Sang Wha

1. Introduction

Having been involved with the Asian Women's Studies network organized by the Asian Center for Women's Studies at Ewha Womans University, I have seen the gradual evolution of new concepts which this paper deals with. The network started with the aim of promoting cooperation among women's studies practitioners in their work of teaching, researching, and curriculum development (ACWS & KWI, 2000). As they proceeded in cooperating, a question arose as to whether this was Asian Women's Studies, or Women's Studies in Asia. The former implied a kind of fixed identity, suggesting some commonality shared by all the constituents, while the latter was understood as somewhat more open or casual (Kim & Kang, 2001: 114; Khullar, 2005: 17-18). There have been discussions on this issue among the participants and this paper is my response, as a philosopher, to these questions.

1 This paper was supported by the Korea Research Foundation Grant funded by the Korean Government (MOEHRD, Basic Research Promotion Fund) (KRF-2005-005-J12501) and published in the *Asian Journal of Women's Studies*, Vol. 14 No. 4 (2008).

The categories of 'Asian Women' or 'Asian Women's Studies,' and the meanings of 'Asia' and 'Asian-ness' have become subjects in need of re-conceptualization and redefinition according to Kim Eun-Shil (2007). In this paper, I first review the meaning of Asia and Asian-ness in terms of their physical vastness and cultural diversity. I argue that in understanding 'Asian Women' we have to maintain both the common features of Asian women and recognize differences among women in Asia. In section two, I try to develop the concept, 'Asian Women' as a 'strategic category' for feminist politics, and bring in 'locational feminism' as an appropriate theoretical resource to discuss Asian Women's Studies after reviewing a rich body of postcolonial debates. As I understand it, locational feminism has adopted a 'genealogical method' for its methodology and the new rhetoric of spatiality and temporality. Since the concept 'location' expresses both different spatiality and multiple temporal-spatiality, it can incorporate multi-positionality, determined in historical and social contexts and women subjects living in these. In section three, I introduce the ontology of becoming, to posit the identity of Asian women changing continuously according to temporal and spatial conditions. In section four, I put forward a summary of some comments regarding my ideas on the 'ontology of becoming,' received during presentations I made in a number of conferences as a way of verifying my new approach. Finally, I conclude with a note affirming various ways for the practice of solidarity among Asian women for Asian women's studies.

2. Meaning of Asia/Asianness and Asian Women's Studies

What is Asia? The following questions arise in the process of defining Asia as an analytical category. What is the reason for including scores of nations and hundreds of languages in the 'region' of Asia? Is it because the various units belonging to 'Asia' share some common characteristics that are different from others outside Asia? Is 'Asia' a region that has cultural and political characteristics clearly distinct from those of other regions? Is the intensity or strength of mutual interactions and communications among countries and units in Asia strong enough to make them 'belong' to one region?

With these questions in mind, I seek to examine how "Asia as a region" can be explained by borrowing a framework of two concepts—geographical space as an objective aspect and cognitive space as a subjective aspect. According to this framework, the concept of 'region' is objectively defined as geographical space, implying contiguity of borders and proximity in space. On the other hand, a region in its subjective aspect is defined as a social construct or an idea created by people who live in the region. Alternatively, it may be viewed from outside by people living outside, who have different backgrounds and motivations (Kang, 2007). However, the following problems appear when this framework is applied to Asia. When considering Asia as a geographical space, the continent appears too huge to view proximity among the countries in it as a measure of belonging to one category. The intensity of cultural, economic, political or security concerns is not always strong enough to speak of Asia belonging to one region.

According to a dictionary definition, Asia consists of 46 countries, often divided into six sub-regions of North Asia, Central Asia, West Asia, Southeast Asia, South Asia, East Asia, or three sub-regions such as South Asia, West Asia, and Central Asia. The number of languages spoken in Asia is innumerable and these are quite distinct and are used by different ethnic groups that also vary within individual countries. For example, while Korea has one language, the Indonesians have more than 600, and the Philippines has more than 100. There is a rich combination of cultural roots: for instance of Buddhism, Confucianism, Islam, Shintoism, and Christianity in the Philippines. The historical experience of colonization differs; France, Britain, Netherlands or United States exerted different influences in the countries they occupied, leaving varied cultural and political legacies. China, Vietnam, Laos, Cambodia, Myanmar, and Indonesia have had communist regimes, which imply a distinct political heritage.

As such, the physical vastness and cultural diversity to be found in the category 'Asia,' and the complexity and dynamics of change within and between its different units reveal continuous changes in geography itself. We may perceive greater differences and diversity, rather than commonalities and identities within the single geographical category of the Asian region. Such differences and diversity make it difficult to clearly demarcate borders, cultural differences and distances between the worlds of Asia and non-Asia. As the geographical space of Asia has continuously changed, so have the meanings of Asia as a conceptual space.

As the notion of Asia presupposes a certain perspective, it cannot be said to be value free (Milner & Johnson, 1984). Looking at the history of the concept of Asia, we find a critical perspective, i.e., a concept imposed by 'westerners,' or 'Asia' as a signifier of the non-western 'Other,' which reflects contents created and communicated via a western perspective (Yamamuro, 2007: 36-37). The concept of Asian Studies, for example, is sometimes regarded as a form of neo-colonialism in the sense that it refers to knowledge about Asia as possessed by westerners. The concept of Asia, created by westerners, in fact, has not always meant the same thing. Orientalism of various kinds operate at various levels in the mystification or marginalization of Asia. On the other hand, the term 'Asia' for Asians can be represented as a more powerful concept with more positive values. The idea and concept of Asia have been understood and used as a powerful expression of resistance against the imperialism of the western powers in the history of colonization. In this continuum, Asia-African solidarity has also been sought after. Sometimes, 'Asia' is taken and interpreted to be an expression of confidence, denouncing negative implications of inferiority or defensiveness and emerging as a power equal to Europe or the USA (Sun, 2003), For example, there have been, for some time very active debates on "Asian values" in Korea as well as in some other Confucian-oriented Asian countries. Asian values were emphasized by some Asian political leaders and male scholars to explain the economic development of the 'non-Western developing countries.' However, many feminist scholars are skeptical of this concept and have said that the notion of "Asian values" has often clouded the diversity and distinctness of countries within Asia. For instance, Kim and Kang assert that "Asian feminist scholars have to pay attention to the way in which Asian values operate to reinforce patriarchy and boost the ego of the male elite … Obviously, we have opposed this male-centered and orientalist idea, which often neglects divisions of class, gender and ethnicity even within one country, let alone all of Asia, and thus freezes society as a timeless entity" (Kim & Kang, 2001: 114). Asian-ness and Asia as concepts, whether they are expressions of confidence or defensiveness, imply something shared by Asians. However, as seen above, it is difficult to say that shared experiences exist among them because of the very varied cultural, political and historical differences in the region (Kosugi, 2002).

We need to pay attention to the fact that Asia as a geographical zone does not imply common cultural and religious values or identical political and economic interests shared in the entire region. Despite the lack of identity or integrity among the units that constitute Asia, we can see the changing evaluation of 'Asian-ness' depending on the intent to essentialize or universalize the cultural identity of Asia as a whole (Sakamoto, 2007). To summarize the above discussion, we can say that, depending on the historical context, Asia is changing the borders of its geographical and conceptual space as a new form of identity and community and as a political formation. However, the common experiences of 'Asia' or 'Asians' are constructed ideas that serve to encourage a more positive sense of homogeneity or homogenizing ideas of 'Asia' or 'Asian-ness.' I understand the term 'Asia' as an idea in the process of being created in accordance with changing historical contexts, wherein the signifier permits a continuous creation of meanings depending on the context. Therefore, to theorize Asian Women's Studies, we need to re-conceptualize the concept of 'Asia' in our feminist theories and practice. In the same vein, such a task of re-conceptualizing Asia in feminist perspectives has to go hand-in-hand with the task of contextualizing feminisms in the perspectives of Asian women. Asia is a concrete category, conceptualized as physical-geographical space as well as a signifying category, which has to be reconstructed as a conceptual space that is 'created' in feminist politics, to which we turn now.

3. Basic Propositions for Asian Women's Studies

3.1 Asian Women

It can be said that researching Asian women implies a postcolonial purpose in the sense that the starting point is to overcome western-centered universalism and to theorize particular concrete experiences of Asian Women. If we agree that women in feminism are not universal subjects but comprise a social group that shares a level of orientation, values and goals, the concept of women as a social group can offer answers to the question of how we can use the category 'women' without assuming the absolute 'sameness' of women. By reconstructing the category of 'women as a social group,' in conjunction with postcolonial perspectives, we can gain the primary identity of 'Asian Women' in relation to other social groups such as 'Western Women.'

The existing debates of postcolonialism have mostly developed around nation states, nationalism, race and histories of western colonization (Brydon, 2001). Postcolonial arguments have presented various new approaches based on critical perspectives about western feminism being disconnected from social and historical contexts (Spivak, 1988; Trinh, 1989; Tae, 2001). But in the process, many limitations have been revealed as a result of the generalizations regarding the dichotomous oppositions of West and Non-West/the Third World (Tae, 2008). 'Asia' as a geographical and spatial region includes many countries with diverse colonial histories and varied politics and economy, which cannot be captured by one criterion or analytic frame, theorized through traditional postcolonial discourses.[2]

As emphasized earlier, if the use of 'Asia' as a category assumes a uniform cultural identity shared by all the units that belong to it, such an 'Asia' does not exist. It is not defined as a fixed geographic location in Asian Women's Studies and the task of critiquing and opposing universalist and essentialist feminisms, so as to exclude the differences among women, is meaningful and necessary. Such a position would apply to both Asian women's studies and western feminisms. In the same vein, I do not adopt the dichotomous approach of global and local/regional in explaining globalization. The exclusive focus on locality, which emerges as an outcome of such a dichotomy and is found in male nationalist or chauvinistic debates, obscures the problematizing of women's oppression and harms their solidarity. We have experienced numerous cases of the suppression and marginalization of women's agenda through the dichotomies of imperialism vs. nationalism.

Nonetheless, I agree with the claim Mohanty makes that "It is possible to trace coherence of effects resulting from the implicit assumption of the 'West' (in all its complexities and contradictions) as primary referent in theory and praxis" (Mohanty, 2003: 17-18). It should also be noted here that western feminist discourses and the political praxis of western feminism do not have any one shared goal or interest. Western feminism is not mentioned here to figuratively imply a unified entity. Mohanty's argument of diverse text strategies is noteworthy—that the concept of "western feminism" can be used to concentrate on the similar effect when writers classify others as non-West, whereby they themselves are coded implicitly as the West. If this in-depth cognition is expanded further, it is very likely that non-western women can take their own culture as the norm, while colonizing the history and culture of women in other groups as that of Others. In this context a postcolonial analytic frame can by applied in

2 Most of the over 100 articles on postcolonialism in the collection by Brydon (2001), for instance, deal with relations between western colonialism and the third world and attention on Asia is focused on a limited number of countries.

any discussion regarding the coding and revival of culturally different others. Thus the project of Asian women's studies requires us to delineate boundaries, as Chandra Mohanty asserts; we have to be "attentive to borders while learning to transcend them" (Mohanty, 2003: 2).[3] It is necessary while constructing Asian women's studies to consider the border between Asia and the West, in order to go forward to a more inclusive and expansive feminist praxis like a global feminist solidarity that goes beyond the boundary of Asia.

The category of Asian women in postcolonial perspectives can be "constructed" as a collective identity in relation to other social groups such as western women or women of non-Asian regions. As stated earlier, the identity of Asian women is not pre-given or fixed by their common experiences or unique characteristics, created through exchanges and meetings of women of Asia and constructed via their differences from women of other regions. To summarize, it is not necessary to assume universal features or a unique patriarchal framework in Asia to consider the particular location of Asian women. Focusing attention on the common features shared by Asian women can lead to a neglect of differences among women in Asia, just as western feminisms have neglected various differences between regions and cultures. Despite these differences, we need to reconsider the meaning of "Asian women" to prove that Asian women's studies or Asian feminism may take Asian women as their basic unit and critically discuss coercive patriarchal ideology, systems and practices against women. This is the very issue of identity of Asian women which must be defined for the establishment of Asian Studies. At the same time, the criterion of "women" must be considered so that the gaps among Asian women can be filled. Therefore, I suggest that the concept 'Asian Women" is to

3 Mohanty further explains 'borders' as follows, "Feminism without borders is not the same as "border-less" feminism. It acknowledges the fault lines, conflicts, differences, fears, and containment that borders represent. It acknowledges that there is no one sense of border that the line between and through nations, races, classes, sexualities, religions, and disabilities, are real- and that a feminism without borders must envision change and social justice work across these lines of demarcation and division" (Mohanty, 2003: 2).

be developed as a 'strategic category' for feminist politics to strengthen the solidarity of feminists and empower them to build collective power to serve common interests.

3.2 Asian Women's Studies and "Locational Feminism": Genealogical Method and Spatial Mode of Thinking

'Asia' in Asian women's studies is a geographical space as a location of concrete daily life and at the same time it is a cognitive space for feminist politics that is trying to solve problems by making its agenda visible and for theorizing agendas and praxis in solidarity.

The concept of 'location,' which I borrow from discourses of "locational feminism,"[4] is not a spatial concept based on divisions of area but a place or situation in which homogeneity and heterogeneity continuously intersect and various differences are produced. According to Friedman, locational feminism "emphasizes that the identity of an individual or a group are shaped at the intersection or crossroads of different systems of social stratification based on race, class, sexuality, religion and nationality. It means the identity of individuals is to be constructed or formed as fluid, situational, and relational subjectivities, which are conditioned in multiple and complex historical and special context" (2001: 18). In this sense, 'Asian Women's Studies' is a praxis of locational feminism that I bring in through a spatial way of thinking and reflecting. Locational feminism was formed basically from a standpoint critical of singular feminism. The theory of feminism constantly analyzes the discourses of men within a concrete context of society and history, performing to clarify the historical and social limitations of such discourses claimed to be universal. In this

4 The naming of locational feminism originated from Adrienne Rich's call for 'politics of location.' Rich asserted that the politics of location, recognizing multiple voices of women in multiple locations, needs to be activated in order to achieve a feminist social transformation (Rich, 1984). Rosi Braidotti, as I understand, also clearly reveals her commitment for locational feminism in most of her major works including *Nomadic Subjects and Metamorphosis* (Braidotti, 2005; 1994).

respect, it can be said that the theory of feminism has adopted a 'genealogical method' for its own unique methodology. This method inquires about an object or the origin (*Herkunft*) of the object, without presuming an identical and universal substance existing in the source (*Ursprung*).[5] It suggests that to examine a certain object or notion in a genealogical manner, we will become aware that at the time of its advent, instead of sacred and inviolable self-identity or homogeneity, essences exist in the tension of constantly-changing powers and the plural orders of fragmented and heterogeneous objects (Lee, 2007: 34-35).

In short, genealogy is a methodology opposed to 'the pursuit of origins.' We can describe two characteristics of the genealogical method. First, it is criticism or it seeks to destroy and criticize a method of pure origin or substance existing as the origin, which is a mere dogma that explores the historical source of object and notion. Second, genealogical method is practical production. Through the notion of invention, presented in opposition to origin, we can infer that genealogy is not a simple disclosure or dismantlement, but connotes a productive practicing concept. In this view, feminism is genealogical by nature. By disclosing how women have been objectified and alienated universally among human subjects, feminism revealed that women existed in reality not as homogeneous and universal subjects, but as humans placed in the social context of gender differentiation. The earliest attempts at feminist theory and practice, however, still maintained a confused territory that was not to be affected by genealogical criticism. In this sense, locational feminism can be described as an intensified genealogical criticism. To sum up, locational feminism applies the genealogical method of feminism proactively to feminism itself, thereby uncovering the following: Feminism in the singular which

5 A genealogical method is the method of investigation Nietzche attempted, in full scale, in *The Genealogy of Morality*. According to Foucault, Nietzche's genealogy investigates the origins of things without assuming identical and universal substance as the origin. Foucault argues that we can discover if we look at things critically we discover the history of things contains multiple elements of fragmented and different entities rather than identical and universal ones (Foucault, 1977; Mahon, 1992: 82).

presupposes universal feminist subjects or female subjectivity, proceeding by focusing on the category of 'Woman' with a capital W, in fact, is merely a local and situated one among the many feminisms that were constructed and developed in a certain specific time and space. In short, feminism in the singular is just a form of feminism which represents only white middle-class women subjects in the West (Friedman, 2001: 16-17).

Through locational feminism we can expect the invention of women subjects and the practice of a new solidarity; the new subject takes into consideration different forms of feminism emerging from various temporal and spatial contexts in which feminisms change or become transplanted. In order to open up a new horizon to practice solidarity among various feminist movements, a new perspective regarding identity itself is required. The invention of a new women subject is possible through genuine praxis of solidarity based on locality. The new concept of subject does not require autonomous subjects presupposed by the western enlightenment. Locational feminism strategically adopts "the rhetoric of space" to thematize differences among women (Friedman, 2001: 18).[6]

A new rhetoric of spatiality effectively distinguishes itself from the rhetoric of temporality; by fragmenting and deconstructing universalization. The homogenization inherent in the rhetoric of temporality is rejected and actively inserts differences. For example, terms like 'contemporary' makes us regard people of a particular period as being evidently placed in a similar, universal problematic situation. Attaching temporal labels such as first generation, second generation or third generation before feminism produces similar effects. Such naming is useful in expressing common feminist agendas and shared consciousness, solidarity and prax-

6 Friedman persuasively explains the ground on which spatiality is introduced in the following quotation, "Locational feminism by its terminology invokes notions of space and spatiality. … Space serves as the prominent source of metaphor for feminist rhetoric of identity. … Where the temporal rhetoric of awakening tends to focus on gender in isolation from other systems stratification, the spatial rhetoric of location emphasizes the interaction of gender with other forms of power relations based on such cultural categories as race, ethnicity, class, sexuality, religion, national origin, age and so forth. … Space, in these terms, is not a static essence, but rather a location of historical overdetermination" (Friedman, 2001; 18-21).

is activated in a particular period. However, it delimits one in capturing the flow of new feminist thinking that sees differences at the core. This requires a shift from the rhetoric of temporality to that of spatiality. The naming of locational feminism effectively conveys through the concept of 'location' the obvious fact that although two women may live in the same time zone, they can be vulnerable to locally contextualized oppression because they exist in different spaces and that there are different consciousnesses and different responses to their problems.

By introducing spatiality, the rhetoric of spatiality reinterprets temporality itself. Time cannot be regarded as universal or homogenous. Though we may accept multi-positionality according to space, there is no reason to distribute a common temporality to multi-positional beings. It would be more reasonable to suppose multi-temporality, just as multi-positionality exists. The concept of 'location' does not simply express different spatiality but brings in multiple temporal-spatiality, determined in historical and social contexts and women subjects living in these.

4. Asian Women's Studies and Ontology of Becoming

While attempting to theorize Asian Women's Studies and to locate it in the contemporary Asian regional context, we should not lose sight of the horizon of global solidarity of feminists. The long-standing dichotomy of identity and differences needs to be replaced by the perspective and politics of difference/becoming. By applying this framework we can overcome the dichotomy of global feminism and exclusive regionalism as a reaction. This is to aim at integration of locality and a vision for the future. In a broad sense, feminism, in itself, can be defined as politics, based on the ontology of differences. Attention was placed, firstly, on the differences between women and men (differences with men/identity of women: politics of difference/identity) and, secondly, on the differences between women (difference between women and men/differences among women:

difference/difference politics) (Young, 1990: 161-163; Arneil, 1999: 152-211; Grosz, 1995).

Now, I think we come to the third stage of paying attention to the ontology of difference/becoming. Excessive emphasis on differences among women runs the risk of fragmentation and conflicts between pluralized feminisms. For instance, the politics of difference/difference has been criticized for being limited in failing to show how women can unite and act together under the umbrella of feminism, while overcoming differences between women. This is because the mere emphasis on differences among women may undermine the foundation of solidarity produced by politics of identity and difference/identity. It is impossible to change local and global orders, which lead to discrepancies in living conditions of women only through recognition and acknowledgement of differences among women.

This problem cannot be overcome via a return to politics of difference/identity. I think it will be a theoretical and practical regression to go back to the concept of identity in order to rebuild a base of solidarity. Rather, we should try to find a new possibility of solidarity, which can be opened by rethinking the concept of difference. In other words, I propose to make differences productive by interpreting them creatively and connecting them to a vision for the future. Politics of difference/difference is a useful strategy for contextualizing a feminist agenda in different conditions and locations of life, taking into account the diversity and particularity of women's experience. However, placing exclusive emphasis on locality in the Asian region may lead to a repetition of the same error of emphasizing difference between men and women and assuming the sameness of women; thus advocating the global solidarity of women (or global sisterhood) may be at the cost of recognizing various differences within the feminist movement.

Given the dichotomous argument, wherein the global is seen as containing homogeneity and undifferentiated commonality/identity, while the local preserves heterogeneity and difference, the true meaning of feminism cannot be realized. Given such a dichotomous view, where the assumptions that local differences must be defended and protected against the invasion of globalization are circulated, may tend to jeopardize the existence of feminism itself. In order to avert such risks, Asian Women's Studies needs to pay attention to the insight of locational feminism in thinking about issues regarding globalization and location in a new perspective. Through the politics of difference, in considering distinctions between men and women and among women, locational feminism tries to find a way for the solidarity of women without stifling differences among women in the circumstances of the globalization era. By not denying the temporal dimension of the historicity of feminism, locational feminism introduces a spatial dimension, that is, the location of feminist theory and practice. Based on such an approach, the limitation of universalistic feminism, focusing solely on gender, is overcome. This stresses that gender creates its identity via interaction with other forms of social stratification. Locational feminism stresses that the identity of an individual or a group is produced under temporal and spatial constraints, and multiple factors of social stratification, such as ethnicity, gender, class, age and sexual orientation, are formulated and defined in a multi-layered interaction.

In order to understand identities with local particularity and global universality at the same time, an individual and a group should be placed not only in the historical and temporal constraints of an era, but also at the complex intersection between the situation and position of the historically-incorporated subject and spatial categories such as networking, zone and territory. Also, such spatial metaphor begins with the premise that a any fixed and essential self- identity, is neither necessary nor possible as a basis for feminist politics. Because locational feminism starts from an ontology of becoming, that is, identity understood as being constructed and changing according to temporal and spatial conditions, and in the process, the identity even of an individual or a single group continues to change. Any attempt to open up a certain new political and ethical horizon necessarily involves the construction of a new ontology. Thus, feminist practice in the globalization era requires a transition to the ontology of becoming, which demands thinking of not only a temporal dimension but also a spatial one. Here, space does not mean a static substance, but the location of historical multi-layered over-determination. In the context of globalization, the global and the local are closely interrelating and interacting with each other, while shaping the living conditions of individuals and groups. The identity of a person cannot be defined by one among numerous factors of social stratification, but is determined by a combination of multiple factors that work differently in the temporal and spatial particularity. Therefore, understanding differences among women in a dynamic process of interaction, within the context of external conditions of local and global levels, opens a way to consider simultaneously the differences and commonalities among women in the interaction between the spatial particularity of their region and the temporal universality of the global era. Through such a mode of thinking, wherein not only do the identities of women keep changing, but so also do the differences and commonalities in the experiences of a woman/women who are continually created. Asian Women's Studies should get over the fixed quality of difference, while embracing the insight of politics of difference (between women and men)/ difference (among women, ethnic, class, race, etc). To sum up, through the ontology of becoming, we need to search for a theoretical basis for the 'politics of solidarity' to work as the driving force for the practice of feminism that, given all the differences among women, should respond to the powers that exercise significant influences on life in today's local area (Buchanan and Colebrook, 2000).

I want to put forward the "ontology of becoming" as a philosophical basis for the theorization of Asian Women's Studies. Ontology of becoming posits that the identity of Asian woman continuously changes according to temporal and spatial conditions. The ontology of becoming does not dichotomize identity and difference, but makes it possible to think paradoxically in search of the possibility of coexistence between the two. Asian women's studies also does not view the meaning of 'Asia' as a fixed space or local community with an essential, fixed, unchanging nature and rejects the approach to globalization based on the dichotomy of global vs. local. The critique on and resistance regarding western feminism, which has overlooked and excluded differences between women, are meaningful and necessary for decolonialization perspectives. However, the overemphasis on the locality that is associated with male nationalism and chauvinism results in not only disturbing and problematizing women's issues, but also hindering the common basis for solidarity and collective praxis between women. We have to remind ourselves that especially in non-western countries, which have had the experience of colonization, women's issues have been always undermined by the sharp opposition between imperialism and nationalism.[7] In this sense, the attempt to theorize Asian women's studies is to locate it on the map of the contemporary global context, maintaining the deepest concern for the future in the global solidarity of feminists.

5. Future Task for Theorizing 'Asian Women's Studies': Re-mapping 'Asia' and the Contextualization of the Postcolonial Perspective

When I gave a summary of the intermediate result of this study I received feedback from a variety of researchers and scholars in and outside

7 The discourse of globalization, which adopts the logic of totalization, disseminates the notion that the world has become homogenized by a dominant process of global integration called westernization. This kind of discourse has been criticized, because according to its logic the site/ space we live in appears to be controlled or dominated by western subjects who live in other places in the world. This discourse assumes the dangerous notion that reduces non-western local subjects into passive beings. With such a simple logic of globalization it is impossible to grasp not only the variety and diversity of non-western nations, states, and cultures but also the complex characteristics and particularities of western cultures. Increasing contact between various nations and cultures of the world have not led to a harmonious space wherein heterogeneous positions reach agreement and become homogenized, but rather it has become a space in which dissonance, conflict and clashes take place among different perspectives and views (Robertson, 2003: 295; Featherstone, 2003: 342-343; Lee, 2007: 41-45; Hardt & Negri, 2001).

of Korea, individually and in groups.[8] As the variety of facts and responses identified and perceived in the process provided very important viewpoints relevant to the task of theorization on Asian women's studies in the future, I will provide a gist of the emerging points. First, responses differed in highly complex and diverse ways regarding the idea of establishing Asian Women's Studies. Differences appeared among Asian women scholars on the one hand and between Asian scholars and non-Asian women scholars on the other. In particular, differences in response among western scholars were visible. In general, responses or points of interest for Asian women scholars were different, depending on the place and contexts where these subjects were discussed. In conferences or workshops only of Korean or Asian scholars or in individual meetings, participants paid attention to 'postcolonial perspectives' and the ambiguity and polysemy regarding the category of 'Asia.' However, they had somewhat skeptical responses as to whether the attempt to theorize these categories would be possible or necessary. Within the sentiment of sympathizing with the difficulty in re-conceptualizing these categories in a feminist way, they responded positively and affirmatively to the necessity and possibility of such an endeavor.

Most Asian scholars, including those from Korea, shared their problems with regard to western-oriented knowledge production structures and so-called 'intellectual coloniality' and they agreed that they needed spontaneous theorizing instead of 'imported theory' in order to break through such situations. But, at the same time, questions arose regarding whether it would be possible to theorize frameworks for conceptualizing and analyzing differences and diversity in each Asian country, given the

8 I made presentations in the following conferences; Korean Association of Women's Studies, Seoul, Korea (November 3, 2006), Gender 2007: East meets West, York University, UK (July 3, 2007), Nanjing University, China (November 2007), and AAWS Inaugural conference, Seoul, Korea (November 16, 2007). I had interviews with participants in the conferences as well as professors of International Christian University, Hitozubashi University of Japan, (October 2-6, 2006) and scholars who attended conference in Tenzin Normal university in China (October 20, 2006).

enormous differences between these countries. On the one hand, even though this may become possible, what methods and concepts would be able to deal with such a huge concern? On the other hand, in conferences in which both western and non-western scholars participated, differences in response were observed between the Asian and western women scholars. The former predominantly expressed affirmative responses rather than skeptical ones with respect to the fundamental direction and intent of this study. Such sympathetic sentiment was found not only among Asian scholars but also among those who were from other non-western countries. In particular, young Asian scholars who were engaged in conducting studies in western countries regarded this study as a very encouraging challenge, expressing strong support and willingness to participate in it. The sympathy among Asian women and those from other non-western countries was interpreted not only as favorable interest and theoretical support for the argument of this study, but also as a demonstration of emotional 'postcolonial sensitivity affected by the environment. This also can be seen as a reflection of the current situation of intellectuals who have experienced a degree of marginality or invisibility in the context of a globalizing academia with no national borders. While there is helplessness and tension involved in knowledge production work that is evaluated by criteria inherently colored by 'intellectual coloniality,' nonetheless, no one is entirely free of self censorship given the reality of cultural and mental coloniality.

Thereafter, we can pay attention to differences in critical thinking revealed in discussing key terms like 'postcolonial perspective' or 'postcolonialism' in relation to the category of 'Asian women's studies.' In these conferences, while Asian women identified issues from the participants' viewpoint, western women scholars viewed the subjects of 'postcolonialism' and 'foundation of Asian women's studies' from an objective and observer's standpoint. This is because western feminist scholars, who are acquainted with long-standing postcolonial discourses and are identified as progressive intellectuals, see concepts related to postcolonialism as meant merely for theoretical debate and not as practical subjects or problematic concepts that are closely related with their concrete reality. It is natural for people who are not involved themselves to regard these discussions as abstract, theoretical and ideological matters. And yet, the implication of the postcolonial perspective of a western feminist, and her prudent and cautious response towards criticism regarding a west-oriented feminist viewpoint can be interpreted as a reflection of stress. This may be caused by critical self-examination as a western scholar on the one hand, and being responsible for 'political correctness' as a feminist researcher on the other. Notwithstanding their differences, western women scholars pointed out that the problems of intellectual and cultural colonization, as those of marginalization, were also the 'problems of East and West' that are visible in the West, especially in Europe,[9] in a broader sense. These indications by western women scholars may imply the question as to why this study is limited to 'Asia' and Asian Women's Studies' while it should be a subject for postcolonial theory and practice as a common agenda to be jointly discussed in the name of 'global feminism that respects differences.'

Therefore, it can be said that the basic valid premise of the 'ontology of becoming,' which is a theoretical and founding principle adopted in this study to initiate Asian women's studies, is verified. This suggests the view of 'Asian women' as one that is not already given, but is in the process of becoming, which can be produced and realized through on-site feminist theory and practice. So, our future task is to develop a methodology to accommodate the politics of difference and politics of identity into a politics of solidarity by studying the analytical category of 'Asian women' in a more concrete locational context, and to theoretically expand exploration areas to western feminism. Critical inquiries that are frequently raised when discussing the postcolonial perspective in Korea are about why they still care about 'postcolonization' when it was liberated from Japanese co-

9 A European feminist scholar who attended my presentation session at the University of York said that the problem of East-West within Europe was surfacing as a very serious issue.

lonial rule over 60 years ago? A very negative viewpoint lies at the core of these skeptical inquiries against the attempt to use the 'imported theory' of 'postcolonialism' for analyzing and explaining the situation we live in. But, given the implication of the term, 'imported theory,' the fact that all sorts of studies that use or apply western theoretical frameworks are facing such criticism, paradoxically shows that 'intellectual colonialism' or 'cultural colonialism' still exists and is reproduced in the process of creating culture and producing knowledge in Korea.

The question, "Why do you adopt the standard framework of a postcolonial perspective in theorizing Asian women's studies now?" is believed to be raised because they interpret the term 'post' in postcolonialism as something 'after,' understood as a concept of time. So these questions can be answered by asserting that Asia is still colonized in reality with the support of a proper basic argument that can explain the reasons. In other words, the concept of postcolonialism should suggest the basis for combining Asia as a category with the premise of a common identity despite the enormous differences that exist in Asia. Therefore, the key point is how to define the meaning of 'colonization' or 'coloniality.' Postcolonialism as an analytical category is polysemic and flexible. Discussion on the subject of postcolonialism as an analytical framework in this era of globalization is based on the view that colonialism and colonization are still underway in the present historical context, although colonial rule ended in the middle of last century.

In the course of reviewing the discussion patterns of Asian/ non-Western scholars and Western ones on the postcolonial perspective, I identified that difference in conditions where discussions were made such as contexts and places when identical group of women participated caused difference in their positions, while difference in living environments of women scholars caused differences in positions when discussions were made under identical conditions. From this, it is seen that there is no 'difference' and 'commonality' or 'identity,' considered to be essential attributes that can be vested in the fixed subjectivity of an individual or a group and these concepts are always relational and are variably formed according to historical and spatial contexts.

Coloniality here should be understood as an extended concept that comprises various types of colonial rules, and historical passages that were subordinate to new colonial domination as well as the present conditions and the ongoing situation of globalization under the hegemony of the West. Asian countries have widely varying experiences and histories of colonization that may be covered by the homogenized concept of "colonization." Therefore, in order to discuss postcolonization in Asian women's studies, we need to re-conceptualize and remap Asia by expanding coloniality to include the seizure of a nation state, loss of sovereignty, economic exploitation by colonial rulers, and so on.

6. Conclusion

I have emphasized that the meanings and significance of Asian women's studies are created and constructed in the multi-dimensional contexts of Asia as the location of concrete experiences of Asian women. I believe that the founding of the Asian Association of Women's Studies constitutes an act of producing and constructing a genuine praxis of solidarity based on locality.

Exchanging ideas, intervening through meetings of Asian women's studies scholars and women's movement activists is pivotal to the process of producing women subjects who are more political and aware. This implies a process whereby Asian Women are constructed as subjects who think about their own issues and problems in the location, are aware of global inter-connectedness with political sensitivity and do not fall into the trap of regional limitations. In other words, new women subjects are produced and invented through the academic praxis of Asian women's studies and the solidarity of women's movements. This also means that by inventing women subjects or Asian women as agents for change, a new horizon of feminism opens up.

Finally, the more active the solidarity and practice around various real issues in concrete locations, the more likely it is that women will become compassionate and capable subjects. Then, we will be more powerful in a political sense to capture unique problems while responding more concretely and sensitively toward the global tasks in the process.

References

Arneil, Barbara (1999), *Politics & Feminism*, Malden: Blackwell.

Asian Center for Women's Studies & Korean Women's Institute (2000), "Report: Building Women's Studies Curriculum: 8 Country-level Workshop," *Asian Journal of Women's Studies*, 6(2): 106-120.

Braidotti, Rosi (1994), *Nomadic Subjects, Embodiment and Sexual Difference in Contemporary Feminist Theory*, New York: Columbia University Press.

______ (2005), *Metamorphoses, Towards A Materialist Theory of Becoming*, Cambridge: Polity Press.

Brydon, Diana (ed.) (2001), *Postcolonialism, Critical Concepts in Literary and Cultural Studies*, Vol. I-Vol. V, London and New York: Routledge.

Buchanan, Ian and Claire Colebrook (eds.) (2000), *Deleuze and Feminist Theory*, Edinburgh: Edinburgh University Press.

Featherstone, Mike (2003), "Localism, Globalism and Cultural Identity," *Identities: Race, Class, Gender and Nationality*, Linda Martin Alcoff and Eduardo Mendieta (eds.), Malden: Blackwell: 342-359.

Foucault, Michel (1977), "Nietzsche, Genealogy, History," *Language, Counter-Mempry, and Practice: Selected Essays and Interviews*, Donald Bouchard and Sherry Simon (eds.), Ithaca: New York: Cornell University Press: 149-64.

Friedman, Susan Stanford (2001), "Locational Feminism, Gender, Cultural Geographies, and Geopolitical Literacy," *Feminist Locations, Global and*

Local, Theory and Practice, Mariannne DeKoven (ed.), New Brunswick: Rutgers University Press: 13-36.

Grosz, Elizabeth (1995), "Feminist Difference and the Problem of Essentialism," *Space, Time and Perversion*, London: Routledge: 83-57.

Hardt, Michel and Antonio Negri (2001), *Empire*, Cambridge: Harvard University Press.

Kang, Sang-jung et al. (eds.) (2007), *Asia New Century* (*Ajiia Shin Seiki) Series,* Vol. 1-8, originally published in Japanese, Tamotsu Aoki and Kang Sang-jung (eds.), Tokyo: Iwanami Shoten Publishers (2002-2003), Korean translation published, Seoul: Hanul Publishing Company Group.

Khullar, Mala (2005), "Asian Journal of Women's Studies: Ten Years and Beyond," *Asian Journal of Women's Studies*, 11(4): 7-31.

Kim, Eun-Shil (2007), "A Direction in Feminist Research in the Glocal Era: The Rise of Communities for Discussing 'Asian' Women's Studies," unpublished paper presented at the International Conference in Commemoration of the Korean Women's Institute's 30th Anniversary, November 1, at Ewha Womans University, Seoul.

Kim, Hyun Mee and Kang Sun-Mi (2001), "Achievement and Challenge of an Asian Women's Studies Project," *Asian Journal of Women's Studies*, 7(4): 106-121.

Kosugi, Yasushi et al. (eds.) (2007), *Identity: Deconstruction and Reconstruction (Jungcheseong: Haeche-wa Jaeguseong), Asia New Century (Ajiia Shin Seiki) Series*, Vol. 3, Hwang Young-Sik (trans.), Seoul: Hanul Publishing Company Group.

Lee, Sang Wha (2007), "Locational Feminism in the Age of Globalization: Ontology of Difference and Prixis of Solidaity (Giguwah Sidae-ui Hyeonjang Yeoseongjuui: Chai-ui Jonjaeron-gwa Yeondae-ui Silcheonron)," *Locational Feminism in the Age of Globalization (Giguwah Sidae-ui Hyeonjang Yeoseongjuui)*, Lee Sang Wha, Kim Eun-Shil and Huh Ra-Keum et al., Seoul: Ewha Womans University Press: 31-56.

Mahon, Michel (1992), *Foucault's Nietzschean Genealogy*, Albany: State University of New York Press.

Milner, Anthony and Deborah Johnson (2004), "Idea of Asia," http://dspace.anu.edu.au/bitstream/1885/41891/1/idea.html (November 1, 2007).

Mohanty, Chandra Talpade (2003), *Feminism without Borders, Decolonizing Theory, Practicing Solidarity*, Durham & London: Duke University Press.

Rich, Adrienne (1984), "Note towards a Politics of Location," *Blood, Bread and Poetry: Selected Prose 1979-1985*, London: Little Brown & Co.: 210-31, Reprinted in *Feminist Postcolonial Theory*, Reina Lewis and Sara Mills (eds.) (2003), Edinburgh University Press: 29-42.

Robertson, Roland (2003), "Globalization as a Problem," *Identities: Race, Class, Gender and Nationality*, Linda Martin Alcoff and Eduardo Mendieta (eds.), Malden: Blackwell Publishing: 295-310.

Sakamoto, Hiroko et al. (eds.) (2007), *History: How Asia was Made, How to Make Asia (Yeonksa: Asia Mandeulgi-wa Geu Bangsik), Asia New Century (Ajiia Shin Seiki) Series*, Vol. 2, Park Jin-Woo (trans.), Seoul: Hanul Publishing Company Group.

Spiva, Gayatri Chakravorty (1988), "Can the Subaltern Speak?," *Marxism and the Interpretation of Culture*, Cary Nelson and Larry Grossberg (eds.), Urbana: University of Illinois Press: 271-313.

Sun, Gur (2003), "What does Asia Mean?," *Conceptual Space 'Asia' (Asia-raneun Ssayu Gonggan)* Ru Pil-jun et al., Seoul: Changbi Publisher: 59-106.

Tae, Heasook (2001), *Postcolonial Feminism (Talsikminju-ui Peminijeum)*, Seoul: Yeoiyeon.

_______ (2008), *Counter-Globalization and 'Asian Feminism' (Daehang Jiguhwa-wa Asia Yeoseonjuui)*, Seoul: Ulyuk Publishing Co.

Trinh, T. Minh-ha (1989), *Women, Nature, Native, Other: Writing Postcoloniality and Feminism*, Bloomington: Indiana University Press.

Yamamuro, Shinichi (2007), "Expansion and Transformation of Conceptual Framework of the Space 'Asia' (Gonggan Asia-l Dulreossan Insik-ui Hwakjang-gwa Byeonyong)," *Space: Questioning Asia (Gonggan: Asia-l Munneunda), Asia New Century (Ajiia Shin Seiki) Series*, Vol. 1, Kang Sang-jung et al. (eds.), Lee Kang Min (trans.), Seoul: Hanul Publishing

Company Group: 21-60.

Young, Iris Marion (1990), *Justice and the Politics of Difference*, NJ: Princeton University Press.

Chapter 3

The Politics of Institutionalizing Feminist Knowledge:

Discussing "Asian" Women's Studies in South Korea[1]

KIM Eun-Shil

1. Introduction

This paper seeks to explore the epistemic interface of Korean Women's Studies with respect to the West where it had its origin and "Asia" as a newly rising context for feminist knowledge production in South Korea. With the first undergraduate level women's studies course started in 1977 in Ewha Womans University, it has been more than 30 years since women's studies has been taught in universities and feminist research carried out in Korea. In this over 30 year period, the circumstances of women's studies have been constantly changing. In this paper, I would like to address the frames of feminist research—which started out in the context of the nation/state development and the process of modernization—in today's globalization process, characterized by the evolution of transnational multilateral relations and the challenges before Women's Studies that Korean feminist scholars are trying to deal with in the glo/cal era.

1 This paper was supported by the Korea Research Foundation Grant funded by the Korean Government (MOEHRD, Basic Research Promotion Fund) (KRF-2005-005-J12501) and published in the *Asian Journal of Women's Studies*, Vol. 16 No. 3 (2010).

Women's Studies, after being introduced and received in Korea within western theoretical frameworks and those of the modernization model and an internationalist perspective centered around the UN as its standard reference, has worked on creating agendas for women's status, role and development. At the same time, it has continuously questioned what kinds of beings women should be in Korean society. This question corresponds with the dispute regarding "Is Women's Studies Korean or Western?" Called upon to function as critical discourse and a new world-view to criticize and deconstruct patriarchal traits and male-centrism in Korean society, women's studies is caught in a trap between nationalism and modernization, which sees Korean women as a subject for modernizing in Korea. This has also been tied with the question of whether Women's Studies should illuminate and construct Korean society within the world/Western-centric order of universality or justify the particularity of Korea? Such were the questions on the agenda pertaining to the universality and particularity of Korean Women's Studies since its beginning and, through the early 1990s. Subsequently, Korean intellectual communities became critical of the discourses regarding the modern/West; as globalization and the glo/cal era emerged, the perspectives of feminist scholars about the world and Korean society began to change. From 2000 onwards, as multilateral exchanges of knowledge and information have grown and many channels opened up to feminist scholars to access a variety of knowledge and information and form diverse networks of human exchange. Opportunities emerged as well for experiencing the limitations of knowledge based on western-centrism built around the nation/state order and regionalization. This provided momentum to Korean feminist scholars to criticize and reflect on feminist knowledge produced in their country and to expand its base for comparison and contemplation. Questions began to be raised in Korean women's studies such as, "How do we locate the West and form relationships with women of the world, particularly Asian women?" and "How do we become each other's reference groups?"

In this paper, I would like to touch on three points. First, I point out changes in the epistemology of women's studies in Korea, from the time it was introduced and received within the context of Korea's modernization and development. This also relates to the epistemic framework of universality and particularity of Korean Women's Studies, which subsequently entered the era of globalization. Second, I deal with the rise of "Asia" as a new category for criticizing western knowledge systems or theoretical frameworks which had been considered universal and to show instances of how the category "Asia" is being used. Third, I suggest cross-cultural comparison as a research methodology to provincialize the West and think of Asia as a new community for our discussions. The data for this paper came from my own and my colleagues' experience of building the women's studies community at Ewha Woman University and of teaching and researching women's studies over 15 years in South Korea.

2. Development of Women's Studies in Korea and its Epistemic Framework: "Universality and Particularity of Women's Studies in Korea" (1984-1994)[2]

There are many ways of explaining the development of women's studies in Korea (Cho, 2000; Kim and Lee, 2006; Chang, 2008). But I believe that the International Women's Year (1975), declared by the UN and the 1995 World Conference on Women in Beijing, provided important benchmarks for the institutionalization of women's studies in Korea. For example, a women' research institute and a women's studies course was set up in Ewha Womans University in 1977. Also, with the gender mainstreaming policy adopted by the central government in the late 1990s, the founding of a Ministry of Gender Equality, the implementation of active

2 This was the title of an academic conference held in 1994 on the 10th Anniversary of the Korean Association of Women's Studies. As the title suggests, Women's Studies in Korea started out from the framework of universality and particularity, general and case-specific, and in that sense has been largely a western-centric modern(ization) project.

measures for women's employment and promotion, legislation of various women-related laws and the advancement of feminist agendas by government organs were important factors that contributed to the status and authority that women's studies would come to have in Korean society. This historical background enables us to understand the scenario and the kinds of political possibilities and limitations before the feminist epistemic framework, which relates to US-centered international feminism and the pursuit of modernization/development of nation-state.

Women's Studies began in Korea as a multidisciplinary course undertaken through team teaching at the undergraduate level in Ewha Womans University in 1977. At the time, a strong economic modernization project was underway in Korea and an oppressive and authoritative political system was subjugating all areas of society under the economic development program. In 1982, a graduate program in women's studies was established in Ewha for the first time in the country and in 1984, the Korean Association of Women's Studies was launched. Once it entered the sphere of the university, women's studies began to contest, negotiate and combine with the knowledge and resources of existing disciplines and came to be identified as a new academic field. In the 1990s, women's studies was taught in most Korean universities as a liberal arts course. Masters programs in women's studies were set up in a number of universities and a Ph.D. program was begun in Ewha Womans University, making women's studies a new discipline and much more visible. Currently, several universities have Ph.D. programs in women's studies.

From the moment it was introduced into the university in teaching and research, women's studies was criticized as a conceptual and theoretical tool based on western experiences, made for explaining western society. Consequently, women's studies was under constant pressure to answer questions on the particularity of Korea. The underlying social ethos of the 1970s and the 1980s in Korea was characterized by a defiant nationalism, accompanied by the democratization movement against the military dictatorship. Given the pervasive sentiments of the social democratization groups, women's studies also aimed at social change and so could not shake off the burden of Korean particularity. Scholars of non-western societies who began women's studies under the influence of the UN's International Women's Year in 1975 carry this kind of burden or constraint when representing their research in their own society as well as in the West.

The launching of the Korean Association of Women's Studies and the publication of the journal, "Korean Women's Studies" in the 1980s created a space for intensive discussions on the identity of feminist knowledge produced in Korea and women's studies as a politics of knowledge, distinct from the existing knowledge system. The initial focus of women's studies in Korea was to introduce feminist perspectives begun in the West to the academic world and to expand them. Feminist knowledge in Korea was thus sought by using an interdisciplinary approach, introducing general theories on patriarchy and carrying out empirical research on women's subordination. In the 1980s, women's studies in Korea laid emphasis on introducing and spreading feminist perspectives throughout academia. In line with this, general theories of patriarchy, as well as various signification systems such as Confucianism and Buddhism, were seen to underlie patriarchy in Korean society. As more and more women scholars with feminist understanding entered the academy in the eighties, concrete and empirical feminist research in diverse fields was activated. Scholars in fields such as Philosophy, English Literature, Anthropology, Sociology, Education, Psychology, Theology, Korean Literature, Social Welfare, Economics, Home Management and Nursing embarked on research, combining their respective fields of study with women's studies and they were the ones who built the early body of women's studies scholarship in Korea. As such, the early stages of women's studies in Korea provided an opportunity to discover women in each academic field.[3]

The Graduate Department of Women's Studies in Ewha Womans Uni-

---

3 For example, Jaekyung Lee (2003) explored how the category or the variable of women was accommodated in the discipline of sociology in Korea.

versity implemented the first women's studies curriculum and established a framework for feminist knowledge in Korea. The curriculum was divided into three major fields of study: Sexuality, Labor and Family. Women's studies knowledge in Korea was partitioned and accumulated within this conceptual framework. The field of sexuality was critically problematized and made an issue on the social, political and cultural agenda by graduates of the women's studies program in Ewha. This characterized and defined a direction in the feminist movement and research in Korea in the 1990s, highlighting issues of the double sexual standard, sexual violence, military sexual slavery, sexual harassment, pornography and prostitution for the social policy agenda and achieving legislation relating to some of these concerns.

In the sphere of labor, there were persistent research efforts tackling the most urgent tasks—Equal Employment Law, protection of motherhood, equal pay for equal labor, measures for hourly labor and marginalization of female labor—as well as seeking a philosophical approach to labor and reconstructing feminist notions of work (Cho, 2001). Here, the way in which the meaning of work has been constructed in the Korean modernization process was dealt with and questions on the relationship between labor and women's citizenship were raised (Kim, 2000). In the early up to the mid-1990s women's issues in diverse areas including cultural representation, the relationship of women's studies, women's movement and women's policy began to emerge as tasks before Korean feminism.

Until the mid-90s, women were seen as victims of patriarchal control in studies on women. But soon, voices of women who were not fully incorporated within the control mechanisms of the system began to be heard. Discussions on sexual politics began growing in universities in 1995 and questions were raised on minority sexualities, women's sexual pleasure and censorship of pornography as part of the politics of sex, challenging the feminist politics of defining women as a category (Kim,1998).

Within the framework of feminism for universal ideal, feminist research in Korea addressed questions of particularity and universality of Korea through the 70s, 80s and 90s.[4] Here, particularity refers to the norms, experiences and value/meaning system that make traditional Korean society as truly "Korean" and, in particular, different from the so-called modern West; universality implied that which conforms with theory, in other words, western theory or shares in the western modern experience. Facing the criticism that women's studies in Korea was imposing and reproducing western perspectives and value systems, many feminist scholars began to question what is "Korean" and "western," and what is "traditional" and "modern." Being very aware of the politics of such criticism, many feminists thought over these and considered that the positive values of Korean society might be transformed into universal principles for all people. This was the situation of the mid-1990s that demanded so-called "Korean" theories, which was expected to explain Korean circumstances in the rationale of overcoming coloniality and western modernity.

Gaining visibility in academe and society in general did not necessarily mean that women's studies would establish an identity as a discipline or be readily accepted into the existing knowledge system. But the institutionalization of women's studies as a discipline and the creating and naming by feminist activists of concepts such as violence against women, sexual harassment, scholars achieved the effect of causing discomfort for existing disciplines and destabilizing the existing order. Nevertheless, the usefulness and acceptability of that knowledge within Korean society was to linger on, doubting the identity of women's studies in Korea. It was in this context that I posed the question in 1994 of "What is 'Korean' feminist inquiry and how should it be raised?" While doing so, I also discussed the conflicts, differences and contestations between feminism and nationalism, criticizing the nationalist framework within which fem-

4 After the establishment of Korean Association of Women's Studies in 1984, the idea of universality and particularity was the main piece of thinking; the annual conference of the Association of Korean Women's Studies from 1986 to 1988 was titled like "The Universality and Particularity of Korean Women's Studies (I), (II), (III), (IV)."

inist knowledge and questions in Korea were defined and formed. So, I requested feminist intellectuals to politicize the feminist discourse and to call in women subjects who were excluded and disembodied by the Korean nationalist discourse (Kim, 1994). Needless to say, my argument met with strong resistance from many feminists at the time, who claimed the national subject as the primary bearer of inequality and contradictions in Korea rather than women. They criticized me as an internationalist with no regard for Korea's reality and a follower of western feminist logic.

Encountering the dichotomy of us/Korean/nationalism versus feminists/western/internationalist, feminists were very keenly aware of a need for a third reference point from which to reflect upon or look at the subject position of women in relation to the nation-state. In response to this desire for a new reference community, "Asia" would soon come into focus.

3. Institutionalization of Women's Studies and the Professionalization of "Gender" in Korea (1995-2004)

In the 1980s, the only instance of women's studies existing as a department or program in Korea was in Ewha Womans University. But by the 1990s, more precisely after 1995, there were 12 Masters programs and four Ph.D. programs in women's studies across the country. Also, many universities set up interdisciplinary women's studies programs at the undergraduate level. And, there were a variety of other social institutions providing women's studies knowledge. During the period of 1995-2004, the most important issues were to define and establish the academic identity of women's studies and how to apply it to real life. That is why Theory and Policy were added to Sexuality, Family and Labor as new areas in women's studies curriculum in Ewha. The main theoretical and epistemological question in this period was how to differentiate Korean women's studies from women's studies in the West, and how to integrate women's studies with the government's gender mainstreaming policy and the women's movement to resolve women's problems in reality.

After the World Conference on Women in Beijing in 1995, the Korean government began to include women's issues in its agenda, work these into the budget and employ personnel to implement them, all under the banner of gender mainstreaming. Accordingly, the central government, local governments and many related organizations began to recruit specialists in women's studies or women related fields. At the same time, a series of government commissioned research projects on women's policy started to appear. Such gender mainstreaming undertaken by the government led not only to an increase in women's studies programs, but also the adoption of Women's Policy as a subject of major in the curriculum (Kim, 2008). In addition, the Kim Daejung government (1998-2003) undertook "gender mainstreaming" as an important item on the agenda of its regime and considered the development of women's status as an indicator of social development. The creation of a social space accommodating graduates from women's studies through the "gender mainstreaming policy" was the direct impetus for universities to set up more programs in the field. Ironically, establishing these was considered "good business." This also created a contest among existing disciplinary fields such as social welfare, law, administration and psychological counseling, and women's studies.

It was during this period that faculty evaluations and promotional decisions came to be based on the amount of research results and procured research funds, while the evaluation of academic journals was conducted according to the classification of disciplines by the Korea Research Foundation. When the Korean Association of Women's Studies registered women's studies as an independent discipline under the classification of the Korea Research Foundation in 1999, it was officially placed within the category of academic disciplines, finally attaining institutionalization.

Women's studies met with positive response in the Korean universities, starting from the 1990s into the 2000s, both at popular and ideological levels. But, faced with the financial crisis, or the so-called "IMF crisis" in the late 1990s and due to difficulties in finding employment, women became more conscious of the job market and turned away from the politics for a new society, choosing fields of study geared toward employment and acquiring professional knowledge as the surest ways to become independent individuals in the neo-liberal global market. It is at this point that "Asia" made its appearance as a new reference or point of view as opposed to the West. This had two aspects: one was the product of pride in the cultural particularity of Asian values derived from the explanation of the unique characteristics of East Asian capitalist development. This was a sort of counter-discourse to western modernity, but taking the form of capitalist power gathering, based on local solidarity and it also signifies the return of fathers outdone by the West (Kim, 2001).[5]

The other aspect was the rise of Asia as a new solidarity of groups which have never been representatives of nation-states. Asia functioned as a network of solidarity and mutual referencing for victims of violence by the state during the Cold War, groups fighting for the issue of military sexual slavery where governments avoided involvement and women's studies scholars carrying out exchange projects (Kim, 2005).

Thus, women's studies, which had swayed back and forth between the universality and particularity of "Korean" women's studies discovered "Asia" as a new international environment and reference group. The exchange and joint development of women's studies curriculum by feminist scholars from eight Asian countries, led by the Asian Center for Women's Studies in Ewha since 1997 had culminated in the publication of country textbooks on women's studies in 2005. This may be considered as one beginning for interactions and communications between feminisms in the Asian regions, sharing the "particularities" of Asian states, yet distinct

5 The rise of "Asia" discourse in the 1990s was closely related to the growth of Asian Capitalist development especially in East Asia, including Hong Kong, Singapore, Taiwan, and South Korea. During this period, the Korean film industry began to produce Korean blockbuster films in which foreign women such as migrant women from other Asian countries and the Korean diaspora women began to appear. Here in cinematic representation the subject position of the Korean man was constructed as the self in relation to the foreign woman as the other. This was a time in the late 1990s that the Korean man was portrayed as father, brother or lover in Korean-style blockbuster films.

from the West/universal. The 9th International Interdisciplinary Congress on Women held in 2005 in Korea was largely based on this experience, and intended to open up a space to subvert the framework of universality and particularity.

4. Problematizing Women's Studies in Korea (2005-present)

Following the IMF crisis and overcoming it, Korean society has radically changed into a neo-liberal market regime in which economic rationality comprises the frame for measuring the value of life. Along with neo-liberal policies, the polarization of the rich and the poor was exacerbated. In 2005-2006, there has been a preposterous increase in the national real estate prices, widening the gap between home-owners and tenants. Many feminist activists and lecturers, so-called "young feminists," who had created the young feminists' group in Korea since the mid-1990s have been attempting to get started on their independent lives. Many of them are tenants, and a lot of them are employed in irregular jobs. In 2006, they said, "the definition and politics of feminisms that they have advocated for years to be minor and powerless in this enormous market capitalism and the competitive world of speed and profit."[6]

Among young college women who think that the devil in "The Devil Wears Prada" is more attractive and beautiful than young Emily, feminism seems to have lost its place. Women students in their 20s say, "We get strength from the shopping mall, by consuming. We are redeemed through a brunch, like in 'Sex and the City,' and shopping on the Internet."[7]

In these social circumstances, feminist knowledge seems to be thought to be dragging young women down to the level of women who are worse off, rather than empowering them. In contrast, in the year of 2005, many

6 This story is from feminist cultural activists working in the International Women's Film Festival in Seoul in 2006.

7 This data came from interviews with several women in their 20s in 1997.

Korean feminists experienced a transnational feminist gathering and participated in the multi-centered and multicultural feminist discursive community by meeting non-Western feminists and listening to non-western voices of feminist politics. In June of 2005, the Women's Worlds (the 9th International Interdisciplinary Congress on Women) was held in Seoul, Korea and 2,271 feminist scholars, activists and policy makers came from 75 countries. Of these, 1,061 were Korean participants who had the experience of articulating their own national feminist causes on international stage (Final report of ww05, 2006). From this event, Korean feminists and activists learnt to be confident in networking, especially with Asian women and being involved in many transnational settings.[8]

In 2006-2007, there were several meetings held to discuss the dilemma and limits of feminist knowledge production and feminist politics organized by the Korean Association of Women's Studies and Korean Social Forum etc.[9] I made several points related to the boundary of knowledge production and practices: (a) the contestation of institutionalization of women's studies in universities and "gender" mainstreaming in government; (b) need to include lesbians, women with disabilities and transgenders in women's studies and the lack of epistemology, experience and the perspective of Korean women's studies to deal with differences; (c) colonization of Korean women's studies by western women's studies and postcolonial feminist or transnational feminist epistemology as an alternative.

---

8 Many of these stories are from personal communications.

9 In March 2006, at the Korean Social Forum, feminist activists invited from several progressive organizations debated about the crisis of Korean women's movements and diagnosed that the problems of movements derived from a lack of critical mind and autonomy in women NGOs, despite their successful effort for the legislation and reform of laws. In 2006 and 2007, Kyunghee Kim and Yoon Jungsuk, Juhyun Jo and Eun-Shil Kim raised concerns about the impasses before women's movement and feminist inquiries in Korea.

5. Institutionalization of Feminist Knowledge and the Contestation of Feminist Politics and the Professionalization of "Gender"

The most important context for the contestation of feminist politics and the professionalization of "gender" is the neo-liberal market in which knowledge is becoming a capital and the government sponsored gender mainstreaming policies through which the numerous government projects and positions require gender specialists. From this stems the crisis of women's studies education, namely that the feminist approach and women's studies knowledge as a perspective is valuable, but concrete and professional knowledge cannot be provided by education in feminist studies. This kind of criticism comes mainly from government officials with single discipline backgrounds or scholars of single disciplines. Further, tensions arise among women's movement and activist groups when they see that Korean society pays little attention to their work and experience, while giving much more value to a paper presented by a women's studies scholar. In Korean society, discussions and criticisms of women's studies and feminist knowledge do not take place only in universities and academic conferences; numerous women's groups, women's social education institutions, local women's organizations as well as government organs and grass-roots groups are in need of the knowledge of women's studies or feminist knowledge, and many are in fact running their own women's studies workshop or lecture programs. The focus of their programs is on what feminist perspective and knowledge activists should have and these programs are sometimes run jointly with women's studies courses in a university such as the Feminist Practice Program of Sengkonghue University. In society, there is a premise that women's studies or feminist knowledge is needed and should be provided wherever women are, in order for them to understand their realities and experiences. The role of a feminist intellectual is in especially high demand when the government adopts progressive policies on women.

Public officials in charge of women's affairs and women activists often experience confusion regarding the identity of women's studies, the characteristics of feminist knowledge, and the question of professionalism regarding "gender." They are asking who are more professional, women's studies' graduates or gender specialized scholars within sociology or social welfare etc. At the institutional level, women's studies has an identity in the universities, but in its relationship with other academic disciplines, that institutionalization is not stable at all. It seems that the key point here, as of now, is not whether women's studies is situated in the university system but rather what its relationship is with the Ministry of Gender Equality and Family, which is in charge of the government's gender mainstreaming policy and budget. Accordingly, the curriculum and knowledge production of women's studies also becomes more closely related with policy. The women's studies department in Ewha has been institutionalized as a single discipline within the university, but looking closely at the content of the courses, it becomes obvious that the institutionalization is merely at the structural level and is always shifting.

It is said that the crisis there is caused by radical individualism brought on by neo-liberalism and the consequent view of understanding discrimination in individual terms rather than social ones. There was also a critique of the politics of identity based on the victim mentality, a change in college culture due to globalization (accountability becoming an important discourse in college administration and less marketable elements being abandoned), and the disappearance of the progressive social atmosphere of the 60s and 70s in which women's studies was born.[10]

Strategies suggested to overcome this state of affairs were such as name changing from women's studies to gender studies, combining and restructuring the program and more emphasis on theory building in order

---

10 Many feminists in Korea including Cho Haejeong and Chang Pilwha have expressed their concern on the relationship between younger generation's attitude toward progressive politics, including women's studies and neoliberal social environments. Many points were mentioned in the dialogue printed between H. Jeong and H. Chung (Jeong and Chung, 2006).

to survive in the university. Asia, in contrast, is an entirely different case and attempts are being made for institutionalization again (Wang, 2005; Du, 2005; Hsieh and Chang, 2005; Zhang, 2005).

6. The Question of Differences among Women

The question of differences among women has been mentioned almost didactically in feminist discussions in 2000s. But, in most gender politics based on the difference between men and women for gender equality, women as a group are emphasized and all differences among women are eliminated. In this sense, the appearance of the Ministry of Gender Equality in 2001 (later Ministry of Gender Equality and Family, as of 2005) in Korea has been beneficial to women but at the same time, it has overridden any politics or principle to deal with differences among women (Kim and Yun, 2006; Jeong and Chung, 2006; Cho, 2006).

Differences in sexual identities, physical disabilities and conditions of employment have been some of the concerns for minority resistance, rejecting the monolithic category of women. But with the appearance of government organizations with public funding such as the Ministry of Gender Equality, much of the resistance has been institutionalized and many minority groups are becoming NGOs. And NGOs are turning into something in the way of interest groups for gaining public social funds (Kim, 2008).

7. Post or De-Coloniality of Knowledge: Politicization of "Asia" Category in Women's Studies in Korea

Since the modernization project of the 60s, Koreans have embodied a perspective of modernization vis-à-vis the world, and a perspective of nationalism vis-à-vis us/themselves. As such, they have pursued a strictly nationalist position in areas such as Korean History and Korean Literature but in the Social Sciences and Natural Sciences, they have taken a western-centric view, constructed the bodies of knowledge that take the subject position to be the West. In Korea, not only in Women's Studies but in all modern knowledge originating from the West, the adjective "western" is largely omitted. What meanings lie beneath the relationship between Women's Studies and Korean Women's Studies? The underlying implication is that women's studies in the West deals with general/universal/theoretical things, while Korean Women's Studies is bound to the individual state of Korea. Is Korean Women's Studies then a counter discourse or alternative discourse to Western Women's Studies? If the West is provincialized and a counter discourse to the West is to be created, what is the political category of that counter discourse? Nation-state, East Asia, or Asia? Or the entire world except the West?

Feminist knowledge in Korea, which had been discussed and produced in terms of western/universality and Korean/particularity, under globalization has come face to face with questions such as "What is Korean and what is Western?" "What is tradition and what is modern?" "What is particular and what is universal?" The political implications of the terms, universality and particularity, are being probed and questions are being raised on whether what are deemed as positive values of Korean society are actually equitable and universal principles for everyone. The breakdown of the world's cold war structure, the globally unifying market capitalism, and the pre-modern, post-modern, postcolonial and post-constructionist discourses have begun to place problematizations of Korean women and interpretations regarding their experiences that were formerly restricted to the space of the nation-state, into a transnational space. If the early focus of feminist research in Korea was on inquiring into the particularity and universality of "Korean" Women's Studies, in the mid- 1990s, the scope of interdisciplinary research and the West as the basis for the particularity of Korean Women's Studies began to be problematized. This led to the rediscovery of a region as a reference and communicative space for communicating and interpreting Korean experiences; that is, "Asia." This is certainly not a natural process. There is a political and economic background to this, which lends itself to many debates (Chung et al., 1995, 2000; H. M. Kim and Kang, 2001).

In the mid-1990s, Ewha Womans University's plans to establish the Asian Center for Women's Studies and publish the Asian Journal of Women's Studies met with a considerable amount of resistance. Questions on Asia as a region, such as "Why Asia instead of World or International?" were raised. Asia implied a closed and restricted region and a culturally heterogeneous quality. Therefore, it was assumed that the content of an Asian institution would be too empirical and limited. Even though Korea was part of Asia, Koreans sought to be different from the rest of Asia, linked instead with the West/ modern. Until the 90s, Asia was understood as the Third World, an unstable region with a complicated political culture or a poor and underdeveloped economy. Asia was never considered a partner in cultural exchange. A similar view of Asia was to be found in many other countries in Asia as well (Yoichi, 2002; John, 2005; Sun, 2003). Even the Korean professors who had started women's studies in Asia didn't have identities as Asians. If they did, it was "Asian," called in and subjectified through its relationship with the West, and their interactions with other Asians were mostly mediated by the West in various ways. For Asians to know each other, one only needed to read books in English and one could also communicate with them in English. What could be found out through such communication was little more than a confirmation of existing knowledge. Even though we were close geographically, Asians were culturally and imaginarily further apart, compared with westerners. Even in direct contact, there were too many historical, social and cultural interventions of the West in between them.[11]

11 There were so many formal and informal meetings talking and discussing about our subject positioning of "Asian" in terms of white westerners, colored westerners, Japanese, Chinese, other South Asians etc. I really enjoyed talking about the dislocation of identity and subject positioning with friends and colleagues, Chang Pilwha, Lee Sang Wha, Hyunmee Kim, Mala

In the mid-1990s, however, with the development of Asia's local economies, there was the emergence of multi-culturalism throughout the academic and political spheres (Choi, Kim, Chung, Yu, 2004), and the issue of military sexual slavery across many Asian countries; feminists began to talk about an Asian feminism or Asian feminist solidarity beyond the boundaries of the nation-state (Cho, 1996; Chang, 2008; Yang, 2006; Kang, 2006). This was when the issues of the nation-state and women, unequal gender relations in respective societies and international solidarity all came pouring out, at the same time.

In this situation, women's studies in Ewha and elsewhere felt the need to visualize the experiences of Asian women and turn them into knowledge, challenge the frame of "western feminisms" and empower alternative feminisms. Professors in the Ewha women's studies community started to discuss ways of representing those Asian women who had been regarded as victims and markers of tradition as subjects, in what could be a counter discourse to the Western feminism. The Asian Journal of Women's Studies was launched in 1995 as a medium for creating knowledge out of Asian women's experiences (Khullar, 2005). They also embarked upon the Asian women's studies project for promoting the solidarity of Asian feminist scholars. This project started out as a network of 8 countries, Korea, Japan, China, Taiwan, Thailand, Indonesia, Philippines and India, for women's studies curriculum development and had a conference on "Asian women's studies curriculum development and practice" was held in October 2000 (Kim and Kang, 2001). At the same time the project for the publication of women's studies text books for eight countries was launched and 8 textbooks came out in 2005. They have also created a space for the exchange of graduate students as well as senior scholars through these networks.

Asia came to be viewed as a context in which Korean women's expe-

---

Khullar, and Youngok Kim, Suwanna Satha-Anand, Tani Barlow, Ruri Ito, Haeung Yi, Elain Kim and so many other friends.

riences can be interpreted and a new space for solidarity and change be created. Academic conferences on East Asian women's experiences began to be held in growing numbers in different places and diverse efforts were made for solidarity among Asian feminist scholars after the Korea Research Foundation started to support scholarly exchange programs. The Women's Studies in Asia project, organized by the Asian Center for Women's Studies in Ewha and carried out by feminist scholars from 8 Asian countries, is an outstanding example of such an effort. The 2005 International Interdisciplinary Congress on Women held in Korea was prepared in the midst of this development and can be seen as the beginning of a new space for the framework of universality and particularity to be newly organized and subverted from the position of Korean Women's Studies.

8. Politicization of "Asia" Category within Korean Women's Studies

The emergence of "Asia" in academic discourses is a recent phenomenon in Korea. In the modern academic system which aspires to the universal, the local has always been used to refer to a particularity. And the term Asia has mainly been used within a political discourse or signified as non-western and a not yet sufficiently modernized local. Since the 1990s under the globalization policy of Korea, with the contracting of the Korea-Japan Cultural Exchange Agreement and China's reform and opening that has been underway, there has been a boost in Korea-Japan and Korea-China exchanges and the academic interaction and joint research of scholars have been animated as well. Prior to these, exchange with Japan had been difficult due to the colonization problem and exchange with China due to Korea's conflict with socialism. In post-liberation Korea, exchange with the world had meant exchange with the US or the liberal powers surrounding the US, and this comprised a one-sided relationship.

Research exchange accelerated in the 2000s, when resources for academic conferences and overseas visiting research began to be provided.[12] Initially, such academic conferences were called international conferences, but more and more conferences started naming themselves Asian Conference or East Asian Conference, signaling the emergence of the "Asia" category. Feminist scholars have also been continuously carrying out research exchanges, using the signifier of "Asia." But, other than in conferences organized by Inter-Asia Cultural Studies and held by Women's Studies centers in Ewha, "Asia" or "East Asia" in Korea are mostly considered a given and the category of Asia is not discussed as problematic (Kim, 2005). Since the establishment of the Asian Center for Women's Studies in Ewha in 1995 and the publication of the Asian Journal of Women's Studies, Asia has always been an object of questioning. Questions such as "What does Women's Studies in Asia mean?" or "Is there such a thing as Asian Women's Studies?" have stayed with them persistently. Such questions are similar to those about western feminism always being a subject of criticism in Asian regions, such as "What does 'western feminism' mean and what is 'western'?" or "Is there such a thing as western feminism?" Here, I will describe several ways in which Women's Studies and Asia are being combined and understood and problematize them.

First, women's studies in Asia means the accumulation or synthesis of women's studies in different Asian countries. Women's studies in each Asian country can be called Women's Studies in Asia or Asian Women's Studies since the country belongs to Asia. Thus, the word "Asia" is understood to mean a specific region and it is combined with women's studies being carried out in that region. It is along those lines that women's studies being carried out in Korea is called Korean Women's Studies. But problems arise when we ask, is all "feminism" taking place in Asia "Asian feminism" and all "feminisms" taking place in Korea "Korean feminism?"

12 Many international academic exchanges and foreign research projects are funded by the Korea Research Foundation.

In that case, how are Asia and Korea connected? Are there women's studies practices in Asian regions that are not Asian? Or women's studies practices in Korea that are not Korean? Not all women's studies work taking place in Asia is called Asian Women's Studies and the same goes for Korean Women's Studies. Then, is this related to the region or the local identity of the individual researcher? Neutral as they may seem, such categorizations involve a strong politics of inclusion and exclusion; what is at play here relates to who does the defining and in what context.

Second, there is a commonly perceived idea that the common experience of colonization different from that of the West or the experience of exclusion from the modern world history building as the non-West. But this kind of structural understanding is easily criticized on a closer look at the specific cases. That is, Japan's experience of colonization by the West, Korea's experience of colonization by Japan, China's experience and Vietnam's experience can hardly be tied into one as "Asian." This leads to the question, does exclusion from the western/modern experience necessarily construct an Asian experience?

Third, the term "Asia" can also be used as a discursive practice. Here, the use of the word "Asia" acquires a political performativity, which creates a difference from existing women's studies with its embedded values of "general," "universal" and "western." Thus, using expressions such as "Women's Studies in Asia" can create the political effect of problematizing Asia and Women's Studies. "Women's Studies in Asia" was adopted by the Asian Center for Women's Studies in Ewha first. However, gradually scholars of the institute began to use the title "Asian women's studies," with the aim of critically questioning "western/universal" women's studies and "national" women's studies, constructed within the framework of the nation-state.

Fourth, there is Inter-Asian Women's Studies where "Asia" has cross-border networks. Inter-Asian Women's Studies indicates research practice based on the studies of women in different countries, sharing and appropriating them to build up new kinds of networks in Asia. I think in most cases, the use of the word "Asia" by scholars belongs to one or two of the above cases. But in Asia, "Asia" is not a natural concept but carries historical and political meanings. Nevertheless, I don't think there are many feminist scholars in Korea who take Asian Women's Studies to be an effective alternative or vision for the future.[13] The question remains: what kinds of temporality and spatiality are being drawn upon as the epistemic context of women's studies by Korean feminist scholars in this globalizing world?

9. Conclusion: Lessons from Women's Studies in Korea

There are differences at multiple levels even among people involved in the Asian Center for Women's Studies in Ewha, in their use of the signification of "Asian Women's Studies," which in its broadest sense indicates a new tendency to study Asia and women or women's intellectual discursive community in Asia (Lee, 2008). What is important is that a social, political and cultural environment, in which signifiers such as Asia, women and gender are received as meaningful, has emerged in Korea. What is needed now is to explore in what contexts these signifiers are being received, who uses these signifiers and what kind of space the semantic field comprises in which meanings are created?

Of the multiple layers in the emergence of the discourse of Asia, the most important one is that the globalization discourse, still based on the nation-state development model, has mobilized Asia as a partner in transnational corporate capital and business and a market for more productivity and profit. At the same time, or prior to it in fact, intellectuals were searching for a new reference for constructing themselves, encouraged by the critical arguments regarding the West/modern brought in from the outside

13 Sang Wha Lee (2008) explored what "the Asian" means and can mean in doing women's studies by exploring the experience of networking of feminist scholarship in Eight Asian countries mediated through the Asian Center for Women's Studies.

after the end of the Cold War. In this process, there were some groups who discovered Asia as their reference group. The feminists who founded the Asian Center for Women's Studies in Ewha in 1995 were one such group. After the mid-1990s, the joint activities of NGOs in Asia for the restructuring of the economy, civil society and global society, as well as civil solidarity activities arose. Politically, Asia arose as an important unit of local defense with multiple points for alliance underway, regulating various tensions around the the US, China and North Korea after the Cold War. In these relations, women have been represented as an effective medium to establish the topography of a new Asia, as migrant workers, NGO activists and political refugees, and they are continuing to mediate new regionalizations (Barlow, 2007).

I want to suggest that as feminist scholars of Asian countries, we should discuss how we should construct questions about women who are being represented in such restructuring of new regions and the re-regionalization of Asia and also how we should carry out the role of creating a new space in the process of restructuring Asia. In order to do this, efforts need to be made to transform ways of inquiring about women, based on the nation-state established in the modern order. Recently, in Korea there have been research projects on migrant women from Asia or women in Asia as part of local research. But there is a great risk that without any critical reflection on the epistemology of the nation-state to frame the problematic of such research, women will be treated as signifiers of political and economic inequality between state boundaries. In this way, the women's issue in Korea will be avoided and, instead, the whole issue will be reduced to the problem of "Asian" women who are in worse circumstances than Korean women. For research with mutual reference to grow, more joint projects across state boundaries need to be carried out and a new comparative methodology must be created.

References

Barlow, Tani (2007), "Asian Women in Reregionalization," *Postions*, 15(2): 285-318.

Chakrabarty, Dipesh (2007), *Provincializing Europe*, Princeton and Oxford: Princeton University Press.

Chang, Pilwha (2008), "Feminist Consciousness and Women's Education: The Case of Women's Studies, Ewha Womans University," *Asian Journal of Women's Studies*, 14(2): 7-29.

Cho, Haejeong (1997), "Feminist Intervention in the Rise of 'Asian' Discourse," *Asian Journal of Women's Studies*, 3(3): 127-156.

Cho, Juhyun (2000), "The Direction and the Structure of Producing Knowledge in Korean Women's Studies (Hankuk Yeosunghak eu Zisik Sangsan eu Gucho wa Banghyang)," *Korean Women's Studies*, 16(2): 139-179.

______ (2006), "Crisis of Gender Politics (Gender Chungchi eu Weegi)," *Women's Studies Review*, 23(2): 3-37.

Cho, Soonkyung (2001), *Labor and Feminism (Nodong kwa Feminism)*, Seoul: Ewha Womans University Press.

Choi, Huyp, Kim Seungkuk, Chung Keunsik and Yu Myungki (eds.) (2004), *Minority in Korea: Past and Future (Hankuk Sosooja eu Siltae wa Jeonmang)*, Seoul: Hanul Publishing Company.

Chung, Moonkil, Choi Wonsik, Paik Youngseo and Chun Hyungjun (eds.) (1995), *East Asia, Problems and Perspectives (Dongasia, Munje wa Sikak)*, Seoul: Munhak kwa Jichung Sa.

______(eds.) (2000), *East Asia as a Discovery (Balkyun euroseoeu Dongasia)*, Seoul: Munhak kwa Jichung Sa.

Du, Fangquin (2005), "Developing Women's Studies at Universities in China: Research, Curriculum and Institution," *Asian Journal of Women's Studies*, 11(4): 35-71.

Final report of ww05 (2006), http://www.ww05.org/english3/pdf/WW05_ Report_Eng.pdf

Hsieh, Hsiao-chin and Chang, Chuech (2005), "The Development of the Women's Movement and Women's/Gender Studies in Taiwan," *Gender, Culture and Society: Women's Studies in Taiwan*, Wei-hung Lin and Hsiao-Chin Hseieh (eds.), Seoul: Asian Center for Women's Studies, Ewha Womans University: 21-79.

Jeong, Heejin and Chung Hyunbak (2006), "Dialogue: Putting the Question on the Center of Women's Movement (Daedam: Yeosung Undong eu Chungsim eso Muleumpyoul Makida)," *Changjak kwa Bipyung*, Summer, Seoul: Changbi Publisher: 231-257.

John, Mary (2005), "Women's Studies in India and the Question of Asia: Some Reflections," *Asian Journal of Women's Studies*, 11(2): 41-66.

Kang, Garam (2006), "Possibilities of Transnational Solidarity Weighted through the Women's International War Tribunal 2000: Focusing on the 'Comfort Women' Issue in Korea and Japan," Unpublished MA thesis in the Department of Women's Studies, Ewha Womans University.

Khullar, Mala (2005), "Asian Journal of Women's Studies: Ten Years and Beyond," *Asian Journal of Women's Studies*, 11(4): 7-34.

Kim, Eun-Shil (1994), "The Discourse of Nationalism and Women (Minjok Damron kwa Yeosung)," *Korean Women's Studies*, 10: 18-52.

______ (1998), "Popular Culture and the Representation of Women as Sexual Subjects (Daejung Munwha wa Sungjekjuche roseoi Yeosung eu Jaehyun)," *Korean Women's Studies*, 14(1): 41-77.

______ (2005), "How the Category of Asia is Possible to be a Referential Community for Reciprocal Recognitions," in the Proceeding for the World Forum of Life Culture, Sept. 2-5, Koyang-shi, Kyunggo-do, South Korea.

______ (2008), "Korean Women's Policies and Feminist Implications of Gender Mainstreaming Strategies," presented at the International Conference on A New Global Trend on Gender Mainstreaming and Its Implications for Women's Policies in Korea, held at Korean Women's Development Institute, Seoul, April 24-25.

Kim, Hyun Mee (2000), "Korean Modernity and Women's Right to Work (Hankuk eu Keundaesung kwa Yeosung eu Nodongkeun)," *Korean Women's Studies*, 16(1): 37-64.

Kim, Hyun Mee and Kang Sun-Mi (2001), "(Report) Achievement and Challenges of an Asian Women's Studies Project," *Asian Journal of Women's Studies*, 7(4): 61-108.

Kim, Kyunghee and Yoon Jungsuk (2006), "Differences and Diversity in Women's Movement (Yeosung Undong eu Chai wa Dayangsung)," Presented in the Forum of Korean Women's Studies at Jungang University, Seoul.

Kim, Seung-Kyung and Na Young Lee (2006), "Women's Studies as Interdisciplinary Discipline: Identity and Institutionalization of Women's Studies in Korea," *Korean Women's Studies*, 22(1): 35-77.

Kim, Soyoung (2001), "Disappearing South Korean Women (Sarajieun Namhan Yeosungdeul)," *Korean Style Blockbuster-Atlantis or America*, Kim Soyoung (ed.), Seoul: Hyunsilmunwha Yungu: 29-31.

Lee, Jaekyung (2003), "The Acceptance and the Influence of Feminism in the Field of Sociology in Korea," *Women's Studies Review*, 16: 31-48.

Lee, Sang Wha (2008), "Conceptualizing the 'Asian' and Asian Women's Studies," *Asian Journal of Women's Studies*, 14(4).

Naoki, Sakai (2001), "Dislocation of the West and the Status of the Humanities," *Traces*, Seoul: Munwha Kwahak (Korean Version of Multiligual Journal Traces).

Sun, Ge (2003), *Asia as a Space of Thought* (in Korean), Seoul: Changjak kwa Bipyong.

Wang, Zheng (2005), "Research on Women in Contemporary China, Chaper 5," *Mapping the Social, Economic and Policy Changes in Chinese Women's Lives*, Du Fangqin and Zheng Xinrong (eds.), *Women's Studies in Asian Series*: China, Seoul: Ewha Womans University Press: 115-17.

Yang, Hyunah (2006), "Lasting Postcolonial Trauma in Testimony of Korean 'Comfort Women' Survivors," *Korean Women's Studies*, 22(3): 133-167.

Yoichi, Komori (2002), *Postcolonial*, Seoul: Samin (translated version into Korean).

Zhang, Liming (2010), "Reflection on the Three Waves of Women's Studies in China and Globalization," *Asian Journal of Women's Studies*, 16(2).

Chapter 4

Feminisms in Japan and Transnational Activism with Asian Sisters since 1970

HARA Hiroko

1. Introduction

Since the early 1950s women activists in Japan had been active toward the goal of improving the status of Japanese women to the level of women in Europe and the United States, at least until 1975.[1] The UN First World Conference on Women was convened in Mexico City from June to July 1975 to coincide with the 1975 International Women's Year. Women organized a parallel NGO Forum, called the 'International Women's Year Tribune,' which attracted about 4,000 participants from worldwide.[2] Of those, about 200 women from Japan participated, including Yayori Matsui. Matsui and others joined discussions as free individuals unaffiliated to the Japanese government's delegation and through this experience realized that, in sharp contrast to women in developed countries, women in

1 This paper is a revised and extended version of my presentation on 6 January 2012 at the International Forum: Asian Women's Studies 2011 "Asian Feminisms and Transnational Activism" organized by the Asian Center for Women's Studies (ACWS), held at Ewha Womans University.

2 http://www.un.org/en/development/devagenda/gender.shtml

developing countries were more concerned with eradication of hunger and poverty, having struggled with hunger and poverty and shouldered a long history of colonial rule. After returning to Japan, Matsui and others explored the ways to build solidarity with Asian women and launched their activities in this direction.In this paper, I will take up two women pioneers, Yayori Matsui and Mitchiko Nakamura, and describe their achievements, to examine if WE women at the very start of 2012 can learn from their dedications and adopt their good practices. I will also provide you with an overview of women's/gender studies in Japan.

2. Yayori Matsui[3] (1934-2002) and Asian Women's Association (AWA)/Asia-Japan Women's Resource Center (AJWRC)

In the 1950s, Matsui spent a year in the United States as an exchange student and then went to France for further study. In both countries, she experienced racial discrimination and on the journey home, she was shocked at the contrast between the poverty of Asia resulting from colonization by Western countries and Japan's invasion during the World War II.

In 1961, Matsui began her career as a first women reporter for the *Asahi Shimbun* (Japan's major newspaper), as she respected Agnes Smedley, an American women journalist known for her chronicling of Chinese people's struggle. In the face of discrimination against women in corporate society, Matsui covered public health and environmental problems rampant during the period of Japan's high economic growth, such as Thalidomide birth defects and Minamata disease caused by mercury poisoning and later on Japanese companies exporting environmental pollution to other parts of Asia.

In the 1970s, after encountering the Women's Liberation movement

3 This part is based on http://ajwrc.org/jp/modules/pico/index.php?content_id=7 (in Japanese). See also http://www.ajwrc.org/eng/modules/picol/index.php?content_id=3, and Matsui (1999).

in the United States, she consolidated her position as a journalist able to highlight the perspectives of Asia and women. In 1973, she participated in forming a women's group opposing prostitution tours to Korea and in 1977 organized Asian Women's Association (AWA), the predecessor of Asia-Japan Women's Resource Center (AJWRC). Thereafter, she actively tackled a series of women's issues, such as support for democratization movements in Asia, tourist development, human trafficking, and Japanese-Filipino children of mixed parentage.

From 1981 to 1985, she reported on 18 countries in Asia as a correspondent at Singapore and back to Japan she became an editorial member of the city news section at Asahi Shimbun, where she vigorously worked on human rights, environment, development, and the North-South problem in Asia.

After her retirement in 1994, she founded the AJWRC in 1995 to get fully involved in NGO activities, as witnessed by her success in organizing a number of international conferences, such as the First East Asian Women's Forum in Kanagawa and Tokyo in 1994, an international conference on Japan's ODA and Asian women in Tokyo in 1995, the *International Conference on Violence against Women in War* and Armed Conflicts in Tokyo in 1997, and the *Women's International War Crimes Tribunal* on Japan's Military Sexual Slavery in Tokyo in 2000, which gathered considerable attention in and outside Japan.

The main functions of the AJWRC are: information sharing and networking; education and training; and advocacy and campaign.[4] The following episode demonstrates how Matsui applied her mind to 'information sharing and networking.' After the 4th World Conference on Women in Beijing in 1995, Matsui pointed out lack of concern: "Because the Japanese media gave only scanty coverage on the Beijing Conference, most of the Japanese public were left unaware of the issue of gender (socially determined differences between men and women), one of the challenges

4 http://www.ajwrc.org/eng/modules/pico1/index.php?content_id=1

for humanity in the 21st century along with the North-South problem and environmental problems, not to mention the historical significance of discussing gender in Beijing (AJWRC, 1997: 5).

In 2002, she took her work to her bed because of liver cancer and continued to speak and write about her hopes for the future until her decease on 27 December 2002. In accordance with Matsui's wishes, her friends and supporters founded Women's Fund for Peace and Human Rights[5] and Women's Active Museum on War and Peace (wam).[6] Even after 10 years after her death, she continues to give courage and inspiration to many women activists in Japan and elsewhere; the participants in the Asia-Pacific NGO Forum on Beijing+15 in Manila in 2009 offered a silent prayer to Yayori.

3. Mitchiko Nakamura (1919-)

Another pioneering Japanese feminist who has made significant contributions to solidarity with Asian women is Mitchiko Nakamura, as illustrated by her life history.

In 1949, she joined the Japanese Association of University Women[7] and while in a teaching position, she participated in a number of international activities (Table 4.1). Upon joining the Pan Pacific and Southeast Asia Women's Association (PPSEAWA)[8] in 1984, she initiated a movement for women's empowerment in cooperation with other women in Asia. In 1993, together with Matsui and other Japanese feminists, Nakamura participated in the Asian and Pacific Symposium of Non-Governmental Organizations on Women in Development held in Manila in

5 http://www.wfphr.org/ (in Japanese only)
6 http://www.wam-peace.org/english/index.php (in English)
7 http://www.jauw.org/english/e_index.html
8 http://www.ppseawa.org

1993.[9] This regional conference was convened by ESCAP and the National Commission on the Role of Filipino Women in coordination with APWG (Asia Pacific NGO Working Group). In 1994, she took part in the pre-Beijing Conference as a member of NGO at the ESCAP Ministerial Conference in Jakarta, strengthening solidarity with women in Asia and the Pacific. Upon the foundation of the Asia Pacific Women's Watch (APWW) in 1999 (first chair, Patricia B. Licuanan), she became a member of its Steering Committee representing Japan Women's Watch (JAWW). Since 2001, she has been active as an APWW's honorary member, playing an active key role in exchanging information and views via e-mail and maintaining women's networking.

Table 4.1 Mitchiko Nakamura (1919–): Chronology

1949	Joined the Japanese Association of University Women (JAUW)
1954–84	Faculty member of Seijo University Junior College in Tokyo
1979–80	NGO representative on the Japanese delegation[1] at the 34th and 35th sessions of the UN General Assembly. (She was present in the plenary session on December 18, 1979, when the Convention on the Elimination of All Forms of Discrimination against Women was adopted.)
1983–89	Committee member of the International Federation of University Women (IFUW)
1984–92	Professor at Chofu Gakuen Women's Junior College[2] (1987–1992 President)
1984–2005	Member of the Pan Pacific and Southeast Asia Women's Association (PPSEAWA) (1984–1994 Vice President)
1986–2001	Coordinator of the International Women's Year Liaison Group (IWYLG)[3]
1992–2002	President of the UNIFEM Japan National Committee (NGO)
1995	Advisor to the Japanese Government delegation at the Fourth International Conference on Women in Beijing

9 http://www.apww-slwngof.org/index.php?option=com_content&view=article&id=6&Itemid=21

1999–2001	Representative, Japan Women's Committee for NGO Report Steering Committee Member, Asia Pacific Women's Watch (APWW) *JAWW is a member organization of APWW.
2000	Advisor to the Japanese Government delegation at the 23rd UN Special Session of the General Assembly on 'Women 2000: Gender Equality, Development and Peace for the Twenty-first Century'
2001–as of 2013	Honorary Member, APWW Advisor to JAWW
2002–11	Honorary President of the UNIFEM Japan National Committee (NGO)
2011–as of 2013	Honorary President of the UN Women Japan National Committee (NGO)

Source: Based on (Akamatsu et al., 2007: 110–114) and personal communication.

1. http://www.apww-slwngof.org/index.php?option=com_content&view=article&id=41:closing-message-by-ms-mitchiko-nakamura-honorable-member-of-steering-committee-and-adviser-to-jaww-at-the-closing-of-apww-june-meeting-on-14-june-2009&catid=12:apww-meeting&Itemid=46
2. Tentative translation
3. http://homepage3.nifty.com/iwylg/profile/profile_e.html

4. Women's/Gender Studies in Japan

This section portrays the revolutionary changes experienced by women's/gender studies in Japan and takes a look at a list of Ph.D. grantees at Ochanomizu University, Josai International University, Hitotsubashi University, and Osaka Prefecture University in the field of women's/gender studies. It also surveys three main categories of institutions on women's/gender studies in Japan: academic associations, research institutions within universities, and those outside.

4.1 Research Groups on Women's/Gender Studies

During early years, women's/gender studies in Japan has undergone structural changes.[10] First, it challenged the traditional world of intellect

10 This section is based on Hara (2011).

built upon the assumption that equates human beings with men. Since the latter part of the 1960s, efforts to establish women's studies claiming that "women should also be regarded as part of human beings" came into existence from which emerged gender studies. Even after 50 years, we are still on the threshold of starting studies to examine the relationship between individuals who demonstrate diverse forms of socio-culturally determined gender and diversity of biological sex characterized as homo sapiens.

In many human societies that existed prior to the so-called pre-'modernization' period, examples abound of human beings that cannot be categorized as 'male or female' but nevertheless lived out their life as a legitimate member of society. However, as modern states developed a system of government, which entailed compilation of census and demographic statistics, operation to dichotomize human beings into either sex took hold. Consequently, men's supremacy and domination over women came to be perceived as a matter of course. Hence, the dichotomy of sexuality was imposed on the realms of women's suffrage movement from the end of the 1910s as well as women's studies promoted around the world beginning in the 1960s (Hara and Osawa, 1996: 2-5).

Since 1975, research institutions and associations on women's/gender studies have been founded one after another (Tables 4.2, 4.3, and 4.4), but many feminist scholars affiliated with one of those institutions and associations expressed conflicting views concerning the proper direction of women's studies as an academic discipline (Fujieda and Fujimura-Fanselow, 1995: 164). At a public symposium entitled "What is Women's Studies?" at Sophia University in 1980 with the Society for Women's Studies-Japan as an organizer, Teruko Inoue defined women's studies as a discipline that should be pursued by women for the benefit of women (Inoue, 1981). By contrast, I stressed that the scholarly contribution of women's studies lay in infusing to the study of already existing disciplines a feminist perspective of recognizing both men and women. Sumiko Iwao and I emphasized the necessity of such a new discipline that benefits the whole human beings (Inoue vs. Hara and Iwao controversy) (Hara, 1981).

However, Inoue and I believed that these conflicting views could and should coexist at that time and we still do so as of 2013. Later Sumiko Iwao and I began to call ourselves as scholars in gender studies, while Inoue wrote that gender studies arose as an outgrowth of women's studies and that women's studies and gender studies should coexist and develop independently (Inoue, 2011: 254-255).

The latter part of the 1980s has witnessed the attempts to carry out what we now call 'gender studies' by the efforts of scholars who supported my view of women's studies:

> Recently gender studies began to make more in-depth inquiries into the definition of gender and at same time clearly demonstrate that those discourses and academic research which on the surface seem to be neutral or unrelated to gender essentially require the concept of gender in constructing their key concepts and fundamental premises (Hara and Osawa, 1996: 4).

Table 4.2 List of Academic Associations in Women's/Gender Studies in Japan

	Website	Year Founded	Mission
International Society for Gender Studies	http://isgs-japan.org/index.html	1977– : International Group for the Study of Women 2003– : International Society for Gender Studies	To promote research in women's studies, men's studies, and gender studies from an interdisciplinary approach with an international perspective as well as dissemination of information and knowledge and development of related projects, thereby contribute to achieving a gender-equal society, where women and men can equally participate.
The Women's Studies Society of Japan	http://www.jca.apc.org/wssj/	1977	To break down dichotomies of values, such as academics vs. everyday life and theory vs. practice and create women's liberation movements grounded on both sets of values; to revolutionize one's self and society, through joint discussion, deliberation, and action among members.

Society for Women's Studies–Japan	none	1978	To establish women's studies as interdisciplinary studies through the corporation of the Society's founding members—women researchers majoring sociology, pedagogy, history, psychology, and anthropology and more recently researchers in economics and law. To issue publications on women's studies; past publications include KozaJoseigaku (vols. 4) between 1984–1987 and the Society's journals JoseigakuKenkyu (5 issues) from 1990 and 1998, where the first issue featured gender and sex discrimination and the fifth issue reconstruction of women's studies
The Women's Studies Association of Japan	http://www.joseigakkai-jp.org/index.php	1978	To eliminate all forms of gender discrimination, aim to establish women's studies free from conventional classification in carrying out studies and to exchange information for that purpose. To exchange opinions and information in various fields, including research, education, practice, and movements, and provide a space for all people pursuing women's studies through democratic and voluntary management of the group by participants.
Japan Society for Gender Studies	http://www.s.fpu.ac.jp/tukamoto/gender.htm	1997	To promote interdisciplinary and international gender studies through equal participation of women and men.
Group on Socio-Gender Evaluation, the Japan Evaluation Society	http://evaluationjp.org/activity/subcommittee.html	2000	To contribute to gender equality in global society not to mention within Japan through incorporation of "socio-gender perspectives" (perspectives to promote gender equality in association with diverse social attributes and contexts including class, ethnic groups, race, and age) in evaluation activities and studies concerning policies, measures and development of human resources in those three fields, all of which are steered by the Society. Further to contribute to the development of evaluation studies.

Japan Society for Sport and Gender Studies	http://www.jssgs.org/	2002	To promote publication of research on sports and gender, exchange of knowledge concerning sports and gender, and collaboration among Society members and with related academic associations in and outside Japan for the advancement of studies on gender and sports, and further to contribute to practices to promote gender-equal ("gender-free") sports.
Japan Association of Gender and Law	http://wwwsoc.nii.ac.jp/genderlaw/index.html	December 2003	To carry out more in-depth studies on law from gender perspectives, bridge theory (research) and practice, and develop and enhance education programs on gender and law.
The Gender History Association of Japan	http://www7b.biglobe.ne.jp/~genderhistory/	2004	To conduct research in all disciplines related to the history of human beings and promote its dissemination.
The Japan Association for Feminist Economics (JAFFE)	http://devgen.igs.ocha.ac.jp/jaffe/about/index.html	2004	To conduct research and exchange information with an aim at interdisciplinary development of feminist economics beyond specialized fields.
The Japan Association for Queer Studies (JAQS)	http://queerjp.org/index.html	October 2007	To provide a space for researchers interested in queer studies to have a mutual exchange and share research achievements, and at a space for a wide range of people engaged in various socio-cultural activities to share knowledge and exchange views and opinions.

Compiled by Miwako Shimazu, Dec. 2011.

Table 4.3 List of Research Centers on Women's/Gender Studies outside Universities in Japan

	Website	Year Founded	Mission
National Women's Education Center, Japan (NWEC)	http://www.nwec.jp/ http://www.nwec.jp/en/	1977- : National Women's Education Center	To promote women's education and contribute to realize the gender-equal society, through conducting training programs for regional government officers, educational and group leaders,

		2001– : NWEC as an independent administrative institution	and international trainees and other personnel in women's education, and conducting specialized research and surveys on women's education.
Asia Japan Women's Resource Center (AJWRC)	http://www.ajwrc.org/ http://www.ajwrc.org/eng/	1997– : Asian Women's Association (AWA) 1994– : Asia Japan Women's Resource Center (AJWRC)	To promote information sharing and networking, education and training, and advocacy and campaigns, to end gender–based violence and discrimination, achieve just and sustainable society, and realize alternative politics and empowerment of women.
Kitakyushu Forum on Asian Women	http://www.kfaw.or.jp/ http://www.kfaw.or.jp/index.html.en http://www.kfaw.or.jp/about/index.html.ko (Korean)	October 1990	To promote the improvement of women's status as well as their mutual understanding and cooperation in Asia.
Tokai Foundation for Gender Studies	http://www.libra.or.jp/index.htm	June 1997	To strive for the realization of gender–equal society where people can live free from gender bias through research on gender issues, training and education of young researchers, and consciousness raising of gender equality.

Table 4.4 List of Research Centers on Women's/Gender Studies within Universities in Japan

	Website	Year Founded	Mission
Institute for Gender Studies, Ochanomizu University (IGS)	http://www.igs.ocha.ac.jp/ http://www.igs.ocha.ac.jp/igs/indexE.html	1975– : National Archive of Women's Studies 1986– : Institute for Women's Studies	To develop academic research and educational activities related to gender studies in Japan; to offer postgraduate courses specializing in gender studies in social science; to promote the expansion of academic networks, with domestic and international scholars collaborating on research projects.

		1996– : Institute for Gender Studies	international symposia and public seminars.
Institute for Women's Studies, Tokyo Women's Christian University	http://lab.twcu.ac.jp/iws/home.htm http://lab.twcu.ac.jp/iws/home_e.htm	1976– : Committee for Women's Studies 1988– : Center for Women's Studies April 1990– : Institute for Women's Studies	To contribute to the promotion and development of women's studies; to widen the sphere for environmental problems which have been lost in the male-oriented culture; to envisage the role and the future prospects of women's universities; and to build up a network of cooperation, both at home and abroad, uniting the people of the same aspiration.
Kobe College Institute for Women's Studies	http://www.kobe-c.ac.jp/gender/	1985	To promote research on women's studies and gender studies and publish research findings; to be utilized as a space for discussion and research on all issues concerning women/men and gender.
Fukuoka Women's University Research Center for Women's Lifelong Education	http://www.fwu.ac.jp/rcle/index.html http://www.fwu.ac.jp/rcle/index-english.html http://www.fwu.ac.jp/rcle/index-korean.html (Korean)	1985– : Women's Lifelong Education Resource Room April 1997: Research Center for Lifelong Education April 2006 Research Center for Women's Lifelong Education	To promote women's career education and lifelong learning; to support the education of women during their working lives; to provide a venue for ongoing education for everyone in the region, including those in their later years, both men and women.
Research Institute for Gender Studies, Showa Women's University	http://content.swu.ac.jp/jyobuken-blog/	May 1986	To promote studies on women and culture in undergraduate and graduate programs and the junior college course within the university and contribute to the creation and development of women's culture in and outside Japan.
Women's Studies Center, School of Humanities and Social Sciences,	http://www.human.osakafu-u.ac.jp/w-center/index.html	1990– : Women's Studies Data Room, Osaka Women's University 1996– : Women's Studies Center,	To aim to create society free from gender discrimination where every individual can live equally; to conduct comprehensive research on gender equal participation on the basis of women's studies and Osaka Prefecture's regulations

Osaka Prefecture University	http://www.human.osakafu-u.ac.jp/w-center/index_e2009.pdf	Osaka Woman's University April 2005: upon integration of Osaka Women's University into Osaka Prefecture University, became a research institute of Osaka Prefecture University	to promote gender equal participation and thereby play a role as a space for networking of researchers in and outside Japan; and to offer education programs in women's/gender studies at Undergraduate and Graduate Schools of Osaka Prefecture University.
Institute for Women's History and Culture, Kyoto Tachibana University	http://www.tachibana-u.ac.jp/official/iwhc/index.html	1992	To elevate women's position in society today through analysis and research on the women's current position in society and the historical and cultural environments in which such women's position was formed; to reevaluate history from women's perspectives so as to fill in the gaps in history and add depth and depth to history studies as a whole.
Institute for Gender and Women's Studies (IGWS), Aichi Shukutoku University	http://www2.aasa.ac.jp/org/igws/index.html http://www2.aasa.ac.jp/org/igws/english/index.html	April 1994	To reevaluate the fixed roles assigned to women and men in society, gather information on cases of gender-based discrimination worldwide; present related materials for educational and research purposes; and to contribute to the realization of a better society where women and men live and participate in equality.
Rikkyo Gender Forum, Rikkyo University	http://www.rikkyo.ac.jp/aboutus/philosophy/activism/gender	April 1998	To serve as a base for education and research activities and develop the University into the one that can respond to the demands of the times towards the realization of gender-equal society.
Institute for Gender and Women's Studies, Josai International University	http//www.jiu.ac.j p/igws/	1999	To gaze into the future vision of the 21st-century world and Japan on the verge of dramatic change and examine women and society, and culture and gender structure, through international conferences, lectures symposia workshops joint research with researchers invited from abroad and publication.

Gender Studies Institute, Project Research Institutes of the Compre-hensive Research Organization, Waseda University	http//www.kikou.waseda.ac.jp/WSD322_open.php?KenkyujoId=P4&kbn=0&KikoId=01	2000	1. To bring together faculty members teaching gender-related subjects in each department to enable them to exchange opinions and information that would be helpful in preparing diverse and enriched curricula at Waseda University. 2. To bring together all teachers and graduate students interested in gender studies at Waseda University and in its vicinity and serve as a space where they can conduct joint interdisciplinary research on various common themes. 3. To publicize academic insights thus obtained both within and outside the campus, thereby contributing to the realization of equal gender relations in Japan and utilize them for the development of gender studies both in Japan and the world.
Gender Forum, Wako University	http//www.wako ac.jp/gender/	2001- : Gender Free Space 2007- : Gender Forum	To enable people to deepen their awareness of gender issues and help them acquire the skills to deal with gender issues; to expand friendship exchange among faculty members and students and between the faculty and office staff and between students and faculty. To bridge academic research and practical activities concerning gender.
Research Center for Gender Equality and Multi-cultural Conviviality (GEMC) Tohoku University	http//.www.law.to hoku.ac.jp/gemc/ http//www.law.to hoku.ac.jp/gcoe/ko (Korean)	- December 2003: Gender Law and Policy Center January 2009- : Research Center for Gender Equality and Multicultural Conviviality	To perform education and research activities as a base of Tohoku University's global COE(GCOE) program "Gender Equality and Multicultural Conviviality in the Age of Globalization" adopted in June 2008. Cf. Purpose of the GCOE program: to analyze social issues occurring throughout the world and to present solutions by integrating our findings and interpreting them from the two viewpoints of gender equality and multicultural conviviality; and to foster young researchers who can present effective countermeasures in regard to such issues.

Center for Gender Studies, International Christian University	http://subsite. icu. ac.jp/cgs/ http://web. icu.ac.jp/cgs_e/	April 2004	1. To break away from passive strategies that rely mainly on consuming information from the western world and work to actively collect and convey relevant information in Japan to the rest of the world. 2. To build networks with and among people in Asia who are interested in women's/men's/gender studies. 3. To support the Program in Gender and Sexuality Studies of ICU, which has launched a new stage of gender studies including the natural sciences.
Center for Gender and Women's Culture in Asia, Nara Women's University	http://koto. nara- wu.ac. jp/gender/ index.html http://koto. nara-wu. ac.jp/gender /en_top.html	November 25, 2005	To promote research on Asian gender issues, in particular contributing to the development of higher education in Asia, and to become a center of a network of female researchers in Asia, by making use of the University's position both within the Asian nation of Japan and as a women's university within Japan.
Meijo University Gender Studies Institute	http:// gender. meijo-u. ac.jp/	April 2006	To promote and enhance research and education based on gender perspectives today when realization of gender-equal society is considered as one of the goals of Japanese society; to expand activities that contribute to society especially local residents around the University.
Center for Gender Research and Social Sciences (CGraSS), Hitotsu-bashi University	http:// gender.soc. hit-u.ac.jp/	April 2007	To create an interdisciplinary research field through integration of gender studies with social sciences and thereby to set trends toward new, advanced social science research incorporating gender perspectives; to establish and practice new gender education on the basis of such research; and to contribute to the training and education of advanced researchers as well as highly technical professionals capable of creating a gender-equal society, as a base of education and research.

Compiled by Miwako Shimazu, Dec. 2011.

4.2 My Involvement in Women's/Gender Studies and Asia

I became involved in women's/gender studies in relation to Asia and other parts of the world back in 1985 when I was teaching at Ochanomizu University as Professor at the Department of Home Management. (In 1986, I became Professor at the Institute for Women's Studies (IWS)[11] (reorganized as the Institute for Gender Studies (IGS) in 1996). In that year, I was approached by an editor of the Public Relation Department at Esso Standard Oil Co. Ltd. who asked me to compile a booklet chronicling the history of women in the world. I dared to accept the offer and sought support from three of my colleagues. We four began to work on a mini encyclopedia entitled Sekai Joseishi (History of Women in the World) which was published in 1986. Its revision was published in 1987 for a wider readership.

The editing team of these two books shared the following recognition:

> At the Third World Conference on Women in Nairobi in 1985, Western feminists proposed a 'multilateral approach to discrimination against women,' whereas more and more women activists in the Third World came to regard struggles against male domination (patriarchy) as part of their action programs along with struggles against neocolonialism and dictatorship. Thus, global feminism, where women in the West and the Third World, however diverse situations they may be in, saw a common root of women's oppression and joined hands together, is being established as the predominant trend which cannot be reverted (Hara et al., 1987: ii).

Just before the publication of the book, I wrote that the experience of editorial work was rewarding in that those Japanese scholars specializ-

11 The Institute began in 1975 as the first national archive of women's studies and reorganized as the Institute for Women's Studies in 1985.

ing in the studies about women in the West and those in the studies about women in the Third World enjoyed a valuable opportunity in getting acquainted with each other and exchanging information (Hara et al., 1987: 9-10).

4.3 Ph.D. Degrees Granted in Women's/Gender Studies in Japan

Ochanomizu University stands out in the number and diversity of research fields among universities in Japan which have been granting Ph.D. degrees in fields related to women's/gender studies, whereas Josai International University, where I have been teaching since 2005, was the first university in Japan to offer an undergraduate program in women's studies with MA and Ph.D. programs. As of 2012, a few other universities in Japan grant Ph.D. degrees on topics related to women's/gender studies; however they are easily overlooked because the names of those classes/courses do not necessarily include the term gender/women.

(1) Women's/Gender Studies Ph.D. Program at Ochanomizu University

The Graduate School of Humanities and Science (doctoral program) was established within the university campus in 1976, and one Ph.D. dissertation related to women's/gender studies was submitted and granted Ph.D. degrees in 1985 (Ohinata, 1985). In 1993, women's studies was officially recognized as an independent field of study. In 2007, the division of Interdisciplinary Gender Studies was added to the doctoral program. Since then, Ph.D. dissertations of subjects covering a wider range of subjects have been submitted and granted degrees. Between 1985 and 2012, a total of 142 Ph.D. degrees were granted within the field of women's/gender studies, each differing in its approach (Table 4.5). Of those 144, 18 dealt with issues in Asia (excluding Japan and Japanese), 5 with China, 4 with the Philippines, 3 with Korea (including Koreans in Japan), and one each with Bangladesh, India, Indonesia, Samoa, Taiwan, and Vietnam.

Table 4.5 Number of Ph.D. Dissertations related to Women's/Gender Studies from Ochanomizu University (1995–2012)

year	total	psy-cho-logy	litera-ture	human develop-ment	social science	educa-tion	physi-cal science	history	humani-ties	natural science	cultural studies	geo-graphy	econo-mics	food science	lingui-stics
1985	1	1													
1986	0														
1987	0														
1988	0														
1989	0														
1990	0														
1991	0														
1992	1		1												
1993	0														
1994	1			1											
1995	3			2	1										
1996	6			3	2	1									
1997	1						1								
1998	6	1	2		1			2							
1999	4		1		3										
2000	6			1	5										
2001	8	1	2		3			1	1						
2002	5	1	1		1	2									
2003	5	1			3					1					
2004	7			1	4	1			1						
2005	10	1	2	1	4		2								
2006	12		1	1	6	1			1		1	1			
2007	12	1	3	2	4	1					1				
2008	16	3		2	8					1	2				
2009	8	1			2		2	1				1	1		
2010	11	1	1		4	2					1			1	1

2011	12			1	5	1		2			1			1	1
2012	9		1		6									1	1
total	144	12	15	15	62	9	5	6	3	2	6	2	1	3	3

Source: http://www.lib.ocha.ac.jp/gakui.html (in Japanese) (accessed on 24 December 2012)

Compiled by Hara Hiroko and Miwako Shimazu (Dec. 2012)

Note: For a short history of the Graduate School of Humanities and Sciences, see http://www.dc.ocha.ac.jp/history_e.html (in English)

(2) Women's/Gender Studies Ph.D. Program at Josai International University

Josai International University in Chiba Prefecture started an M.A. program in women's studies in 1996 and a Ph.D. program in 1998. Eighteen Ph.D. degrees in women's/gender Studies have been granted since 2007 (Table 4.6). Among those 18, 3 dealt with China (Chinese linguistics, Chinese demography, and Chinese Americans).

Table 4.6 Number of Ph. D Dissertations related to Women's/Gender Studies from Graduate School of Humanities, Josai International University (2007–2012)

calendar year	total	physical science	literature	linguistics	archeology	social science
2007	4	1	2	1		
2008	2				1	1
2009	3		3			
2010	4		4			
2011	2		1			1
2012	3		2			1
total	18	1	12	1	1	3

Compiled by Hara Hiroko (Dec. 2012)

Note: For an overview of Graduate School of Humanities, Josai International University, see http://www.jiu.ac.jp/englishsite/g_program/humanities.html (in English)

(3) Other Women's/Gender Studies Graduate Programs

Apart from the two above, women's/gender studies-related graduate programs have been established at Hitotsubashi University in Tokyo (Dr Fumika Sato) and Osaka Prefecture University in Sakai, Osaka (Dr Kumiko Ida and Dr Yasuko Tama).[12]

5. Before the Beijing Conference

In my personal view, two events which took place before the Fourth World Conference on Women in Beijing have social and academic significance in the history of women's/gender studies in Japan: the establishment of the Kitakyushu Forum on Asian Women (KFAW) and Asian Women's Conference.

5.1 Kitakyushu Forum on Asian Women (KFAW)[13]

Kitakyushu City, where KFAW is located, is a cosmopolitan city in terms of the number of foreign residents and the amount of citizens' interest in exchanging with people in every part of Asia. Therefore, the fact that KFAW is based in Kitakyushu is significant as Japan's gate to Asia.

The Kitakyushu Forum on Asian Women (KFAW) was established in 1990 with a special government fund for revitalization project of local community with additional donation by ordinary citizens in the City. The purpose of KFAW is to promote the improvement of women's status as well as their mutual understanding and cooperation in Asia.

KFAW aims to foster citizens' participation through grassroots activities related to Asia; to study and research broadly, deeply and comprehen-

12 Hitotsubashi University has granted 11 Ph.D. degrees in women's/gender studies-related fields since 1997 (two of which are related to Korea), whereas Osaka Prefecture University granted the first Ph.D. degree in 2012.

13 http://www.kfaw.or.jp/about/index.html.en

sively women's issues; by promoting international exchange and cooperation, to create a new identity for Kitakyushu City; and to contribute to 'Gender Equality, Development and Peace' while respecting the diversity of Asian cultures.

To consider the problems of women in Asian countries and promote the empowerment of Asian women, KFAW holds the Kitakyushu Conference on Asian Women annually, with the first Conference held in 1991.

5.2 Asian Women's Conference

In 1992, Asian Women's Conference 'Recreating Women's Asia 1992' was convened in Japan by Asian Women's Organizing Committee. This Conference grew out of organizing members' earnest aspiration to deepen solidarity between women across Japan and women in other parts of Asia. The Conference Coordinator Kuniko Funabashi[14] wrote in the preface of the Conference Report II:

> The plenary session of Asian Women's Conference was held from April 2 to 4 at the National Women's Education Center in Saitama Prefecture, followed by local sessions in Yokohama, Sendai, Sakai, Hiroshima, and Osaka ... Besides 18 speakers from 13 countries and 1 region in Asia, a total of 1,500 women participated in the plenary session ... we participants learned from each other's diverse experiences, particularly the movement and research conducted to overcome the situations women in various parts of Asia are facing. We also succeeded in creating wide networks among women within Japan as well as women in various parts of Asia, through which we can encourage each other, talk with each other and empower ourselves.

14 She is one of the 200 Japanese women who attended the 1975 International Women's Year Tribune in Mexico City and attached importance to the relationship between women in Japan and the rest of Asia.

6. After Beijing, 1995

Many women in Japan participated in the UN Fourth World Conference on Women in Beijing in 1995. Those participants from Japan were mainly members of women NGOs and local women who applied for a study tour to Beijing offered by each local government. They were led by public servants in charge of women's issues and their travel expenses were partly paid by the local government. (At that time local governments in Japan had a budget for such programs because of nation's economic prosperity.) Reflecting this nationwide situation, research activities, international exchanges, and publishing activities in the area of women's/gender studies gained momentum.

6.1 Joint Research Project by NWEC and IWS, Ochanomizu University

In 1993 and 1994, the then Ministry of Education subsidized a joint research project on "Women and Gender in Asia-Pacific: Policy Development and Women's Studies in Eight Countries" to be carried out by the National Women's Education Center (NWEC) and the Institute for Women's Studies (IWS) at Ochanomizu University. The Research Team was comprised of the following members:

1. Korea: Mari Osawa (University of Tokyo), Chung Chin-Sung (currently Seoul National University), and Mizue Maeda (NWEC)
2. China: Mizue Maeda, Yasuko Muramatsu (Tokyo Woman's Christian University),[15] and Huang Yufu (Chinese Academy of Social Sciences)
3. Indonesia: Yasuko Muramatsu and Rie Taguchi (Ph.D. candidate at Ochanomizu University)

15 One of the members of the editorial committee of the *AJWS*.

4. Thailand: Hara Hiroko, Chikako Uemura (NWEC), and Sae Eto (Ph.D. candidate at the Tokyo University of Foreign Studies)
5. India (case study on Mizoram Hmeichhe Insuihkawm Pawl (Mizo Women's Federation and on mahila mandal in Rajasthan): Maravika Karlekar (Centre for Women's Development Studies, New Delhi.[16]
6. New Zealand (on Maori women): Chigusa Kimura-Steven (Visiting Scholar at IWS)
7. Australia: Kaoru Tachi (IWS) and Chieko Seta (NWEC)
8. New Zealand: Chigusa Kimura-Steven, Kaoru Tachi, and Chieko Seta

Through this research project, the members of the research team realized the importance of highlighting the interconnections among gender, ethnicity, and class and perceived the necessity to transform knowledge by developing concepts and theories in light of reality and clarifying those interconnections in terms of women's/gender studies[17] (Hara and Osawa, 1996: 15-16).[18]

6.2 Network on Women's/Gender Studies in Kitakyushu

The Network on Women's/Gender Studies in Kitakyushu was formed in 1996, headed by Keiko Tamura (specialized in international relations and Southeast Asian studies) and Masami Shinozaki (specialized in family sociology, women's/gender studies). Seven members from this group contributed to a book entitled Ajia no Shakaihendo to Jendah (Social Change and Gender in Asia) with those two as editors which was published in 1999 in Japanese. The book covers such topics as "aging in Singapore and China," "women in Singapore and their families," "rural women in Pakistan," "jobless women in China," "violence against wom-

16 Another member of the editorial committee of the *AJWS*.
17 The outcome of the Project was published as (Hara, Maeda, and Osawa, 1996).
18 This particular section was written by Mari Osawa.

en coming to Japan from other parts of Asia," and "Nepali women and their NGOs."

Shinozaki says in its afterword that the book was written primarily based upon the following two premises. First, Asia demonstrates diversity in various facets and factors, and levels of industrialization, not to mention climatic and geographical conditions, but at the same time it is also full of dynamism. Second, towards the end of the 1990s, studies on social change and gender were confronted with the East Asian financial crisis which coincided with the period when the latest developments in gender issues were reported. Given the two premises, Shinozaki says the editors felt it necessary to examine how the economic crisis and the ensuing political crisis had impacted women and men in every country/region in Asia from diverse perspectives, including employment, social security, political process, education, migration, family, and health and body.

6.3 Book Review on Gender and Development

Highly recommended as an introductory book on gender and development is a book entitled Kaihatsu to Jenda: Enpawamento no Kokusaikyoryoku (Gender and Development: International Cooperation for Empowerment) edited/co-authored by Yumiko Tanaka, Mari Osawa, and Ruri Ito (Tanaka et al., 2002). In the book written in Japanese, a total of 6 men and 38 women of various ages offer multi-faceted explanations on gender and development based on what they experienced as a member of a development project all over the world. The book covers a wide range of Asian countries, namely (parentheses showing the number of case studies): Bangladesh (3), Thailand (3), the Philippines (2), Afghanistan (1), Cambodia (1), East Timor (1), Korea (1), and Nepal (1). Some of the papers that cannot be categorized by country address cross-boundary issues, such as the disabled in Asia, genital mutilation, the Asian economic crisis, and networking between women's centers and NGOs in Asia.

The excellent quality of the book owes to the three editors' mastery over each topic which they acquired over the years. Yumiko Tanaka[19] is a Senior Advisor on gender and development at JICA. Mari Osawa is a professor in economics at the Institute of Social Science (ISS), the University of Tokyo, whereas Ruri Ito was a professor in sociology of migration at the Institute for Gender Studies, Ochanomizu University as of 2002 and a professor at Hitotsubashi University as of 2013.

6.4 Activities at the Science Council of Japan (SCJ)

SCJ is composed of 210 scholars from various disciplines including Humanities, Social Sciences, Basic Natural Sciences, Agriculture and Forestry fields, Engineering, Medicine/Pharmacology, and Nursing.

(1) 'Gender' and the Grants-in-Aid for Scientific Research funded by the then Ministry of Education [20]

In 1997, I became a member of the First Division of the Science Council of Japan (SCJ) representing the field of cultural anthropology. Around that time, the Ministry of Education began to consider revising the disciplines and research fields for the Grants-in-Aid for Scientific Research to be introduced in fiscal 2003 and called on SCJ to prepare and submit a report on its findings. During the 1980s, applicants for the Grants-in-Aid for Scientific Research wishing to conduct their project in women's/

19 Yumiko Tanaka's short bio: After obtaining a master's degree in development studies from the Graduate School, the University of Manchester, Yumiko Tanaka held several administrative posts, including an officer at the UNIDO Field Office in Thailand between 1981-83, an officer for Women in Development at UN-ESCAP between 1983 and 1990, a planning expert on gender issues for the Community Development and Forest/Watershed Conservation Project in Nepal between 1994 and 1996, and Manager, Office of Evaluation and Post-Project Monitoring, Japan International Cooperation Agency (JICA) between 1998 and 1999, and Executive Director, Social Development Cooperation Department, JICA between 1999 and 2001. From 2002 and onwards she serves as Senior Advisor on Gender and Development, JICA to further promote gender and development. (She has acquired Ph.D. in Development Studies from University of Tokyo in 2014.)

20 Reorganized as the Ministry of Education, Culture, Sports, Science and Technology (MEXT) in FY 2001.

gender studies, gender-specific medicine, and women's literature tended to choose law, sociology, medicine, literature, and other disciplines that they thought closest for their application, but it was not easy for them to obtain understanding from the referees (mostly men). Alarmed at this state of affairs, Chizuko Ueno, I, and others had been requesting the Ministry to add 'women's/gender studies' as a new discipline for the Grants-in-Aid and suggested to categorize it as a multidisciplinary research field. Thanks to our efforts, in the FY 2001 revision of a List of Categories, Areas, Disciplines and Research Fields for the Grants-in-Aid, the discipline 'Gender' was newly awarded a status in the area of new multidisciplinary fields under the category of Integrated Science and Innovative Science.[21] Fourteen keywords of the discipline are enumerated in the List, and in 2003, it became possible to determine the allocation of the Grants-in-Aid according to this revised List.

(2) Science Council of Asia and 'Gender'

The Science Council of Asia (SCA) is composed of eligible academic organizations in 11 member countries in Asia.[22] However, only Indonesia, the Philippines, and Japan have a national organization covering the entire disciplines as SCA's member organization.[23] Member countries are to host annual Conferences and send its Chairperson on a rotational basis. The SCA Secretariat is housed at the Science Council of Japan. SCA's Joint Project on Gender originated from the two keynote speeches by Stephen Hill of Jakarta UNESCO and me[24] and a review on gender studies in Asian countries by Sjamsiah Achmad (LIPI, Indonesia) at the Third Conference

21 Cf. http://www.jsps.go.jp/english/e-grants/data/09_2011/06_e.pdf

22 For details, see http://www.scj.go.jp/en/sca/organizations/structure.html

23 Namely, the Indonesian Institute of Sciences (LIPI), the National Research Council of the Philippines (NRCP), and the SCJ.

24 "The Gender Studies/Women's Studies in Asia" by Hara Hiroko (the Science Council of Japan (SCJ)) and "Connecting the Unconnected: Science and Technology Policy Challenges for Asia in the 21st Century—the Gender Dimension and Poverty Alleviation" by Stephen Hill (Jakarta UNESCO Office).

held in 2003 in Denpasar, Bali.[25] At the Fourth Conference held in Seoul in 2004, the Steering Committee urged Sjamsiah and me to present an official proposal to include 'Gender' as one of SCA's Joint Projects for annual SCA Conferences for the duration of 6 years. With the acknowledgement of our proposal, we held a Gender Workshop at annual SCA Conferences in Hanoi in 2005 (Fifth), in Delhi in 2006 (Sixth), in Okinawa in 2007 (Seventh), in Qingdao, China in 2008 (Eighth), in Singapore in 2009 (Ninth), and in Manila in 2010 (Tenth) as the last session, each under different titles.[26]

7. Major Research since 2001

Some women scholars in Gender Studies have been successful in receiving large-scale research grants from the Ministry of Education, Culture, Sports, Science and Technology (MEXT).

7.1 Ochanomizu University

A program entitled "Frontiers of Gender Studies (F-GENS)" at the In-

---

25 See p. 39 at http://www.scj.go.jp/en/sca/pdf/7th_proceedings.pdf

26 "A Comparative Study of the Research Conditions of Women Scientists and the Present States of Women's/Gender Studies in Asian Countries Towards the Human Centered Sustainable Development" in 2005 (http://www.scj.go.jp/en/sca/data/5thgender.html).
"A Comparative Study of the Research Conditions of Women Scientists and the Present States of Women's/Gender Studies in Asian Countries Towards the Human Centered Sustainable Development (Gender) in 2006 (http://www.scj.go.jp/en/sca/pdf/6thsummary.pdf).
"Academic Pursuit and Family Life" in 2007 (http://www.scj.go.jp/en/sca/pdf/7th_proceedings.pdf).
"Women, Small/ Medium Scale Enterprises (SME) ICT" in 2008 (http://www.scj.go.jp/en/sca/data/8th_gen.html).
"Grooming Scientific Talent in Asia: from Gender Perspective" in 2009 (http://www.news.gov.sg/public/sgpc/en/media_releases/agencies/astar/press_release/P-20090616-2.print.html?AuthKey=).
"Reproductive Health Issues in the Context of Population Mobility and Climate Change" in 2010 (not yet published).

stitute of Gender Studies (IGS), Department of Gender Studies, Graduate School of Humanities & Sciences, Ochanomizu University was conducted as a 21st Century COE (Center of Excellence) program by the MEXT between 2003 and 2008, with Prof. Tamie Kainou as the Program Leader.[27]

7.2 International Christian University (ICU)

At ICU, a program entitled "Research and Education for Peace, Security and Conviviality" was awarded a 21st Century COE program between 2003 and 2008 with Prof. Yoichiro Murakami[28] as its Program Leader. One of the three research projects, Research Project 3 entitled "Conviviality, Education, Gender" consists of 4 research groups, including a group on "Creating 'Knowledge' on Human Security and Gender: From Asian Perspectives" coordinated by Prof. Kazuko Tanaka and Prof. Yumiko Mikanagi of ICU Center for Gender Studies.[29]

7.3 Tohoku University

At Tohoku University, a five-year 21st Century COE Program "Gender Law and Policy Center" (GELAPOC)[30] was carried out between 2003 and 2008 to promote research on a wide variety of gender issues, with Prof. Miyoko Tsujimura, School of Law, Tohoku University as the Program Leader. This GELAPOC was succeeded by a Global COE (GCOE) Program entitled "Gender Equality and Multicultural Conviviality in the Age of Globalization."[31] Again Prof. Tsujimura serves as its GCOE program leader and Prof. Mari Osawa of ISS, the University of Tokyo as an ISS Collaboration GCOE Program Leader. The Program advances

27 For details, seehttp://www.igs.ocha.ac.jp/f-gens/index_e.html
28 http://subsite.icu.ac.jp/coe/coe/murakami_e.html
29 http://subsite.icu.ac.jp/coe/coe/hyou_e.html
30 http://www.law.tohoku.ac.jp/gelapoc/english/
31 http://www.law.tohoku.ac.jp/gcoe/en/about-gcoe/outline/

the achievements of GELAPOC from a general social sciences perspective and aspires to establish a world-class research and education center on gender equality and multicultural conviviality in the age of globalization. Collaborating with the ISS and other institutions at home and abroad, the Program aims to build a research and human resources development framework that will foster young researchers, legal professionals, and policy specialists in a global arena. In 2011 the Program's achievements were published in English as a book titled Gender Equality in Asia: Policies and Political Participation, edited by Miyoko Tsujimura and Jackie F. Steele.[32] The book consists of two parts: Part 1 "Gender Equality Policies in Asia"[33] and Part 2 "Women's Political Participation in Asia."[34]

7.4 Kyoto University

At Kyoto University, sociologist Dr Emiko Ochiai, Professor, Graduate School of Letters, Kyoto University, led a Global COE Program entitled "Reconstruction of the Intimate and Public Spheres in 21st Century Asia."[35] As of 2012, this Program is being carried out mainly by the scholars in the following fields:

> Sociology, strictly defined: theoretical sociology, sociology of the family, sociology of education, rural/urban sociology, cultural sociology, sociology of knowledge, economic sociology, sociology of information technology, sociology of emotion, and other fields.Related areas: cultural anthropology, area studies, political science, economics, agricultural economics, history of education, and gender studies.

Although 'gender studies' appears at the end of the list above, I believe

32 http://www.tups.jp/book/book.php?id=244
33 Specifically, India, Japan, Filipino women living in Japan, China, and Turkey.
34 Specifically, Korea, India, Japan, Sri Lanka, and Japan's military sexual slavery.
35 https://www.gcoe-intimacy.jp/images/library/File/GCOEProposalEnglishFinal20080630.pdf

this project will give a valuable clue to scholars attempting to understand what should be the future course of Asian feminisms, since they claim:

> Necessity to pioneer a new scientific discipline
>
> The dramatic transformations taking place in the family and private life today transcend national boundaries. The conspicuous *decrease in fertility* taking place throughout East Asia, including Japan, is both a cause and a result of these changes. The rapid spread of *globalization* and neo-liberal ideology has resulted in the disruption of families through unemployment and unstable job conditions on one hand and long labor hours on the other. *A shortage in care services in the societies* with an already aged population structure induces the *transnational migration of women* as domestic and care workers as well as marriage partners, creating a considerable impact on the family life in both the sending and receiving societies. All these changes necessitate a fundamental rethinking of the framework of the *welfare state* and the *citizenship regime* ... There is therefore an urgent need to pioneer new scientific disciplines in order ... to better explain the trends in *the reframing of the intimate and public spheres*.[36]

Prior to this GCOE Program, Ochiai carried out a research project "A Comparative Study of Housewifization in Asian Societies: Gender Change in the Process of Modernization and Globalization" subsidized as a Grant-in-Aid for Scientific Research by MEXT between FY 2006 and FY 2008. Its research methodology was twohold: the research team tried to grasp the current situations through field research while making theoretical analysis by making comparison among various societies in Asia and with societies in the United States and Europe and by integrating historical examinations. The findings of the research team indicated that (1) the

36 https://www.gcoe-intimacy.jp/images/library/File/GCOEProposalEnglishFinal20080630.pdf, p. 3.

transformation of gender in Asia today is taking place in the "reconstruction process of the intimate and private spheres," which involves changes in families, creation of a welfare state and its changes, and globalization and international migration; (2) regional differences could be explained by the connections of these factors; and (3) there could be recognized what they called "familistic welfare regime" that places emphasis on the role of families while adopting the market theory in the midst of globalization. In sum, the research characterized transformation and identified its historical significance. The research team confirmed that even in the age of globalization, the role of a state remains critical. Their research achievements have been published in four languages in English (Ochiai and Molony, 2008), Japanese (Ochiai et al., 2007; Ochiai and Ueno, 2007), Thai and Chinese.[37]

8. Conclusion

In this paper I have sketched how women's/gender studies emerged and developed in Japan as I personally view it. I could not mention several important figures who made a remarkable contribution in this field, including sociologist Chizuko Ueno (1948-) and Keiko Amano (1942-) (a cardiologist who has been the driving force to establish a new field of gender-specific medicine, health policy, and medical practice), except for the remarkable New Year news: On January 1, 2012, Asahi Shimbun reported that Ueno was selected as one of the five recipients of the 2011 Asahi Award for her "research and practice of women's studies, feminism, and

37 วิถีครอบครัวชาวเอเชียในศตวรรษที่ 21 (เอะมิโกะโอะชิอะอิคะโยะโกะอุเอะโนะบรรณาธิการ, วรเวศม์สุวรรณระดาแปลและบทนำฉบับแปล, อรรถยาสุวรรณระดาแปล), สำนักพิมพ์แห่งจุฬาลงกรณ์มหาวิทยาลัย. (21st Century Asian Family, Emiko Ochiai and Kayoko Ueno (eds.) (2011), Worawet Suwanrada and Attaya Suwanrada trans.), Chulalongkorn University Press.
落合惠美子、宫坂靖子、周维宏、山根真理编著（2010），《亚洲社会的家庭和两性关系—中日韩新泰（五国六地）实证和比较研究》，世界知识出版社.

the issue of care-giving."[38]

Reflecting myself on my past and present as a researcher in cultural anthropology, who concurrently became a researcher and activist in women's/gender issues in November 1993 just before the ICPD, I feel that I have been very lucky to have wonderful forerunners and colleagues in Japan, in Asia, and in the world.

For the next two or three decades, I am determined to explore the following questions with Asian sisters whose answers should guide us through the future course of women's/gender studies, although the list is not exhaustive by any means.

References

[In Japanese]

Akamatsu, Ryoko et al. (eds.) (2007), *Mitchiko Nakamura's Life History: A Stretch of Road (Nakamura Mitchiko Raifuhisutori: Hitosuji no Michi)*, Japanese Association of International Women's Rights.

Asia-Japan Women's Resource Center (AJWRC) (ed.) (1997), *To Women in Japan from Beijing: What to Learn from the World Conference on Women (Pekin hatsu Nihon no Onnnatachihe: Sekai Josei Kaigi o do ikasuka)*, Akashi Shoten.

Asian Women's Conference Organizing Committee (1992), *Asian Women's Conference "Recreating Women's Asia 1992" Report Part II*, Asian Women's Conference Organizing Committee.

Hara, Hiroko (1981), "From the Perspectives of Studies on Humankind (Ningenkenkyu no Shitentoshite)," *Creating Women's Studies (Joseigaku wo Tsukuru)*, Joseigaku Kenkyukai (ed.), Keiso Shobo, pp. 67-72.

38 http://ajw.asahi.com/article/behind_news/social_affairs/AJ201201010026 (accessed on January 4, 2012).

______(2011), "Gender Issues in Population, Environment, and Development (Jinko, kankyo, kaihatsu no jendakadai)," *Towards an Equitable Global Community (Koseina Gurobaru Komyunitee wo)*, Mari Osawa (ed.), Iwanami Shoten, pp. 95-120.

Hara, Hiroko et al., (1986), *History of Women in the World (Sekai Joseishi)*, PR Department at Esso Standard Oil.

Hara, Hiroko et al. (1987), *Encyclopedia for Reading, Women's World History (Yomu Jiten, Onna no Sekaishi)*, Shin-yo-sha.

Hara, Hiroko and Mari Osawa (1996), "Women's Studies and Women's Policy (Joseigaku to Joseisesaku)," Hara Hiroko et al. (eds.) (1996), pp. 1-22.

Hara, Hiroko, Mizue Maeda, and Mari Osawa (eds.) (1996), *Women and Gender in Asia-Pacific: Policy Development and Women's Studies in Eight Countries (Ajia Taiheiyochiiki no Joseiseisaku to Joseigaku)*, Shin-yo-sha.

Inoue, Teruko (1981), "Studies on Women, by Women, for Women (Josei no Josei niyoru Josei notamenogakumon)," *Creating Women's Studies (Joseigaku wo Tsukuru)*, Joseigaku Kenkyukai (ed.), Keiso Shobo, pp. 55-61.

______(2011), *A New Invitation to Women's Studies Shin (Joseigakuheno Shotai)*, Yuhikaku, pp. 254-255.

Matsui, Yayori (1999), *Women in the New Asia: From Pain to Power*, translated by Noriko Toyokawa and Carolyn Francis, Zed Books.

Ochiai, Emiko and Kayoko Ueno (eds.) (2006), *21st Century Asian Families (21-seiki Azia Kazoku)*, Akashi Shoten.

Ochiai, Emiko et al. (eds.) (2007), *Asian Families and Gender (Azia no Kazoku to Jenda)*, Keiso Shobo.

Ohinata, Masami (1985), *A Study on the Formation of Motherhood and Its Transformation Process—Situations Surrounding Motherhood and Their Problems—Relationship with Motherhood Studies (Bosei no Keisei oyobi Henyo Katei nikansuru Kenkyu—Koryu wo meburu Genjo to sono Mondaiten—Bosei Kenkyu tono Kanrensei nitsuite)*, Ph.D. dissertation, Ochanomizu University.

Tamura, Keiko and Masami Shinozaki (eds.) (1999), *Social Change and Gender in Asia (Ajia no Shakaihendo to Jendah)*, Akashi Shoten.

Tanaka, Yumiko et al. (eds.) (2002), *Gender and Development: International Cooperation for Empowerment (Kaihatsu to Jenda: Enpawamento no Kokusaikyoryoku)*, Japan International Cooperation Publishing Co. Ltd.

[In English]

Fujieda, Mioko and Fujimura-Fanselow (1995), "Women's Studies: An Overview," *Japanese Women: New Feminist Perspectives on the Past, Present, and Future*, Fujimura-Fanselow, Kumiko and Atsuko Kameda (eds.), New York: The Feminist Press, pp. 155-180.

Ochiai, Emiko and Barbara Molony (eds.) (2008), *Asia's New Mothers: Crafting Gender Roles and Childcare Networks in East and Southeast Asian Societies*, Folkestone: Global Oriental.

Tsujimura, Miyoko and Jackie F. Steele (eds.) (2011), *Gender Equality in Asia: Policies and Political Participation*, Sendai: Tohoku University Press.

Chapter 5

On Research and Practice of Women's Movement and Its New Tendency:

The Case of a Feminist Participatory Action Research in China

DU Fangqin

1. Chinese Women's Movement Seen from the Feminist Perspective

1.1 A Feminist Redefinition of Women's Movement

The main-stream idea usually defines a women's movement as one that, with its own leaders, members, large groups of participants, and unified political creed, is able to paddle its own canoe in making decisions of its targets, schedules and activities, expressing its political demands, and having their political aims realized by exercising pressure in constant and scaled protests.

In 1990s, many feminist intellectuals started to think the possibility of including in the women's movement all the scattered organizations such as clubs, groups, or activities initiated via the Internet. Their reasoning goes as follows: although these groups or activities are not organized under the same political creed, leadership or coordinating system, and some may not even have a uniform agenda or their organization and actions may not directly voice out women's needs, they ought to be taken as an organic component of the women's movement when their targets, tenets, ideas, strategies and results can help improve gender relationship and meet women's needs (like their practical gender needs and strategic gender interests), advance social reform policies favoring gender equality or equality of men and women, and promote changes in cultural and structural ideology, etc.

As a matter of fact, women's movement in its general sense should also include the knowledge-producing activity, for "if the social and political activities initiated by feminist ideas are classified a generalized women's movement, the process of systemizing the animadvert theory of women's studies in the academic world will benefit the women's movement." (Chang Pilwha, 2006). And Li Xiaojiang, the precursor of women's studies in China, simply defined women's studies as part of the women's movement, and named it "women's studies movement" (Li Xiaojiang, 1997). Besides, the 35 years development of women's studies at Ehwa Womans University in Korea also proves that, combined efforts in both research and practice (including policy and law initiating, media advocating, and social and cultural changing) via women's education and women's studies are successful in pushing forward the feminist movement (Chang Pilwha, 2008).

Apart from defining the organizational structure, functioning and goals of the women's movement, scholars have also discussed the more important organizational practice and "autonomy" strategy. Some believe that "autonomy fetish" means that an NGO's autonomy is best protected and nurtured by avoiding linkages with state and market institutions. However, Zhang Naihua, a scholar focusing on the study of the Chinese women's movement, expressed her disagreement, claiming that such standard is improper, or at least does not fit in the situation in China (Zhang Naihua, 2001). For in China, just like the case in most of the Third World countries, there are very few organizations that are free from directed mobilizations (e.g. women's federations) or foreign capital supports (e.g. women's NGOs). So in referring to women's movement in China, we must, first of all, discuss its organizational form, its functioning, relationship and changing activities in practice and efficiency.

1.2 Chinese Women's Movement since the Reform and Opening up: Seeing Its Research Direction from the Perspective of Organizing Practice

1.2.1 The Subjects of the Movement: Organizational Form and Their Operational Mechanism

When the six decades' women's movement since the founding of the People's Republic of China is reevaluated by the above-mentioned definition, great changes can be seen in its organizational forms: women's federations at different levels under the leadership of the CPC were the only one type of women's organizations existing in the first three decades; however, in the three decades of the post-reform period, such outshining type is replaced by diversified women's groups such as women's federations, women's/gender (feminist) educational and research centers attached to universities or social scientific institutes, and the independent non-governmental women's organizations. Both of the latter groups are classified NGOs since 1990s, and the women's federations have been trying hard to identify themselves with the NGOs also, in spite of the fact that the three types of organizations differ greatly in nature. Judging from the operational mechanism, we can easily see that the advantage of the women's federations lies in its ability to integrate all women's groups for taking common actions by functioning in the "top-down" three-level (or from central to local, then to the grassroots) way of quasi-government bodies; meanwhile, the research centers attached to universities and academic institutes are taking part in social movements in an "inside-out" way, that is, earn a living within the formal institutions to support their social work without (members of such groups still work part-time now); and finally, the NGOs outside the formal institutions that target their services at the specific women groups are mainly run in a "bottom-up" way. In fact, it is the networking of women's organizing and movement in the recent decade that has been obscuring the bounds of the three forms of women's groups. One good case in point is that the networks of the Stop-Domestic-Violence (StopDV), Gender-And-Development (GAD), and the Net on Women/Gender Studies (W/GS) are featured in overlapping at organizational levels and memberships, indicating another integrating tendency in the agents of women's movement.

1.2.2 Developing Tendency: Organization, Relationship and Position

(1) Reform and Opening-up: The Outshining Women's Federation (1982-1992)

All China Women's Federation (ACWF), soon after its resumption of activities at the end of the Cultural Revolution, was trying to handle all the gushing women's problems with the three strategies such as "Promoting Women's Qualities," "Safeguarding Women's Rights and Interests," and "Researching in Women's Problems" by following the instructions of the CPC Central Committee. "Quality Promoting" required women to participate in the reform and in "building up the new order of socialist commodity economy" in the "four-self" spirit: namely, self-dignity, self-confidence, self-supporting and self-promoting. As a result, women in the countryside were encouraged to get involved in the "double-learning and double-competing" campaign, while their urban counterparts were urged to take part in the campaign of "women-making-contributions." The intention was to get women adapted to the economic development in the reform and opening up. As for the "Researching or Studying in Women's Problems," it was actually ignited by some leader's important speeches. For example, when a Central Committee leader again brought up the subject of "women's liberation being an important measurement of social liberation," claiming to "take up safeguarding the legal rights and benefits of women and children as the working principle and major task of the Women's Federation" in April, 1983, the women's federations at provincial levels started to set up each of their own "women's research society" or "research society on marriage and family"[1] one after another. And in 1991, the Women's Studies Institute of China (WSIC), was established for the purpose of studying and making proposals to the government on how to protect the rights and benefits of women and children. But, a close examination of the work of the WSIC shows an interest shift from care of the individual cases in the 1980s to that of the systematic and legislative protection of women's rights and interests in the 1990s. The *New Marital Law* came out in 1980 and the *Law of Safeguarding Women's Rights and Benefits* in 1992 are illustrations of such shift.

(2) Moving on the International Tracks: Three Carts Racing Bridle to Bridle, Confusing Identity and Position (1993-1999)

When the 4th UN World Conference on Women was held in Beijing, China, it not only introduced the topic of the international women's movement and the guiding theories for the movement, but also brought into being the folk women's organizations in the country. "NGO," as a new term and a new type of organization, was introduced to the Chinese at the Conference, and is now rooted deeply in this land. Women's federations and their derived research or service groups, studies centers attached to universities and social scientific institutes, and organizations specifically serving women, were growing just like mushrooms after the rain in this period. The International Conference of *Chinese Women Organizing: Cadres, Feminists, Muslims, Queers* held in Oxford University in 1999, was a gather-together at which all these groups communicated and exchanged ideas and research findings. That was a time when the newborn Chinese NGOs were still weak and small. Many were facing a hard struggle of survival. So "big or small, all NGOs are equal" became a strong

1 Chen Pixian, a member of the CPC Central Committee in charge of the work in All China Women's Federation then, published an article entitled "Take Safeguarding Women and Children's Legal Rights and Benefits as the Working Principle and Task of Women's Federation" on the *People's Daily* in April 27, 1983. As a result, the provincial and municipal women's federations had their research centers set up 2 or 3 years earlier than the universities.

appeal at the conference. And the dispute over whether women's federations should be classified NGOs demonstrates the fact that the three types of women's groups were just like three carts racing bridle to bridle but each was operating on its own. In this period, the distinction in the organizational forms did not stop the communication and cooperation among the Chinese feminists as individuals. The intensive information share before and after the Beijing Women's Conference and the discussions[2] at the meeting, cultivated and trained the first generation of Chinese feminist researchers and activists, many of whom are still actively working for the network of the women's federations, at the various women's groups attached to the universities and Party schools, and in the NGOs outside any of the formal institutions.

(3) Gender-Mainstreaming Promotion: From "Multi-Horses-Towing-One-Car" to the New Positioning of the "Entity of Four" (since 2000)

The greatest impact of the UN 4th World Conference on Women, Beijing 1995 was the conscientious action taken in the promotion of "gender-mainstreaming." When Jiang Zemin, then the CPC General Secretary and Chairman of the People's Republic of China, made a speech on "Setting up the Marxist Ideology on Women within the CPC and the Whole Society" on March 7, 1990, he further clarified Marxist ideology on women be the guideline for the mainstream women's movement in China. However, on September 4, 1995, Jiang, on behalf of the Chinese government, made an official commitment at the 4th World Women's Conference, vowing to "take equality of men and women as the basic state policy for the promotion of our social development"; maybe such promise was not an intentional "butt joint" but a contingency to the "gender-main-

2 For example, feminist scholars in China organized the first, second and third conference on *Chinese Women and Development* and women's studies workshops respectively in Tianjin (1993, 1999), Nanjing (1997), Chengdu (1998), and Boston (1999), in cooperation with the China Women's Society Abroad. The preparation for the NGO Forum of the UN 4th World Conference on Women and all the post-conference memorial activities have enhanced the friendship, connection and cooperation among feminists all over the world.

streaming" strategy proposed in the Beijing Platform for Action (BPfA) of the World Women's Conference in Beijing. Just two years later, the UN made a clear definition on gender-mainstreaming, demanding to include in the designing, implementation, and supervision of legislation, policy, and programs at all levels the concerns and experiences of both men and women. Obviously, its purpose is to realize the equality of men and women by evaluating the impacts and significance of the laws, policies and programs on females and males, thus making sure that both can benefit equally.[3]

The "gender-mainstreaming" initiation under the UN framework has brought a chance to the international women's movement in the 21 century. Having taken advantage of its own legal status and multi-access to resources like their dialogues with the international world and connections with the CPC Party Central Committee, the Central Government, the women masses, and the civic groups, ACWF has managed to unify in legislating, policy-making, and programming the two concepts (gender equality and equality of men and women) into one. As a result, the two concepts that are quite different in nature may appear identical in each of its own context. As a matter of fact, disputes and questions are being constantly made over the concept of "gender" in both the academic and the practical arenas. Some scholars hold that the ideas such as "equality of men and women" and "women's liberation" are the core of Marxist ideology on women, whereas "gender" is a Western feminist discourse ought not to be copied in China; its transliteration *xing bie* is the only correct and proper term if we have to refer to it. Facing such disputes, the ACWF high-level leaders, together with the feminists active both in and out of the women's federations, have creatively coined new Chinese words such as "*xin bie zhu liu hua* (gender-mainstreaming)," "*xin bie ping deng* (gender equality)," and "*xin bie wen hua* (gender culture)," by way of grafting in, diverting, and refitting. These strategies not only "thinning off" but also "clearing up" the political sensitivity resulted in the translation of "gen-

3 http://www.un.org/chinese/esa/women/mainstreaming.htm

der" into "*she hui xin bie*," literally meaning "social sexes." And what's more significant is that the period witnessed unprecedented advance in lawmaking that cares more for women and for gender equality.[4]

Legislation and policy-making need the backup of research in the same way that gender-mainstreaming is in need of the enlightenment by experts from different fields. By setting its Women's Studies Institute (WSIC) as the Standing Secretariat in December 1999, ACWF succeeded in integrating all the research institutes attached to universities, social scientific institutes (at the municipal, provincial or national levels) and women's federations into the Chinese Women's Research Society (CWRS), one that is registered in the Ministry of Civil Affairs. The new organization has gradually expanded its forces and influence by organizing varieties of activities like the annual symposiums, trainings, special topic workshops, consultations, and awards to attract the participation of more community groups or individual members. By 2010, there are as many as 113 community group members and 177 Board of Trustees (most of them are the persons in charge of the organizations). For further integration, 21 community group members were named as women's research/training bases (13 from the universities, 2 in the social scientific institutes, 3 at the Party schools, and 3 from the local women's federations) by a public appraisal in 2006. They are expected to become the nucleus, through which, ACWF/CWRS expect to unite scholars, experts and activists in promotion of legislation and policy-making for the progress of women's movement.

4 High-level ACWF leaders and feminists have been doing such "discourse-graftting" in the 15 years after the World Conference on Women in Beijing. At one conference in December 2010, Peng Peiyun, who used to be Vice Chair of the National People's Congress, Chair of ACWF, and the initiator of the Chinese Women's Research Society, made a keynote speech, in which she not only made juxtaposition of the two terms ("the equality of men and women" and "gender equality"), but also emphasized that "Government is the responsible subject for the implementation of the prime state strategy of men and women being equal. A state mechanism should be constantly developed in completion to secure and advance the equality of men and women, as well as to facilitate women's development, vigorously motivating the gender-equality awareness into the mainstream policy-making course." Tang Meiling. A Summary to the "Conference on Marxist Ideology of Women and the Development of the Awaiting Gender Theory," Women's Research Series, p. 93, 2011. (1).

What makes it possible for ACWF to unite the "three-carts" into a combined force to pull the one "gender-mainstreaming" carriage and to act as the agent to voice out and defend women's interest and guide such actions in a male-dominating political, economical and cultural structure? Obviously, three factors are quite indispensable: steadiness in targets, flexible strategies and indigenous creativities. The number of different forms of organizations is growing drastically in the 21 century. These organizations were greatly isolated from one another as they were so different in locations, conditions, tenets and specific targets. For a certain period in China, the academic feminists and the actionist feminists were taking respective ways simply because the foreign funded projects were heading to different orientations and concerned with different interests.[5] For example, such comments as follows were frequently heard: "The scholars are engaged in studies, the women's federations in movement, and the grassroots in activities." It is a matter of fact that academic feminism has the tendency of being disjointed from both the mainstream international women's movement and from their own society. For instance, the academic feminists have initiated their efforts in getting women's studies into college classrooms with the intention to turn it into one of the formal research disciplines. However, many of the women scholars did not know the 12 fields of of BPfA or The Convention on the Elimination of All Forms of Discrimination against Women (CEADW). Similarly, the women's NGOs engaged in facilitating development, helping the poor, offering legislative

5 NGOs in China have apparently split in two under the funding orientations since the year 2000, namely: the academic scholars vs. the actionists. In October, 2003, Du Fangqin proposed to start the "Cross- boundary Gender Studies and Practice" and organized a relating conference on it. In 2006, under the influence of Chang Pilwha's idea of the "Feminist Knowledge Community," Du began to separate the academic research carried out at colleges, universities, and the social scientific institutions from curriculum teaching and the NGOs focusing on the initiation of law- and policy-making, press publicizing, and service offering, naming the former academic feminists and the latter actionist feminists. Relating descriptions and articles can be found respectively in "Practice and Reflections on Bridging the Gender Activists and Scholars," (Du Fangqin and Wang Zheng (eds.). *Gender Studies*,Volume 2, p. 3-31) and on the website of www.gendercommunity.org set up by the Institute of Gender and Social Development Studies at Tianjin Normal University in 2007.

help, job training, psychological consultation, and health care and services, would not accept the statement of these women scholars, criticizing them as doing self-talking, or publishing essays just to get promoted for professional ranks; claiming that their research was irrelevant, incomprehensible and useless in practice. The fact is, scholars have yet put up no studies or courses that the actionists are badly in need of, whereas the latter have to compose their own training materials and reporting their own findings all by themselves. Similarly, the activities organized by the actionists were not always successful, some programs became mere formalities or even ran into resistance due to a shortage of indigenized theories or methods that could meet the local needs.

Up till now, China does not have a university like Ehwa Womans University in Korea that has been engaged in women's education for as long as a hundred years, and in women's studies for about 40 years. In fact, there is not even an institutionalized all China women's studies society now. The reasoning logic commonly accepted from up to the bottom is just as follows: the issue of gender means the issue of women, and women's issues and problems are in the care of the women's federations. According to such reasoning, it wouldn't be too difficult to understand why in China the gender issues are often attributed to women, and women's issues to the women's federations.

In their efforts to have the research forces integrated in the name of "gender-mainstreaming," ACWF and CWRS were, besides having in their mind the intention of serving the needs of the state legislation, policy-making, survey and demonstration of women's work, also thinking of getting the gender awareness into the mainstream domains like the social sciences and education respectively, considering of the isolation between the academic and the actionists. Since 2004, CWRS has run a series of forums on getting gender awareness into the mainstream education and social scientific institutes. The efficiency was obvious especially in the social scientific domain. A good case in point is the State Social Sciences Funds under the control of the Propaganda Department of Central Committee of the CPC. A total of 139 project proposals on women/gender have been approved between 2005 and 2011, the average yearly number climbs dramatically, from 5 in 2005, when no intervention was taken, to 20 between 2006 and 2010, culminating to 33 in the year of 2011 alone. The project proposals approved are concentrated in fields like Marxism, scientific socialism, the CPC history and construction, applied economics, sociology, law, demography, and politics. Apparently, project proposals on women/gender studies in pragmatic fields are more likely to be approved than that of the basic research in theories, although the latter is the foundation of women's studies. The problem we are facing now is that, the women's research in China has rushed into law and policy making for building up a harmonious society and a harmonious gender culture before having sorted out in all aspects the current and historic conditions of China's patriarchy, or making a profound and in-depth research on the feminist implements such as ontology, epistemology, and methodology, or on the indigenization of all these tools, which are considered of the most criticalness. Fortunately, the slow progress of Gender Mainstreaming gained in education by CWRS and women scholars at colleges and universities has finally led to feminist reflection on the hindering factors: the more superficial one is that women's studies is not yet classified the first or second level disciplines in registeration owing to the confinements of China's higher education in academic, disciplines and degree systems; and the more hidden problem perhaps comes from the fact that China's universities that once shrouded in ideology are presently soaked in marketing principles. They sure find it hard to admit the spirit of criticism embodied in women's studies. The theoretic, social and administrative legalizations or Trio-Legalization of women's studies[6] dreamed by feminists working at colleges and universi-

6 Wang Jun was the first to put forward the idea of Trio-Legalizations in the disciplinary construction of women's studies: gender legalization means to gain a legal positioning in administration, social legalization means to gain social recognition, and theoretical legalization refers to the completion of an independent theoretic system. She also pointed out that "in reality, women's studies could not expect a wider space of development until we have essentially included women's studies as a branch of learning with a completion of the

ties, are left with space in the first two although the realization of administrative legalization is meeting setbacks now. Perhaps the pragmatically oriented disciplinary integration and research cooperation could offer a way out.

What should be noted is that, the alternative way of NGOs' mainstreaming—networking is getting popular in this period. The need of NGOs' organizational development, of course, is one reason, but the greater pushing hands are coming from the foreign foundations. For a time, all the NGOs in China seemed to be netted in, their frequent activities displaying impressive power and influence. However, the financial crisis in 2007 led to shrinking in both the funds and social space. Some NGOs with powerful backing, including a few of the national networks were forced to shift to business registration as they were either "unhooked" from their backings or their supporters "had their boss replaced." As a result, one national network is registered in the district of a city and runs in the name of a " Training Center."

In spite of all the difficulties, feminists are still firmly convinced that nothing can stop the cause of gender equality. For instance, the Anti-Domestic-Violence Network that was set up as early as 2000 under the Chinese Law Society, has been working unremittingly for 12 years and succeeded in having the item of "forbidding domestic violence" included in the 2001 edition of the Revised Marital Law; its network members such as the women's federations at the provincial levels, have actively facilitated the local law-making for the prevention of domestic violence. The drafting on The Law of Preventing and Stopping Domestic Violence that has gained the support and participation of ACWF in its investigation and research, will be presented to the National People's Congress for Approval in 2012. The other women's groups that also have made great contributions to the Chinese women's movement include: The Women's Me-

---

discipline, accepted by the government, society, and insiders of the higher educational system, and won a fundamental legal status in the disciplinary administration." (Wang Jun, 2005).

dia Watch Network, The GAD Network (2001), Shaanxi Women/Family Research Society, and Henan Community Center for Education and Research. The last two are well-known women's NGOs in China that have not only exercised great influence at home and abroad, but also won the trust of women at the grassroots.[7]

1.3 Check on the Law- and Policy-Making in the Decade of Gender-Mainstreaming from the Relationship between Research and Practice

A significant turn in Chinese women's movement started in the year 2000 when ACWF, under the banner of advocating gender mainstreaming and in way of discussions and counsels, began to "join hands " with feminist researchers and actionists, as well as specialists and experts working within the legal and policy-making institutions, to make surveys, give counsels and proposals, or even directly put forward drafts for the government. By doing so, ACWF has expanded its influence on the law and policy making institutions. As a result, "gender" and public policy-making experts are listed in the think tank of the ACWF and the relating ministries and commissions of the Central Government.[8] What is more, ACWF not only took the lead in promoting the revision of the *Law of Securing Women's Rights and Benefits* (2001) and *The Marital Law* (2001),[9] but also taking an active part in bringing out and implementing the *Law of Land Contracting in Rural Areas* (2002), and the *Law of Population and Family*

7 The experience of the six independent women NGOs is a great combination of research and practice. Please refer to *Chinese Women NGO in the Progressive Tense* ed. By Gao Xiaoxian and Xie Lihua, published by Jincheng Publishing House in Beijing, 2009.

8 Nowadays, "experts" relating to issues like women/gender cover a wide range of fields, including scholars engaged in studies of women and gender, or of law and policies, as well as technical official in execution of legislature, administration of laws, and policy making and performing.

9 *Women's Equity Safeguard* was first drafted under the initiation of the Women's Federation and approved by the People's Congress in 1992, and revised in 2005; the 1983 version of the Revised Marital Law was again revised in 2001. A historical view proves that the Women's Federation were playing a leading role in the coming on and revision of the two laws.

Planning (2001), which are composed of 100 legal items closely related to the guarantee of women's rights and benefits. It will again submit for approval of the drafts for setting up or revising the laws such as *The Approaches for Preventing and Curbing Domestic Violence, and the Regulations for Female Workers' Protection* when the "two conferences,"[10] or the NPC and CPPCC conferences are being held in March 2012. Additionally, ACWF takes an obvious turn in viewing policies concerning women and state development, it is a shift from the state or government perspective to that of gender-sensitivity. A case in point is the three-phase *Chinese Women's Development Outline.*[11] Initiated in 1995, the Outline in application has witnessed a gradual promotion of its targets and refining of its index, making it easier to perform in fields such as women suffrage (from the grassroots level at the village to the upper level of authorities), women employment and health, and turning it into what the government has to draw on with in making the law for women/gender equality and formulating the national development.[12] Another case is that ACWF succeeded in preventing the inclusion of "setting up the sectional-employment system" in the National 15th Five Year Planning by initiating a joint-signing among the scholars just before the "two conferences" in 2001. And its success lied heavily on the surveys and studies made by feminist researchers within and without the Women's Federations. As for women suffrage, the Constituent Act of Villagers' Committees revised in 2011, has clarified that the ratio of women representatives shall take up at least 30% of the total. Replacing the vague term of "a proper proportion" with a definite number has made the suffrage target more feasible in performance. Judged by the social impacts, we can see that the legislative policies in favor of

---

10 It refers to the National People's Conference and the Chinese People's Political Consultative Conference held regularly in March.

11 The Five Year Outline (1995-2000) made previous to the World Women's Conference in Beijing, and the two Ten Year Outlines for 2001-2010 and for 2011-2020 are accounting more and more in the making laws and policies that favor gender equality.

12 Jiang Yongping has summarized the whole process of the arguments in her essay "The Discussion on 'Sectional Employment' and 'women going back home' ," please refer to Women's Studies Series 2001 (2).

safeguarding women's rights and benefits are quite popular thanks to the advanced mass media and promotion of people's awareness of rights. When their economic rights concerning land, stocks, or house are violated, a majority of the rural women will turn to the law for their protection.

In the recent decade, the legislature advocating is making great progress with ACWF taking the lead and scholars participating in. Now the Women's Federation is focusing more on taking advantage of "combining research with the application of legislative policies, and continuously turning the women's studies into laws and regulations, policies and measures for the promotion of gender equality."[13] However, in spite of the achievements, a "breakage" is still there in the law text and its application. Sometimes, even contradictions arise in legislature, judicial or policy domains. For example, the 2001 version of the revised marital law has included terms like "the right of spouse" and "the right of birth" regardless of the fact that they are unfit in China's historical context, and the conflicts[14] resulted from the "judicial interpretation (3)" of the Marital Law coming on in 2011, are indication of the juridical logic confusion and a shortage of gender perspective in legislature and judiciary. Besides, with the intensified performance of "capital going down to the countryside and peasants going up in apartment buildings," women are facing more and more new challenges and problems while trying to protect their economic rights of land, housing, and inheriting as well as their rights in political participation. Take land loss as an example, the recent data reveal that: 21% of the rural women lost their land in the year 2010, of which 27.7% were caused by marriage mobility (marriage, divorce, spouse decease),

13 The speech made by Chen Zhili, Chair of ACWF at the Annual Meeting of Chinese Women's Studies on November 22, 2011.

14 With the dominating idea of maintaining family harmony and protecting individual rights, the revised 2001 version of the Marital Law included the "spouse right" and the "birth right." However, in the traditional Chinese cultural inertia, such legislation turned out to offer legal basis for a husband to control his wife's body and secure his right to have sons; The disputes over the Legal Interpretation (3) in the 2011 version of the Marital Law are still going on as such interpretation is suspicious of trying to protect the man's pre-marital housing.

meanwhile, the percentage of men losing their land was as low as 3.7%.[15] These have forced the feminists to reflect on the problems the women's movement has neglected in legislative policy making.

The author hereby believes that inadequate research is the key cause to all the problems. The gap not only exists in applied studies, but also in the basic research in women's studies, and such a gap has been neglected for quite a long time. Two reasons are found responsible for such shortage and negligence: one is that women's studies has not yet been formally admitted in the higher education; the other is the shortage of resources. The limited resources from foreign foundations are heavily action-oriented, thus resulting in shortage of systematic knowledge criticism in academic and disciplinary studies and in its reconstruction. For instance, a lack of studies in women's history will sure lead to the decontextualization in making policies for legislation; the absence of Legal Women's Studies, shortage of theory supports, and insufficient survey of the established legislative policies, all show their results in the pragmatic legislation, that is to consider each case as it stands; and finally, insufficiency in the reception of feminism and subsequent changes in the academic system has crippled the creativity and criticism capability of local feminists, thus leaving a smooth passage for such fashionable term as "building up a harmonious gender culture" to come out easily. As for the experts, there are usually two problems: gender experts generally know little about the law or the science of law, whereas the legal experts have little knowledge of gender, thus leading to the plight in legislative policy making, which can be described as "no ceiling" (lack of theoretic directing) and "no grounding" (decontextualization resulted in difficult implementation). Guo Huimin, a feminist scholar in law, has pointed out the three-ungear in theoretic studies and legislative application worth in-depth thinking: (1) the ungear between theoretic research and the methods of advocating in making legislative

15 *Data Reported of the 3rd Phase Survey on Chinese Women's Social Position* published by ACWF and the National Bureau of Statistics in October 2011.

policies, which leads to focus on equality in form while neglecting the inequality in reality; (2) the ungear between legal case promoting and legislative impelling has resulted in inadequate "case" accumulation in "movement or application," in another word, it is a lack of integration between the actionists and professional academic researchers; (3) the idealization of the gender relationship in Chinese history and culture (like infinitely exaggerating the legend of the "harmony between yin and yang") is off gear to the reality of serious sex prejudice (i.e. the continuous rising in unbalanced sex ratio at birth) (Guo Huimin, 2005). All these problems need feminist researchers and actionists to take serious and in-depth reflections.

2. A New Way for the Indigenous Women's Movement: The Case of a Feminist Participation Action Research

2.1 Background, Issue, and Team

High imbalance of sex ratio at birth is witnessed in China for the past 20 years. But how to handle it? The approach put forward by the Research Group for Promoting Gender Equality at the Central Party School gained supports from The National Population and Family Planning Commission (NPFPC). The proposed approach goes as follows: commence the experimental feminist action research and intervention to explore the more holistic approach that combines the efforts of promoting the gender equality policy and changing the attitude and behavior towards gender at the community level. And since 2008, feminist scholars (in sociology, politics, history, management, and development studies) have joined hands with their activist counterparts in forming a gender research team (hereafter referred to as "the gender team") to work cooperatively with the government organizations (GOs) on specific "issues" in the name of a project. The associated linkage formed between the GOs and the loosely composed gender team proved effective in application. With joint efforts, they have explored ways for promoting gender equality in the rural communities together with the villagers at the grassroots, then extending the experience horizontally to other communities while advocating it in the policy-making authorities. As for the masses, particularly women at the grassroots level, the gender team emphasizes more on extensive participation and mutual empowerment at multi-dimensions (mutual empowerment among women, among the male and female villagers, among village cadres, and between the research team and the villagers). The empowerment of women and the villagers' participation in changing their communities, have not only made it possible for the deprived to regain their lost rights and benefits, but also enhance the results of gender equality achieved in community reconstruction. In the process, the indigenous feminist knowledge production is not only tested but also gaining a rare opportunity for creation and catering to society.

2.2 Strategy, Operation and Effects: Combination of the Bottom-up and Up-down Strategies, and of Research and Applications

2.2.1 Finding the Problems and Causes in Surveys and Research to Locate the Targets and Acting Strategies

Why peasants insist on having sons? Why is it so hard to put into practice the equality of men and women that is defined by the law? What is the relationship between women's current conditions and the imbalanced sex ratio at birth? The gender team has found the structural and comprehensive ills in the system that resulted in the violation of rural women's rights and benefits as follows: negligence of the economic rights of survival and of the participatory rights in communal affairs is the most critical one. Researchers at the gender team have discovered, by tracing down the current Chinese patriarchic mode in its continuous operation to its historical origins at both micro and macro levels, that for the rural women, family and communal patriarchy are the key elements in the well-knit (Private) Individual→Family (Clan)→Administration→Market patriarchic chain.

Starting with the two may perhaps open up a way for both the bottom-up and up-down action studies. So the team planned its action research strategy as follows: to reform the institutional structure of the family and communal patriarchy by having the village rules revised. Here is the roadmap: having the gender institutional structure at grassroots communities changed through cultural transform and ideological renovation, and participatory empowerment—that is to work out the revising scheme together with the villagers.

2.2.2 Empowerment and Action: Exploration in the Promotion of Gender Equality Awareness and Transformation of the Patriarchy at Grassroots

The first tryout community selected by the gender team for gender analysis and participatory empowerment is Zhoushan Village at Daiye Town of Dengfeng City in Henan Province. By empowerment we mean to analyze and deconstruct the currently applied rules of the collective and family patriarchy in the community based on the villagers' living environment and conditions, and their individual experience so as to illustrate to the villagers the structural factors that lead to the violation of women's rights and interests.

First of all, we took efforts to find the gender discrimination loop a woman suffers in her life cycle by tracing down the cause and effect of the discrimination performed under family patriarchy: selective abortion before birth; abandonment or discrimination after birth; becoming an "outsider" of her own family and of her husband's family, while it is considered her duty to bear sons to carry on the family line for her husband; but her own intention is also to bear boys, for fear that a girl will suffer another round of discrimination. The result is: most families with daughters think " daughters are 'useless' " as they can neither carry on the family line nor provide for their aged parents, nor attend upon their funerals. The data collected at the participatory training in Zhoushan Village illustrate that 100% respondents in the research agree that only sons can carry on the family line, and that 96% accede that sons are the life insurance of their parents.

Secondly, we inspired the villagers to find gender discrimination embodied in the community rules of participating public affairs, intending to find a way of change from the grassroots. For instance, when it comes to issues like resource allocation and participation of public affairs, the collective patriarchy at village level has not only copied and extended the family patriarchic rules in marriage, gender-based labor division, and inheritance of property, but also had women in marriage mobility (marriage, divorce, spouse decease) derived of their economic and public affairs participating rights. Their excuse is that these women have lost their "villager identity" according to the legal provisions of the National Household Register (national administrative patriarchy). The fact that women are not allocated homestead because they must move out when getting married, proves that it is marriage mobility that leads to their vulnerable position in the community. And the gender blindness in the community decision making process is conspiracy of the public patriarchy and family patriarchy, which has not only ruled out any possibility for women born in the village to become the mainstay of the community, but also given them the excuse to exclude the married women in participating public affairs by the traditional gender-based labor division. A comparison of the visible village rules with that of the invisible regulations in applications has enabled the villagers to see how women have always been treated unfairly. And the result is an action, which is started with a revision of the village rules and regulations.

Women turned out to be the main force in propelling the transform. The first case in point is the "Women's Handiwork Association." Established in 2003 under the support of the Henan Community Center for Education and Research (HCCER), the Association has been engaged in activities aiming at empowering women of their awareness and capabilities, though their initiative was just to make income. It is the female sensitivity of gender that enabled the Gender Team to find out the illegal items existing in the old village rules and in the invisible regulations. For example, the abolished old Village Rules were composed of 10 provisions primarily aiming at punishment (fines); and of the 13 Provisions applied for allocation of grain cash, one defined that "none of the married women whose household register still remains in the village shall enjoy her share of the grain cash ," and another discriminative provision was "anyone who does not live in the village shall not enjoy the treatment even though the household is registered here."

The ideological transform was set on advocating new marriage trend as the break. And the selection of such a break was again the result of discussions held between the Gender Team and the Women's Handiwork Association. All the Association members worked together to prepare a big wedding ceremony for Hao Zhi's daughter. This was the first of its kind in which a man moved into his wife's house upon marriage here. The wedding, that marks the overturn of the patriarchic marital system, has played an positive role in publicizing the masses, self-educating, and igniting activities of change (see the illustrations).

In March 2009, villagers at Zhoushan succeeded in having their Village Rules revised, and it is celebrated the first Village Rules revised by Chinese peasants themselves that featured in gender equality and safeguarding women's rights and interests. Its main breakthrough lies in gender equality in the community public affairs. As far as women's economic rights are concerned, it has all the provisions in the *Law of Safeguarding Women's Rights and Benefits* and in the *Land Contracting Law* really work at the grassroots. For instance, the liberty in marriage (residency) now defines that any man that lives in his wife's house after marriage will enjoy the same treatment as all the other villagers; the divorced, the widowed, as well as their children shall be treated the same as all the other villagers once they have their household register moved back. As for the communal participating rights, the revised Village Rules provide that the ratio of women representatives at the villagers' conference shall be no less than 50%, and women to be elected in the decision-making group will be no less than 1/3. Meanwhile, the communal transform has advanced gender equality within the family by advocating the following ideas: children have equal obligations for providing or nurturing their parents and enjoy the equal rights of inheriting their properties, men and women are equal in participating social activities, they should both do housework and take common efforts to stop domestic violence.

2.2.3 The Impacts of One Village's Change

The work has been carried out from 1 pilot village in 2009 to 10 different pilot villages, and finally expanded to the whole city of Dengfeng in 2010. And there are two missions to be done in the year 2011, one is to put into practice the revised pro-gender-equality village rules in the tryout counties by the villagers' self-organizing, self-managing and self-servicing; the other is persuading the state authorities to expand the pilot communities. Now the authorities has agreed to a program that will start the campaign of revising the village rules in 100 pilot counties and cities.

From virtual to practical: the pro-gender-equality village rules have turned what is beautifully written and spoken, or even what is conflicting, into something that is operational, feasible, realizable, enjoyable and fairly practical. That is a real preservation of rights and interests. Besides, such process participation is in fact a democracy of self-rule that can help rebuild values and new community management in the rural areas. Needless to say, changes from the grassroots are the true forces to challenge and crack the patriarchic linkage. It can hopefully liberate both men and women villagers, and change the managing pattern of the rural communities.

From villagers to officials: The voluntary changes of grassroots teach a good lesson to government officials at all levels. Many of the officials used to govern by issuing orders or with punishment and fines, as they were suspicious of the villagers' consciousness and creativity. Now they have changed their ideas. One official responsible for family planning at Daiye Town made the following comment: "Revising the village rules and constructing the new village by villagers' self-rule, what we are doing is of the same significance as what happened 30 years ago in Xiaogang Village, Anhui, when the land contracting started; theirs was an economic reform in ownership, whereas ours is initiating an in-depth revolution in the culture and institutions!"

From bottom-up: high authority advocating plus a few years' experiment in wider practice may bring out new policies and laws. Zhao Baige, head of the National Population and Family Planning Commission, laid emphasis on the "masses" (especially women's) participation and on their being well informed at the High Authority Advocating Workshop organized by the Research Team at the end of 2010. She said: "Great plans, decisions, policies and institutions could hardly be put into practice or bring real benefits to the people without the participation of the masses." She hoped that the work could "push forward the progress and change in culture, and finally lead to institutional innovation."

Combination of research and action: Liang Jun, a feminist actionist engaged in community education and development, keeps saying that "However hard I might try, I could not have the peasants generate such power for change if the patriarchic research had not found a solution to abolish the old idea of 'having a son to carry on the family line'!" And I myself have, in observation of the transform facilitating, seen the necessity of transforming disciplinary and academic knowledge into public knowledge before it can be understood and used by the media, decision-making authorities, and the general intellectuals; similarly, public knowledge needs to be popularized via propaganda and education before it can be accepted by the ordinary people for a change of their attitude, which in turn, will lead to changed behaviors. In a word, only the knowledge and strategy that can call on common people's will to change, and that are helpful to the change can be held as knowledge or learning of real availability.

A close cooperation between feminist actionists and researchers can create a perfect match for theoretical studies and their application in reality.

Four years have passed, and it is still hard to predict the result of the transform. But judging from the changes that are taking place in China's rural regions, we can tell that the attractive combination of studies and practice will seduce more people to follow.

References

AACWF and the National Bureau of Statistics (2011), *Data Reported of the 3rd Phase Survey on Chinese Women's Social Position.*

Chang, Pilwha (2006), *Joys and Pains of Women's Studies Institute Building in Asian Countries*, International Conference of Women's Studies between China and Korea, Tianjin, China.

______ (2008), "Feminist Consciousness and Women's Education: The Case of Women's Studies, Ewha Womans University," *Asian Journal for Women's Studies,* Vol. 14 No. 2, pp. 7-29.

Gao, Xiaoxian and Xie Lihua (2009), *Chinese Women NGO in the Progressive Tense*, Beijing: Jincheng Publishing House.

Guo, Huimin (2005), "Gender and Women's Human Rights: Also on the Legal Analytical Methods of Gender," *Gender Equality and Law Studies as Well as the Countermeasures*, Tan Lin and Jiang Xiuhua (eds.).

Jiang, Yongping (2001), "The Discussion on 'Sectional Employment' and 'Women Going back Home'," *Women's Studies Series*, 2001(2).

Li, Xiaojiang (1997), *Women's Studies Movement: A Case Study of China*, Hang kang: University of Oxford Press.

Wang, Jun (2005), "Women's Studies" Seen in the Perspective of Disciplinary Institutions, *Women's Research Series* (Supplement).

Zhang, Naihua (2001), "Searching for 'Authentic' NGOs: The NGO Discourse and Women's Organizations in China," *Chinese Women Organizing*, Ping-chun Hsiung (ed.), University of Oxford Press, pp.165-168.

Chapter 6

Asian Feminist Pedagogy and Women's Empowerment:

A Case of Ewha Global Empowerment Program[1]

LEE Myoung Sun

1. Introduction

It has been almost 40 years since the first women's studies course was opened at Ewha Womans University. Corresponding with recent global trends, interest in women's studies has flagged markedly in South Korea, with expressions of worry that the social backlash against feminism may increase. At the same time, women's studies is moving beyond university campuses and showing signs of gradual outward expansion in avenues such as adult education, women activist training by NGOs, women's leadership programs, gender equality education programs for public officials, and various other international programs for women. Scholars and instructors teaching women's studies and feminist courses at universities and adult education programs remark on the many changes feminism has produced in terms of sharpened awareness of gender discrimination and the numerous social advances in empowering women individually and socially

1 This paper was published entitled "Asian Feminist Pedagogy and Women's Empowerment: A Preliminary Analysis of EGEP" in the *Asian Journal of Women's Studies*, Vol. 20 No. 2 (2014).

and contributing to the beginning of real life changes (Lee, 2013). That is, Women's Studies has contributed to the formation of 'women subjects,' allowing women to reconstruct their lives and create changes in their world.

The practical attributes of women's studies and feminist education programs are connected not only to the ideological characteristics of feminism but also to the praxis of feminist pedagogy. The latter is the field where feminism and feminist theory are practiced and comprise not just teaching skills that remain in the classroom, but a process and an experience where the theories of feminism are realized, and a locus of praxis that brings change to individuals and society with attributes of a social movement (hooks, 1994; Weiler, 1995; Larson, 2005; Hur, 2013). Accordingly, feminist education sites, as well as research on feminist pedagogy, demonstrate the praxis and impact of feminism and are very important for expanding feminist women's education.

Regrettably, many stories about the concrete experience and results of feminist education are told at the informal and individual level rather than in the domain of research. Despite the almost forty-year long history of women's studies in South Korea, actual case studies and empirical research on feminist pedagogy and feminist educational sites are very limited and mostly restricted to theoretical reviews and epistemological approaches.[2] This stems from the limitations in quantifying or objectively measuring changes in awareness and women's experiences of feminist education, and the difficulty in analyzing the impact of feminist education on individuals and groups, as well as identifying factors of change. But to make the achievements of women's studies education visible and to execute feminist education more effectively, case studies and empirical research relating to such education must be produced and collected on

2 Compared to active research on feminist pedagogy in western feminist academia since the 1980s, in Korea, research on feminist pedagogy is limited both qualitatively and quantitatively. Since the 2000s, there have been some theoretical studies on feminist pedagogy, for example, Nah (1999), Yu (2006), Song (2002), Jeong (2004), Kim (2007), Choi (2008), The most recent studies showing interest in the fields of feminist pedagogy include Jeon (2013), Jeong (2013) and Hur (2013).

an ongoing basis, while a requisite theorization based on these is done as well. In particular, women's studies education taking place in various contexts of the university campuses very urgently require the accumulation of diverse feminist pedagogy-related case studies, module development, and theoretical studies. In this setting, the present study, based on the case of Ewha Global Empowerment Program (EGEP) as a field of feminist pedagogy, will look at the concrete makeup of EGEP and analyze the effects of this praxis of feminist education on its Asian women activist participants. With this objective, the study is presented in three parts. The first will briefly review the concept and theory of 'Asian feminisms,' which makes up the epistemological backdrop and theoretical framework of the EGEP. The second part explains how the concept of Asian Feminisms is being implemented and practiced on-site as feminist pedagogy. The third part analyzes the experiences of the Asian women activists who have participated in EGEP to show how the program empowers women and produces 'Asian women subjects.'

This is only a preliminary analysis because, at present, it is certainly too early and perhaps too close to the implementation of the program to do a comprehensive evaluation of the program itself and its impact. Nonetheless, an interim analysis and review would be essential for improving future practice. The objective of EGEP is stated as "the empowerment of Asian women activists and fostering of future women leaders." EGEP was initiated by Kim Sun-wook, a former member of the steering committee of the Asian Center for Women's Studies and the 13th President of Ewha Womans University. Her understanding of the significance of Asian Women's Studies and her commitment to the cause of women's empowerment led to the creation of such program.

Since its initial operation in 2012 until the present, EGEP has been offered 5 times with 20-25 participants in each term, totaling 103 women from 33 countries joining in the program so far.[3] There are likely be many

3 Currently, as of the program's fifth term, a total of 103 women activists from 33 countries

different theoretical approaches to review programs such as the EGEP but this study focuses on the aspect of pedagogy, utilizing diverse qualitative data about the participants such as survey data,[4] essays, evaluation reports, recordings of group talks, proceedings from the Open Forums, participants' papers published in the *Asian Journal of Women's Studies (AJWS)*[5] etc. This is based on my own experiences of planning the program, participating in it and observing the total process as an EGEP faculty member and organizer.

2. Epistemological Background: 'Asian Feminisms'

'Asian Feminisms and Transnational Activism,'[6] EGEP's first program theme, epitomized its theoretical and practical framework theme. This was created three years ago, but the context of its emergence was the construction of 'Asian feminism' that has been developing through the growth and institutionalization of women's studies at Ewha Woman's University since the 1970s and in some projects of the ACWS for 'Asian Women's Studies' since the 1990s (Miske et al., 1998; Kim & Kang, 2001). Asian Women's Studies began, as Chang Pilwha, one of pioneers who developed Asian

have participated. Of the 103, there were 96 Asian participants from 27 Asian countries, also including 7 participants from Africa and Central and South America from the fourth term. Age range spanned from early the 20s through mid-40s with those in their 20s and 30s comprising the large majority (85 women: 84%). As for educational background, participants holding MA degrees were 56 (54%), BA degrees 38 (37%), Ph.D.s 8 (8%) and high school diploma 1 (1%), indicating that most were highly educated. The reason why this trait appears was because the total applicant pool itself was mostly a highly educated group. The fields in which they were engaged were diverse, including education, development, VAW, children, reproductive/health, as well as immigration, labor, government, environment, religion, media, agriculture, etc.

4 A questionnaire survey conducted in 2013 of 57 EGEP participants from terms 1 to 3 received 28 responses. The survey was a post-facto investigation of EGEP experiences and effects of the program.

5 Some EGEP participants' papers (Ame, 2013; Cai, 2013; Jurado, 2013; Patria, 2013; Vedhanayagi, 2013; Kunwar, 2013; Khanis, 2013; Ying, 2013; Akhter, 2014; Aryal, 2014; Jayarathne, 2014; Valerio, 2014) were published in the *AJWS*.

6 From the fourth term, EGEP expanded the scope of participating countries to Africa and changed its pedagogical theme to "Transnational Feminisms and Women's Activism."

Women's Studies, has stated, as critical-reflection about doing women's studies as a Korean feminist (Chang, 1996, 2006, 2007) and gradually developed into joint projects in partnership within an Asian feminist community.[7] Asian Women's Studies was attended by conceptual disputes such as whether it should be 'Women's Studies in Asia' or 'Asian Women's Studies'; the raising of various debates and issues such as whether solidarity between Asian women was possible and whether the concept of 'Asian feminism,' was to be understood in opposition to so-called 'western feminism' or as an alternative to it (Kim & Kang, 2001; Lee, 2008; Kim, 2010). Ultimately, these disputes politicized the concept of Asia (Kim, 2010) and became the force behind the development of theories of 'Asian feminisms.' Rather than a macro-discourse or concrete theory, Asian feminism is still an ongoing project and a form of feminist praxis. EGEP is a project within this process, an actual field for practicing the epistemology of Asian Feminisms, as well as a feminist space for producing 'Asian women subjects' (Lee, 2008). In the following pages some core concepts relating to EGEP's epistemological background and theoretical frame are gleaned from some feminist scholars' thoughts about Asian Feminisms (Chang, 2007, 2008; Du, 2005; John, 2005; Cho, 1997; Kim, 2005, 2010; Lee, 2008).

First of all, Asian feminism is not a local or regional feminism, opposed to global feminism or western feminism, but rather aims to be both a critical reflection on existing western feminism's Eurocentric hierarchy and an alternative discourse that is critical of the 'Othering' of Asian wom-

7 From the founding of the Asian Center for Women's Studies in 1995, the *Asian Journal of Women's Studies (AJWS)* was published (Khullar, 2005) and afterwards pushed forward with a project called "Women's Studies in Asia: Knowledge, Exchange. Theory and Practice" jointly with eight Asian countries including China, the Philippines, and Thailand, over three years, this project has had the participation of female scholars from eight Asian countries as researchers, as workshop and conference organizers and participants. The result of the project was the publication of feminist textbooks for seven countries (Miske et al., 1998; ACWS & KWI, 2000; Kim & Kang, 2001). The partnership and networking of these Asian women's studies scholars continued through various projects of the ACWS. This served as the springboard for the founding of the Asian Women's Studies Association in 2007.

en. Asian feminism is not a feminism based simply in the physical geographicality of 'Asia,' but is a feminist perspective and theory interpellating the agency of othered and relativized women subjects. Asian feminism critiques western perspectives that view Asian women as 'Other' and as passive, while emphasizing the agency and subjectivity of Asian women as subjects of change. As subjects, women are not given, but exist in a process of formation, produced through praxis based in the actual circumstances of their lives (Lee, 2008). In Asian feminism, Asian women are not simply victims of patriarchal society, of biased representation by the West, or victims of patriarchal oppression. Instead, they are subjects who create change, who produce knowledge and praxis (Kim, 2005, 2010).

Asian feminism does not demand or require an essential or universal base or commonality, regionally, culturally or historically. On the contrary, 'differences' that appear in women's lives encompass not only gender but also race/ethnicity, class, and sexual orientation, and from that viewpoint account for diversity and differences among women that emerge in concrete reality. Asian feminism respects differences and diversity among women and aims for solidarity/alliance based in the same. In other words, Asian feminism is a praxis that transcends a single theory and connects with values that aim for communal change. Even if women's problems vary by local context, it is true to say that in most societies they share the experience of victimization, violence and discrimination. Violence, the trafficking of women, political and economic inequalities, that is, the so-called problems of gender inequality, intersect and correlate with social problems like poverty, economic development-related issues, environment, peace and immigration. Moreover, as globalization rapidly advances, women's issues transcend local problems, become intimately connected, and impact each other globally. To resolve these problems, a transnational solidarity/alliance of women that eclipses regional borders is necessary. This transnational solidarity of women respects mutual 'differences' among women, signifying a formation and practice of a feminist community transcending the borders between states based on understanding and sympathy for difference (Kim, 2005, 2010; Lee, 2008).

The perspectives and aims of Asian Feminisms form an epistemology that imbues EGEP's educational program, and shape the theoretical background for the feminist pedagogy implemented by EGEP. From this perspective, EGEP is a space that produces Asian women subjects through Asian women's praxis. That is, the program is a praxis of Asian feminisms, a process producing political, socially-conscious awakened women subjects, a site made up of Asian women who are not caught up in regional limitations but are subjects who also grasp political sensitivities at the international/global level.

3. EGEP's Feminist Pedagogy

3.1 Creating 'Asian Feminist Pedagogy'

As a field where Asian women subjects are produced, what is EGEP's educational curriculum like? What attributes make up the feminist pedagogy it implements? What are EGEP's educational curriculum and feminist pedagogy like and how do these contribute to the production of Asian women subjects? As a general definition, feminist pedagogy is an educational theory that explains and contests the structure perpetuating gender inequality against women and seeks solutions for it. At the same time, it is also a pedagogical method for practicing that theory (Song, 2002). Feminist scholars have commonly argued that the objective of feminist pedagogy is women's empowerment, criticizing the *othering* of women as passive existences in educational curricula, and that women need to be reconstructed as subjects of education (hooks, 1994, 2003; Weiler, 1995; Shrewsbury, 1993). In feminist pedagogy, empowerment is an important principle for liberating women from the oppressions they experience (Parry, 1996). That is, empowerment is understood as competence and strength allowing us to interpret our lives more critically and to reconstruct our social identities, and initiate change in our lives. Empowerment includes the ability to lead individual and collective social change (Shrewbury, 1993; hooks, 1994; Larson, 2005).

The major principles of feminist pedagogy are rooted in the women's movement, particularly 'consciousness-raising' (CR) as one of the activities of women's liberation movements in the West during the 1960s and 1970s. CR groups were collective, leaderless groups in which women shared their oppressed experiences in androcentric society. They discussed women's issues such as sexuality, work, family and participation in public arenas and pursued to address these problems through social and political actions (Evans, 1979; Weiler, 1995). In the 1980s, as women's studies became institutionalized in the universities, feminist pedagogy began to be theorized in earnest. The pioneer theorist of feminist pedagogy was a feminist scholar and activist, bell hooks, whose feminist pedagogy placed importance on 'dialogue,' 'participation,' and 'experience' (hooks, 1989, 1994, 2003), and her theories are still influential among researchers of feminist pedagogy.

Principles being applied to the field of feminist pedagogy are not fixed or systematized. Diverse concepts and methodologies have been newly created and displayed depending on educational background, objective, and locus of activity. That is, the educational praxes of feminist pedagogy are not any single approach theorized by a particular researcher or academic, but include experiences and praxes created together by teachers and students, by women activists and feminists at their many sites of activity, and in women's studies classrooms. As a site of feminist education, EGEP adopts the core values and concepts of feminist pedagogy in a general sense. At the same time, it has developed some of its own core educational concepts and practices based in Asian Feminisms which is implemented through the program. In this sense, EGEP is charting a new territory for 'Asian Feminist Pedagogy' and broadening its scope.

3.2 Educational Practices and Principles

EGEP's main objective is fostering women leaders through the empowerment of Asian women activists. Given this goal, the program is targeted at 1) Asian women activists, that is, professional women's groups or feminists active in gender or women's NGOs; 2) It is a short-term, two-week program with 70 hours of instruction, including sub-programs such as Lectures Seminars,, the Open Forum , a Study Tour, Action Plan sessions, and Social Hours; 3) It is a residential education program in which participants and EGEP faculty members (as facilitators) reside together at the Ewha campus dormitory; 4) EGEP faculty members are feminist scholars, women activists, experts from international organizations, not only from Korea but from all over Asia and elsewhere; 5) Participants number 20-25 in each course and are selected through a public call for submissions and a screening process; 6) Participants come from diverse national, ethnic, and religious backgrounds; 7) The ages of the participants are also varied, ranging from the 20s to the 40s. The majority are in their 20s and 30s and hold a BA or higher degree; and 8) English is the medium of communication.

The EGEP has an educational praxis centered in concepts like 1) reciprocal learning; 2) participatory education; 3) relevance of Asian women's experience; 4) integration of theory and praxis; and 5) women's solidarity. Of course, these do not represent a fixed and unchangeable system but are minimal, flexible principles that may be revised and supplemented.

First, EGEP is oriented for reciprocal learning. Not only participants, but all those involved in the program, including faculty members and organizers, respect equality and reciprocity. Feminist pedagogy critiques the dichotomous hierarchy of traditional teaching methods in which the teacher embodies knowledge and authority and the student exists only as knowledge recipient (Larson, 2005; Nah, 1999; Choi, 2008; Song, 2002). Furthermore, feminist pedagogy views the teacher-learner relationship as fluid, where each learns from the other. In such a pedagogical environment, teachers and learners constitute a relationship in which they invest power in one another and offer reciprocal support for mutual empowerment (Song, 2002). Of course, in the real world, hierarchical difference between teachers and students cannot be eradicated completely, but at EGEP, faculty members and organizers, while acting as educational curriculum facilitators, share in the identity of the learners. Inasmuch as participants are neither authorities with absolute knowledge nor simply recipients of knowledge, they interact with teachers; and insofar as both teachers and students learn from and impact one another, they exist on equal terms.

Second, we are oriented towards participatory education. All participants are subjects of education, of knowledge production and praxis; therefore, a participatory educational environment for that purpose must be supported. The educational curriculum encourages maximization of the participants' active educational participation and values debates, presentations, and group activities. Participants are encouraged to participate in the educational curriculum using their own initiative, but they are also encouraged to take care that a few people do not dominate or take over the lead in debates and group activities. A teacher's lecture is not a unilateral imparting of knowledge but a process which prompts debates and questions. The utmost consideration is also given to environmental factors, such as the arranging of desks or seats in a circle to encourage face-to-face communication between teacher and participants and among participants, sometimes two-way, sometimes multi-directional.

Third, we respect women's experience as an important dimension of education and knowledge production. Feminist pedagogy values women's experience and experiences of oppression, rather than objective, rational knowledge given in books as an important source for producing knowledge (Foss & Foss, 1994; Parry, 1996). Feminist education also does not discourage expressions of emotion (Larson, 2005), and in the feminist classroom, tears, anger, silence, joy and enthusiasm co-exist and are accepted as a natural part of the learning process (Morgan, 1996). The valuation of women's experiences is an important aspect of the epistemology in the women's movement and feminist academia as manifested in the representative feminist tenet, 'the personal is political.'

It is viewed in the program that individual experiences, particularly of an 'Asian woman activist,' and experiences of women's oppression are important repositories of knowledge production and pedagogical resource. We arrange programs, including presentations, group debates and group discussions so as to integrate women's experiences into the educational curriculum. In this, participants talk about their lives and experiences as women activists and feminists and analyze them together. In this space, the participants must be encouraged to speak and their differing experiences and perspectives are respected and supported rather than judged or critiqued. This environment allows these women's experiences, often devalued in patriarchal society, to be re-interpreted. Moreover, it allows us to understand our respective differences and commonalities in the context of Asia through experience-sharing with other women. Also, in the process of analyzing our own experiences, alongside those of other women and searching for practical alternatives, they experience individual and collective empowerment.

Fourth, various attempts and efforts are made to encourage integration of theory and praxis. The linkage or integration of theory and praxis reflects the valuation of an old tradition in the feminist camp, that is, that knowledge and theory production are not separate from praxis and, especially, that feminist knowledge is intimately connected to the actualities of the women's movement. We not only conduct on-site visits to Korean NGOs but seek to integrate theory and praxis through a variety of programs. For instance, lecture seminars include theoretical instruction and debates on transnational women's activism, which lead on to field work. Participants have opportunities to join in at the Wednesday Demonstrations,[8] meet military comfort women, and make public statements before

8 Since 1992, the 'Wednesday Demonstration' has been held every Wednesday in front of the

the gathered demonstrators. Also, concrete action plans are established for transnational activist initiatives and for women's solidarity on the military comfort women issue. Finally, we emphasize generating women's solidarity and alliance. While the participants are all women activists, most come from diverse familial, cultural, religious, class, and national backgrounds and are active in a variety of women's movements. The program respects their diversity and differences, and based on these, creates local/global networks and alliances. We ensure that EGEP becomes a feminist space based on women's friendship, trust, and sisterhood.

3.3 Tensions between Feminist Ideals and Reality

While putting the program together, the EGEP organizers held several rounds of debates, seminars and advisory meetings with domestic and overseas consultants.[9] In this process, many issues were raised and deliberated on, such as: How is EGEP distinctive from other international education programs? Would the positionality of the program's host country (South Korea) operate as a hierarchy between nations in the curriculum? What/Who is a feminist leader? Who are more suited to be participants in the program, the so-called 'talented, superior women,' or women who may require more training opportunities? And would it be politically correct to use English as a common language for Asian women activist education?

These issues represent standards and values to be carefully weighed when thinking about the perspective of Asian feminisms and for implementing feminist pedagogy. For example, discussions about its distinc-

Japanese embassy in Seoul to censure the colonial military 'comfort woman' system and to seek an apology from the Japanese government.

9 From EGEP's inception until its full-operation, the program benefitted directly and indirectly from a resource group of women's studies scholars and feminists from Korea and other Asian countries, acting as advisors and faculty members. ACWS hosted a specialist workshop in April 2011 with the objective of developing the program. At the workshop, 20 feminist scholars from seven Asian countries (Korea, Philippines, Thailand, China, Indonesia, Vietnam, and India) participated. Also, several expert advisory meetings were held with feminists, women's policy experts and women activists from South Korea.

tiveness from other educational programs and the positionality of the host country included concerns about how an international program geared toward women from so-called developing countries could 'Other' the participants as candidates for 'enlightenment.' Discussions about participants addressed not only the issue of whom the program was to target but also, in a competition-driven world, how EGEP will realize the values of feminism. In fact, the selection process[10] for choosing the 20-25 women every term from among the several hundred applicants has sometimes produced conflicts and dilemmas in which the feminist values of 'cooperation' and 'community' clash with 'competition.' The use of English also remains another point of political contention, illustrating the contradiction between the standpoint of 'Asian feminisms' and reality.

In reality, there was no single answer to be applied in all situations. Some of these points are still being debated today or have been shelved as unresolvable. But through these debates, EGEP organizers engaged in a process of opinion-sharing regarding such points as: 'EGEP is a feminist community for reciprocal learning,' 'Women leaders are feminist subjects who create change for gender equality in society,' and 'As an international program we cannot avoid the use of English, but the participants' English skills should not outweigh other standards, such as passion and dedication to women's activism.'[11] The process of raising and debating these dilemmas, struggles, and issues reflects paradoxes in which feminist pedagogy collides with reality, but at the same time, it illustrates that feminist pedagogy is a negotiation, a process of feminist praxis.

10 EGEP selects participants through a screening process, following a public call for applications. The demand for education is very high, and for each program term as few as 160 and as many as over 400 applications are received from which 20-25 are selected. More than 1500 applications were received over the course of the first five terms.

11 Minimal selection standards are employed to bolster the objectivity and consistency of the screening process: a career as a woman activist, expertise in women's issues, potential for contributing to the local/global society, potential for growth as a future leader.

3.4 The Experiences[12] of Asian Women Activists: Empowerment and Formation of 'Asian Women Subjects'

What do the participants experience during the process of the program? What meaning do these experiences have? Participants express their experiences, feelings, and transformations in consciousness in various ways. Based on the participants' experiences, the concepts appearing most frequently and commonly are 'confidence,' 'leadership,' 'learning,' 'emotional support,' 'healing,' 'consideration,' 'elevation of consciousness,' 'positive attitude,' 'strength,' 'recharging,' 'courage,' 'hope,' 'connectivity,' and 'solidarity' etc. These experiences are the building blocks of empowerment and at the same time can be its outcome. Furthermore, empowerment experiences are a testament to the ways in which Asian women subjects are produced in the real context of Asian feminist pedagogy. Women activists participate as subjects of knowledge production and education, make their voice heard, and share their experiences reciprocally. Also, they newly interpret their individual and local experiences and search for possibilities for alliance to create change in Asian contexts.

3.5 Participating as Subjects of Knowledge Production and Education

The experience of empowerment is expressed in various ways. Two of the most common expressions used are 'confidence' and 'leadership.' Participants have commonly reported: "This program gave me confidence" or "I've gained new vision for the work I'll be doing." Such self-evaluation suggests a heightened sense of leadership and confidence in their expertise as women activists. Various paths for gaining confidence were

12 The experiences and cases analyzed in this chapter (framed in quotation marks) were partially excerpted from participants' evaluation reports, presentation papers, recordings of Group Talk, and discussions in class etc. Some are stories or feedback recounted to the researcher in individual discussions during the course of the program.

observed. Feminist theory and strengthening of knowledge through education bolster confidence in one's own expertise. Learning and knowledge production are carried out reciprocally and simultaneously in diverse pedagogical settings. For example, Open Forums are spaces where discourses on Asian feminism are produced. At these forums, participants share their papers on various local women's movements and on issues such as violence against women, education, health, reproduction, and patriarchal customs like child marriage. In this process, they listen to each other's presentations and expand their knowledge, while at the same time participating themselves as subjects of knowledge production. Based not on 'theory in texts' but on 'our lived experiences,' participants are able to better and more deeply reflect upon, understand and analyze 'our problems,' not problems of 'othered' Asian women and not from 'the West or a westernized gaze.' The experience of standing on the conference hall stage as a presenter during the Open Forum session, speaking in a public place and communicating her agenda to the public, also becomes a leadership training opportunity. One woman activist said: "I was very active in my local area but always lacked confidence when surrounded by male leaders and just sank into the background. After presenting at the Open Forum, I felt myself stronger, that I grew. I think I can go back and work with more confidence."

3.6 The Meanings of First Experience and Crossing Boundaries

In a patriarchal society, women live under numerous taboos and prohibitions that limit their autonomous choices and their ability to resist/be agents. Even as activists, women live under limitations and difficulties as 'women.' They speak endlessly of their tireless efforts to overcome the taboos and limitations they face. For them, getting past these boundaries, stepping outside the barriers of social oppression against women, represent a challenge and accomplishment. A typical instance is university education. Many of the participants commented that women attaining higher education is a rare exception in their society positioned within the milieu of Asia and related how they overcame the objections of family and relatives. Their stories show that higher education for women is not only a privilege but a challenge and an overcoming of individual and social barriers and oppression.

EGEP is another boundary these women have surmounted. The women participants view the program experience as one of achieving 'first-time experiences,' of breaking taboos, and of meeting challenges. One participant from a province in Pakistan said, "In our society, for a woman to leave home and go to a foreign country on her own can be problematical. Coming to this program required great determination. For me it's been an important challenge and accomplishment." EGEP is also a transnational space that transcends the borders of the state to which the women belong physically and psychologically. Within that transnational space, women are in a 'safe space,' free from political surveillance and oppression. Participants debate with fellow women activists about the impact of political oppression, disputes, wars on women; and women with no experience of political agency such as demonstrations confess to being impressed by the experience of participating in the Wednesday Demonstration for the military comfort women. Crossing borders represents more than the challenge and accomplishment of some limited opportunity.

It also includes the experience of overcoming small norms and taboos of their daily lives. One woman who grew up in an Islamic social setting whispered, "dancing with other participants at farewell party was very impressive to me. Actually it was my first experience. I had never before danced in front of people outside my family." In the Social Hour program, donning training wear and running about playing soccer with colleagues was also a first experience for some. Although the first experiences in the EGEP space recounted might seem trivial or commonplace, these paradoxically demonstrate the oppressive and controlled positionalities they occupy within their patriarchal, androcentric societies. They are 'political' in the sense that their experiments with border crossing, through these first experiences, were opportunities to gain new courage and confidence with respect to their lives. These new ordinary life experiences, some in public settings, allowed the women to "discover desire" hidden within them, and gave them "courage and confidence to go to graduate school" after returning home, and "desire to try more aggressive advocacy" as a feminist.

3.7 Recounting Experience and Mutual Support

The participants' experiences as women activists are highly meaningful and in the EGEP educational curriculum. As suggested by the first group discussions on "My Journey as an Asian Woman Activist" opening the EGEP's first session, women's experiences are seen as an important pedagogical source in all the curriculum's forums and lectures. Not only during the official program but also during tea/coffee break times, or standing in the hallways, or in the dormitory, or in separate get-togethers after class, the participants shared personal stories of their years growing up, family history, parental violence, divorce, and sexual violence, as well as social problems like class and religious discrimination, political oppression and war. This experience-sharing is usually accompanied by emotions like anger, sorrow, sympathy, comfort and support.

By recounting their experiences, women experience 'healing,' 'happiness' and 'recovery.' During a group talk session, a participant from Cambodia said: "I harbored negative attitudes and indignation owing to parental violence in my home as a child and problems with my husband; but coming here, I recovered a positive feeling of happiness through experiencing support, sympathy, trust, intimacy, and friendship." A participant from India who was from an 'untouchable caste' confessed a similar story. She said, "I felt happiness here and gained new hope for the future. I've met many 'genuine' feminists here, and feel I'm respected as a human being and as a woman." These stories are evidence of the experience of healing and recovery found in supportive and intimate relations among women. Also, within EGEP, the experiences of various emotions and feelings do not stop at the outpouring of individual emotion but are newly interpreted and reconstructed as 'women's experience.'

3.8 Awareness of Expansion of Women's Problems and Constructing an Identity as a Feminist

Participants are activists working in domains related to women/gender, but it is not uncommon to encounter women who do not identify themselves as feminists or who feel uncomfortable with such a title. This is because in Asia, as in other parts of the world, a participant discussed in class that feminists are often cast negatively as "dangerous women who lean indiscriminately toward western culture and betray traditional culture/religion/nationalism." Moreover, most participants are not well-grounded in feminist theory and perspectives. Some reported they had never heard of such core feminist concepts as 'sexuality' and 'gender' before coming to the program. At first, some participants even find the feminist activities of others strange. For example, one participant said on the evaluation report: "I heard about the LGBT movement for the first time after coming here. It was unfamiliar to me but gradually I've come to think of it as an important women's issue." On the other hand, one LGBT activist said, "Some people think the LGBT issue is weird. They deal with violence against women but think violence against lesbians doesn't count." These experiences are recognitions of others' differences and at the same time lessons in understanding each other's struggles.

Regarding this understanding and learning process, one participant said, "In the course of sharing stories about women's rights in Asian countries I detected not only commonalities but also differences. I also found a range of differences exist in approaches to finding solutions to problems. But in the time we spent sharing our different thoughts, my vision of women's issues widened and I learned a lot from the rich experiences of other activists." By the end of the program, some participants remarked, "I wasn't a feminist before coming here. Now I am," proudly and naturally 'coming out' about their change of identity. These experiences show changes in awareness of women's problems through reciprocal learning as well as how feminist identity is constructed.

3.9 Discovery of Connectedness and Women's Solidarity

In coming to appreciate differences and commonalities, women discover that women are linked, that women's issues which seem remote in space, time and form are actually tightly 'interconnected' with themselves. The connectedness the participants speak of is experienced at a personal level, and is at the same time an awakening to a communal experience of oppression. Most of all, through their participation in EGEP, participants 'discover' the fact that their own existence and experiences as women and as activists are interconnected. They often say that through EGEP, they came to understand that "we're all connected existences" and that "there are other people in the world who are working as activists and so I don't feel alone." Awareness of the connectedness among women activists is not only a contemporaneous experience but also one that transcends time and nation.

An understanding of connectedness includes awareness that women's issues that appear different are in fact interconnected within the framework of women's oppression. One Indonesian participant's story offers an extreme example of how awareness and the experience of connectedness come about. The following story is a reconstruction from several stories from her Open Forum presentation, article and her private disclosures.

> In the lecture on sexuality, the professor cited some cases in Indonesia where the government used violence against women for the purpose of justifying itself. The Suharto administration in Indonesia rounded up women activists who protested against the dictatorship. The state used sexual violence against them and imposed silence about their actions. While listening to the lecture, fleeting memories of my grandmother

came to my mind. While speaking with the professor after the lecture, I realized my grandmother had been an anti-government protester. When participating in the Wednesday Demonstrations with the elderly military comfort women, I thought of my grandmother again. Coming to Korea and seeing the comfort women, I could understand why my grandmother's life and memory were purged from my family and our society. The military comfort women issue was a government perpetration of organized, ruthless violence on women. Regardless, patriarchal society with its dual standard for women's sexuality imposed shame and silence on the women who experienced it. Through the experiences of the Korean comfort women, I could understand my grandmother's experiences under Indonesia's Suharto administration and realized that the experiences of women in the two regions are closely connected.

Awareness of this 'connectivity' was discovered as an awareness of the need for alliance among women acting in different areas and domains, a solidarity crossing the boundaries of state and issues. That is, through the experience of connectivity, they discovered that the women's issues they engaged with at the local level are in fact connected to international women's issues and acknowledged the need for a transnational alliance.

4. Conclusion: Achievements and Tasks

In analyzing women's experiences within a process of feminist pedagogy as implemented via the EGEP, this paper showed empirically and experientially how the production of Asian women subjects may be achieved in the field of Asian feminisms. Above all, the experiences of the women activists are vivid testaments to EGEP's *raison d'etre* as a site for Asian feminism. Through the program, women activists become empowered in manifold ways, strengthening their identities as feminists and broadening their understanding of Asian women's issues, and based on these processes, seek possibilities for transnational women's solidarity. This conclusion suggests that EGEP is largely fulfilling its objective as a praxis of 'Asian Feminist Pedagogy.'

The EGEP program, however, has several tasks for the future. The most important at hand is how it can continue such educational successes in the long-term. It is operated as a short 2-week program covering a wide range of theoretical ideas and practice of various areas. In order to supplement this limitation, it is necessary for participants to develop related projects and follow-up education, whereby networking and education can be maintained after they return to their organizations and regions. Currently, the Asian Center for Women's Studies steers a variety of projects, publishing participants' papers in the *Asian Journal of Women's Studies*, supporting opportunities to attend international conferences for presenting their ideas and activities and hosting alumni meetings for program graduates in other regions. However, more systematic, multi-faceted projects following on the EGEP program are needed to better maintain and expand the program's achievements in a stable manner.

Additionally, EGEP is "a site for the education and knowledge production of Asian feminists." With over 100 women activists participating in its last 5 programs, many activity reports, action plans, and lecture notes have been collected from a number of participants and faculty members. But unfortunately, at present, EGEP has been focused on 'operations,' while related researches and analytic reviews have not been actively carried out in parallel. For long-term development and expansion of Asian Feminist Pedagogy, there is need for more active generation of in-depth studies and evaluations, the development of new models treating more subject areas, and quantitative and qualitative research for making visible and objectifying the praxes and impact of feminist pedagogy. Also needed are more multi-dimensional research, such as those on Asian women NGOs and Asian women's movements, and analyses of Asian women's issues, and policies for improving the lives of women in Asian locales. These projects are part of the process of the formation of 'Asian feminism.'

References

Akhter, S. (2014), "Endless Misery of Nimble Fingers: The Rana Plaza Disaster," *Asian Journal of Women's Studies*, 20(1): 137-147.

Ame, K. R. (2013), "Overcoming the Curse of Early Marriage in Bangladesh," *Asian Journal of Women's Studies*, 19(4): 150-163.

Aryal, K. (2014), "Women's Empowerment in Building Disaster Resilient Communities," *Asian Journal of Women's Studies*, 20(1): 164-174.

Asian Center for Women's Studies (ACWS) & Korean Women's Institute (KWI) (2000), "Building Women's Studies Curriculum: 8 Country-Level Workshop," *Asian Journal of Women's Studies*, 6(2): 106-120.

Cai, Y. (2013), "Re-vitalize, Re-strategize and Re-politicize the Chinese Women's Movement in the New Era," *Asian Journal of Women's Studies*, 19(1): 113-126.

Chang, P. (1996), "The Rise of Women's Education: Against the Korean Patriarchy," paper presented at the Asian Women's Studies Conference in Seoul, May 10.

_______ (2006), "Women's Studies in Korea," *Women's Studies Quarterly*, 24(1-2): 317-326.

_______ (2007), "A Study on Feminism: Knowledge Production and Challenges for the Future," paper presented at Academic Conference on the occasion of the 30th Anniversary of KWI, Ewha Womans University in Seoul, November 1-2.

_______ (2008), "Feminist Consciousness and Women's Education: The Case of Women's Studies, Ewha Womans University," *Asian Journal of Women's Studies*, 14(2): 7-29.

Cho, H. (1997), "Feminist Intervention in the Rise of 'Asian' Discourse," *Asian Journal of Women's Studies*, 3(3): 127-156.

Choi, S. (2008), "Feminist Pedagogy: Politics, Ethics, Aesthetics (Feminist Pedagogyui Jeongchi, Yunri, Mihak)," *Feminist Studies in English Literature*, 16(1): 167-199.

Du, F. (2005), "Developing Women's Studies at Universities in China: Research, Curriculum and Institution," *Asian Journal of Women's Studies*, 11(4): 35-71.

Evans, S. (1979), *Personal Politics: The Roots of Women's Liberation in the Civil Rights Movement and the New Left*, New York: Knopf.

Foss, K. A. & S. K. Foss (1994), "Personal Experience as Evidence in Feminist Scholarship," *Western Journal of Communication*, 58: 39-43.

hooks, b. (1989), *Talking Back: Thinking Feminist, Thinking Black*, Boston: South End Press.

_______ (1994), *Teaching to Transgress: Education as the Practice of Freedom*, New York: Routledge.

_______ (2003), *Teaching Community: A Pedagogy of Hope*, New York: Routledge.

Hur, S. (2013), "Expanding Women's Studies: The Field of 'Practical Women's Studies,' in a Perspective of Feminist Pedagogy (Yeoseonghakui Hwakjang: 'Silcheon Yeoseonghak' Hyeonjang, Yeoseongjuui Pedagogy Gwanjeomeseo)," paper presented at Academic Conference on the occasion of the 30th Anniversary of Department of Women's Studies, Ewha Womans University in Seoul, February 16.

Jayarathne, S. S. (2014), "Women's Potential in Dealing with Natural Disasters: A Case Study rom Sri Lanka," *Asian Journal of Women' Studies*, 20(1): 125-136.

Jeon, H. (2013), "Feminist Lectures Meet Local Specification: Focusing on Salim Medical Cooperation Feminist School Program (Jiyeokui Gucheseonggwa Mannan Yeoseonghak Kangui: Salim Uiryosaenghyeob Yeosungjuui Hakkyo Programeul Jungsimeuro)," paper presented at Academic Conference on the occasion of the 30th Anniversary of Department of Women's Studies, Ewha Womans University in Seoul, February 16.

Jeong, J. (2013), "Women's Studies as General Education: How to Teach Women's Studies? (Kyoyanggeuyukeuroseoui Yeoseonghak: Yeoseonghak Eotteoke GarchilKeotinga?)," paper presented at Academic Conference on the occasion of the 30th Anniversary of Department of Womans Studies, Ewha Woman's University in Seoul, February 16.

Jeong, M. (2004), "The Meaning of Poststructural Feminism in Education (Habrijeok Daehwaleul Neomeo Chaileul Baeugi)," *Korean Educational Sociology*, 14(3): 183-205.

John, M. (2005), "Women's Studies in India and the Question of Asia: Some Reflections," *Asian Journal of Women's Studies*, 11(2): 41-66.

Jurado, M. C. (2013), "Organizing Urban Poor Women in Securing Housing and Land Tenure in Manila," *Asian Journal of Women' Studies*, 19(3): 172-185.

Khanis, S. (2013), "Human Rights and the LGBTI Movement in Indonesia," *Asian Journal of Women's Studies*, 19(1): 127-138.

Khullar, M. (2005), "Asian Journal of Women's Studies: Ten Years and Beyond," *Asian Journal of Women's Studies*, 11(4): 7-34.

Kim, E. S. (2005), "How the Category of Asia is Possible to be a Referential Community for Reciprocal Recognitions," paper presented at the World Forum of Life Culture in Paju, Korea, September 2-5.

_________ (2010), "The Politics of Institutionalizing Feminist Knowledge: Discussing "Asian" Women's Studies in South Korea," *Asian Journal of Women's Studies*, 16(3): 7-34.

Kim, H. M. & Kang S. M. (2001), "Achievement and Challenges of an Asian Women's Studies Project," *Asian Journal of Women's Studies*, 7(4): 61-108.

Kim, Y. (2007), "Feminist Pedagogy: Educational Discourse and Practice (Feminist Pedagogy: Gyeoyuk Damrongwa Silcheon)," *Practical Education Studies*, 1(2): 25-47.

Kunwar, P. (2013), "Coming Out of the Traditional Trap," *Asian Journal of Women's Studies*, 19(4): 164-172.

Larson, L. (2005), "The Necessity of Feminist Pedagogy in a Climate of Political Backlash," *Equity & Excellence in Education*, 38(2): 135-144.

Lee, M. S. (2013), *Producing Gender Specialists through Women's Studies in Universities*, Seoul: Korean Women's Development Institute.

Lee, S. (2008), "Conceptualizing the 'Asian' and Asian Women's Studies," *Asian Journal of Women's Studies*, 14(4): 28-53.

Miske, Shirley, P. Chang, & S. W. Lee (1998), "Expanding the Network: Building Women's Studies in Asia Workshop," *Asian Journal of Women's Studies*, 4(3): 164-180.

Morgan, K. P. (1996), "The Perils and Paradoxes of the Bearded Mothers," in A. Diller, B. Houston, K. P. Morgan, & M. Ayim (eds.), *The Gender Question in Education: Theory, Pedagogy & Politics*, Boulder, CO: Westview Press.

Nah, Y. (1999), "Feminist Pedagogy," *Andragogy Today: International Journal of Adult & Continuing Education*, 2(4): 55-76.

Parry, S. C. (1996), "Feminist Pedagogy and Techniques for the Changing Classroom," *Women's Studies Quarterly*, 24(3-4): 45-54.

Patria, H. D. (2013), "Uncultivated Biodiversity in Women's Hand: How to Create Food Sovereignty," *Asian Journal of Women's Studies*, 19(2): 148-161.

Shrewsbury, C. M. (1993), "What is Feminist Pedagogy?," *Women's Studies Quarterly*, 21(3-4): 8-15.

Song, H. J. (2002), "A New Identity for Feminist Pedagogy in Korea: A Search for Women's Domain in Education (Daeanjeok Paradigmeuroseoui Feminist Pedagogy: Geu Ganeungseongeul Chajaseo)," *Andragogy Today: International Journal of Adult & Continuing Education*, 5(3): 1-28.

Valerio, K. A. (2014), "Storm of Violence, Surge of Struggle: Women in the Aftermath of Typhoon Haiyan (Yolanda)," *Asian Journal of Women's Studies*, 20(1): 148-163.

Vedhanayagi, P. (2013), "Agro-feminism: An Ideology of Hope for Dalit Women," *Asian Journal of Women's Studies*, 19(3): 186-200.

Weiler, K. (1995), "Revisioning Feminist Pedagogy," *NWSA Journal*, 7(2): 100-106.

Ying, L. (2013), "The Situation of Kachin Women during the Current Political Crisis," *Asian Journal of Women's Studies*, 19(2): 162-171.

Yu, J. (2006), "Feminist pedagogy and the Teaching of Feminist English Novels (Feminist Pedagogywa Feminism Yeongmunhak Jakpum Ilkigi)," *English Language and English Literature*, 46(2): 529-547.

Part II

Transnational Feminist Issues and Asian Women's Activism

Chapter 7

Nation Building and Sexual Politics in Asia

Saskia E. WIERINGA

1. Introduction

Gender issues and sexual politics are related to processes of nation building in Asia in various ways. Several states, such as Pakistan, imagine themselves to be masculine and aggressive nations. In that country this picture is linked to Islam and women are subjected to various forms of oppression associated with that religion, to be seen as the proper feminine counterpart to that nation's masculinity. In Sri Lanka a similar process can be observed, here related to Buddhism. In Indonesia new regional identities are forged based on moral injunctions on women. In that country homosexuality is criminalized in several regions (such as Aceh and Palembang)—which it never was, to 'prove' the Muslim character of those regions. In Taiwan on the other hand, there is a discussion to legalize same-sex marriages, in a move to 'prove' the country's modernity, in relation to the claims of more conservative China on unity.

In this chapter I explore the ongoing process of modernity and nation formation in Asia as a deeply gendered and sexual process. Apart from obvious regulatory tasks that nations have assumed in relation to the sexual, such as marriage and health laws, nations are built on ideas of race/ethnicity, political or religious superiority and a particular sex-gender regime. These are assembled on the construction of a shared history and traditions which are endlessly repeated and hardly questioned. The aspect of sexual politics in relation to nation building has received relatively little attention, in contrast to eg sexual politics surrounding ethnicity and race.[1] I give three examples to illustrate the relevance of sexual politics: the deployment of the sexual panic that gave rise to the militaristic New Order regime in Indonesia, the postcolonial amnesia which fuels nationalist imagination and new debates on sexual citizenship.

2. The Imagined Nation

Anderson famously wrote a 'nation is an imagined political community … it is imagined as a *community* [italics orig], because, regardless of the actual inequality and exploitation that may prevail in each, the nation is always conceived as a deep, horizontal comradeship. Ultimately it is this *fraternity* [italics added] that makes it possible, over the past two centuries, for so many millions of people, not so much to kill, as willingly to die' (Anderson, 1983: 6-7). The legitimacy of a nation, its moral persuasiveness is a fragile construct. Yet when frozen into nation states communities are anchored in the institutions they have engendered such as laws, a regulatory apparatus, an educational system (and the selection of stories that are told in its history classes). Underlying this moral construct are ideas of an imagined, reconstructed past, of the gendered and sexual identities of humans, as well as their subjectivities, and their aspirations for the future. The selection and extent of its spiritual, religious ideas also forms part of this moral fabric.

1 See eg the collection of Brah and Coombes (2000) in which hybridity, ethnic mixing, is discussed in a colonial and postcolonial context.

A nation then is an idea, a cultural construct, a figment of the imagination, based on certain ideas of morality and of humanity. Members of a nation feel connected because they imagine themselves sharing certain notions about themselves, their fellow-nationals, and about the others, those who don't belong, who are seen as perhaps not sharing the same kind of humanity (think of the ease with which those who don't belong can be killed, tortured, exploited—by imperial nations, Nazis, Japanese generals, Maoist cadres, Indonesian generals, Hindu nationalists in India, Sri Lankan Buddhist generals etc). A nation has its pride, which can be wounded, and football and other sports teams. It has a flag, a national anthem which however ugly its music and clumsy its lyrics, may bring tears to the eyes of those who sing it or listen to it. Not only in nationalist movements a national identity is conjured up. Postcolonial struggles over ethnic and religious divisions too are built on identity constructions in which often women's bodies are situated as battlefields (Jayawardena and de Alwis, 1996).

The homogenizing tendency of nation building excludes members of minorities, women, and members of economically deprived groups from claiming the same benefits and rights in relation to those who have arrogated to themselves the power to define the character of the nation. This may lead to violent conflicts, witnessed in many parts of Asia.[2] Armed conflicts in their turn produce an ideology of militarism based on particular notions of femininity and masculinity. These gendered notions of citizenship are massively disseminated via the media, school curricula and non-state actors.[3] Nationalist projects typically portray the women of the own community as more decent, virtuous and modest than the women of the 'other' community. The current form of heteronormativity in a particular society both marginalizes the non-normative 'others' and informs the

2 The collection of essays in Jeganathan and Ismail (1995) is a good example of an early warning of the violence that would follow in Sri Lanka based on decades of exclusions of Tamils, Muslims and women from the national imagination.

3 See Saigol 2013 for a lucid analysis of how Pakistan is produced as a militaristic nation. See also Garon (1997) for an illuminating case study on the construction of the Japanese nation state.

ways how the 'own' women are policed, preferably by women of the own community (Wieringa, 2012, 2015). Rightwing women's groups are therefore a strategic part of the nationalist project.[4]

Not only dominant groups manage to define the character of the nation. The portrayal of victimhood is also able to sway nationalist sentiments.[5] This happens when in armed conflicts the rape and murder of a woman is classified as an honor killing and the perpetrators are portrayed as 'barbaric'—whether in an ethnic or religious sense. Marital rape, or daughter rape, on the other hand are hardly ever prosecuted—these crimes are committed by the 'own' patriarchs. Likewise homophobia may be exploited. While gay men and lesbian women face persecution in many countries, the execution of two young males in Iran in 2006 was singled out for international outcry. This case led Puar (2007) to analyse the configurations of sexuality, race, gender, nation, class and ethnicity in relation to counterterrorism with its security concerns and nationalism.[6]

In an early analysis Yuval-Davis and Anthias (1989) listed a number of ways in which women are involved in nationalist projects, for instance as biological reproducers, as reproducers of the boundaries of ethnic/national groups and as 'cultural carriers.' This was a rather functional analysis of the ways women served the nationalist cause. Since then analyses have appeared which offer a more nuanced picture. West for instance (1997) pointed out that feminism also constructs nationalism: gender is not only an effect of nationalist projects but women's movements also are active agents redefining the communities they are involved in.

Yet nationalism is primarily seen as concerned with the construction

4 See Wieringa (1985) and Sarkar and Butalia (1995).

5 See the discussion on Korea's comfort women by Jonson in this volume.

6 Whether the young men were hanged because they had had consensual sex or because they had raped a younger boy remains unclear. Puar introduces the term homonatiomalism, in which 'properly homo' patriotic US identities are poised against racialized 'others.' In Holland a similar process is underway in which the country has reinvented itself as ''always-already' tolerant, while Muslim migrants are framed as homophobic. This debate is exploited by rightwing populists claiming to defend (and define) Dutch national culture.

of male status hierarchies, and of male bonding, as becomes clear in the above quote by Anderson. As Enloe stated: 'nationalism has typically sprung from masculinised memory, masculinised humiliation and masculinised hope' (1990: 44). Connell pointed out that this process not only entails subjecting women to strict controls, but also rests on the construction of hegemonic masculinities (Connell, 2005). Every nation state has its own way to imagine itself, based on a morality rooted in what is seen as tradition or natural culture. In this process culture and tradition are naturalized and essentialized. That they are based on constantly changing unequal gender regimes and on other enforced hierarchies, of class and ethnicity for instance is often forgotten.

Foucault's analysis of biopolitics and disciplinary power added to our understanding of how subjectivities are moulded to create coherent societies (Foucault, 1977, 1978).

Apart from subjecting individuals to the regulatory power of the discourse on sexual morals prevailing in a particular society, social cohesion is created and maintained by 'othering' those delegated to a minority status and/or having particular ideas. States that consider themselves democratic and based on some form of religion 'other' those that they consider undemocratic, either because they adhere to a socialist state form or to a state based on different religious principles. Thus the US had no qualms to kill members of the Viet Cong or to support Suharto's troops which were killing hundreds of thousands of suspected communists. And its ordinary soldiers didn't feel morally disturbed about sexually torturing Iraqi prisoners in Abu Ghraib.

Constructing the nation state is an ongoing process—with deeply gendered connotations and far ranging effects of people's sexual life. As McClintock wrote, 'all nationalisms are gendered, all are invented and all are dangerous … in the sense that they represent relations to political power and to the technologies of violence … all nations depend on powerful constructions of gender (McClintock, 1995: 252-353). This also applies to the building of socialist nations. An example is the gigantic changes China underwent since the Maoist victory.[7] The one child policy for instance had deep consequences (forced abortions and sterilizations, femicide) as powerfully illustrated in the novel Wa (frogs) by the 2012 Nobel prize laureate Mo Yan. It was only revoked in 2015 when it no longer served the nations' interests. Another example is the fierce persecution of anybody engaged in a form of non-marital sexuality during the Cultural Revolution, while the more recent opening of the economy with its attendant emphasis on individualism led to a relaxation of these norms and to the emergence of LGBT organizations.[8]

Women in most nationalist projects are usually constructed as the symbolic bearers of the nation but they are denied direct access to national agency. Postcolonial nations are typically presented as timeless or rather as bound in tradition yet as modern and progressive where men are seen as the agents of progress and women as the bearers of traditions. This is similar to what Chatterjee (1999) analysed in relation to nationalism in South Asia. Men occupied the 'material' world, of economic progress and western-inspired ideas of individualism and nationalism, while they located women in the 'spiritual' world. The material world was to be conquered, and British superiority in this field was accepted, to be emulated. On the other hand, South Asian nationalist men saw themselves as superior in the 'spiritual' realm of the home, family and religious traditions. Here no change was foreseen, at the most certain customs (such as sati and child marriage) needed to be reformed.[9]

While the divide between the material and spiritual worlds as Chatterjee saw it illuminates many of the tensions in the male-led nationalist world, it cannot do justice to the complexities faced by the Asian women's movements during the pre WWII period After all, the main points of struggle for women, education, suffrage and against patriarchal injunctions

7 See Pan Suiming (2005).

8 In 2015 political control of feminist and LGBT groups increased again.

9 See for an exploration of this theme in India the edited volumes of Sarkar and Sarkar (2008) and Sangari and Vaid (1989).

straddled both the public (material) and the private (spiritual) worlds. This is valid for both colonial nations and for nations that were never colonized by Western powers but which sought to emulate the 'energy' of those powerful nations.[10] The educated 'new women' of Japan, Korea and China were faced both with public ridicule and great resistance in their natal families. They triggered men's fears and were either repudiated but were also seen as a source of inspiration. Their situation was complex as they also found themselves at odds with their nationalist movements, as women's education and female suffrage were seen as western imports—which seemed to have different consequences for women than for men. Men could aspire to education without being seen to betray their nation's culture, while educated women fighting for suffrage were variously seen to conspire with their western sisters against their own brothers. Women's education was seen as a threat, linked with amoral materialism and sexual promiscuity. This produced in women a conflict of loyalty.[11]

Though women played major roles in the nationalist or modernist movements and in the various nationalist wars that were waged on the continent, their demands for equal rights were not met after national independence. Though some progress was made (suffrage, education) other contentious issues did not change; polygyny for instance was not ended in Muslim countries. Instead the new male national leaders pursued similar sexual/gender politics as their orientalist, colonial predecessors And conveniently ignored several rights women and members of other minorities enjoyed in pre colonial times. By this process of postcolonial amnesia (Wieringa, 2009) typically respect for transgender practices that was lost through the import of western patriarchal essentialist theories was not restored (instead LGBT issues came to be seen as western imports). Also, women's economic and political power (land rights, inheritance rights for

10 See Frühstück (2003) for Japan.

11 See Edwards and Roces (2004) for a number of case studies in which these and other dilemmas faced by women in the prewar women's movements in Asia were faced. See also Kim and Choi (1998), on Korea, Wieringa (2007a) on Japan.

women, women as political leaders or rulers) that was taken away or reduced by the colonial administrators was not restored.

The classic study about the interconnections between nationalism and sexuality is Mosse (1985). He analysed how modern European society was based on stereotypes of bourgeois respectability. This was an essential element for the maintenance of social stability, security and order. Religion, politics, morality and economics are intertwined phenomena not only in the creation of modern nation states but also in the creation of colonial empires. The British empire was not only created on the basis of commerce but also entailed the spread of Christianity and its sexual morals. The colonial enterprise was primarily based on greed and sex, morality became an afterthought, so to speak. The supposedly freer sexual morals as well as the riches to be had, lured western men to Asia. As Hyam lucidly writes 'the expansion of Europe centred around copulation and concubinage.' Orientalist visions of harems and women waiting to be penetrated fed these imaginations. The complicated relationship of race relations and sexual politics are analysed by various authors. As Stoler argues: '… the very categories of "colonizer" and "colonized" were secured through forms of sexual control that defined the domestic arrangements of Europeans and the cultural investments by which they identified themselves' (1995: 14).

The deployment of sexual metaphors and symbols is also a central point in Said's analysis of orientalism (1978). Political and economic interests defined who slept with whom in the colonies (creating a large group of Eurasians in the process). In their search for the 'exotic' other however, Orientalist scholars, both linguists and ethnographers, also usefully (though at times in a very biased way) documented the great variety of gendered and sexual practices they encountered (Wieringa, 2012).

3. Whose Imagination? (Precolonial) Nationalism

> During the Japanese occupation (1910-1945) Korean feminism was entwined with the cause of national liberation. Indeed, the goal of the first women's movement under Japanese protectorship (1905-1910) was to raise funds to pay the debt to Japan that Koreans considered the direct rationale for the protectorship. Although the patriotic women's convention consisted mostly of gentry women, a large number of courtesans participated in the movement, which explains the importance of restaurants as message-relaying posts for the (underground) independence movement. (Kim and Choi, 1998: 2).

Courtesans in the forefront of the guerrilla! Interesting! But were their interests translated into nationalist jargon? Were their voices heard in the nationalist women's movement? Whose voices dominated the Korean nationalist discourse? What image of humanity, of Korean identity was built? The courtesans were thanked for providing money and their work places for the movement. However they were quickly pushed to a place far behind the stage of the long liberation struggle of the Korean population. For the quote continues:

> … at the turn of the century enlightened male intellectuals in Korea during the Japanese colonial period preached about the importance of women's liberation and education to strengthening the nation. However, the nationalist position of the male elite did not separate women from nation and emphasized enlightenment for women only as mothers. Inevitably, the national liberation movement was hostile to the New Women's movement of the early 1920s which stressed women's explorations of their own sexuality and emancipation from the patriarchal household … (Kim and Choi, 1998: 2).

These themes resonate all over the region. Sexual symbolism was rife. In India the nation was evoked as 'Mother India,' the sanctity of marriage for women and motherhood was upheld (see Sangari and Vaid, 1989). Preserving women's chastity became a prime concern during the bloody Partition with the bewildering result that women were raped and abducted in large numbers. The raped women of course were always the 'other' women. Gandhi could rise to such mythical dimensions partly through his emphasis on sexual abstinence—which indicated self-control, and which would ultimately, it was expected, lead to political power (Alter, 1994). Women supported the Gandhian movement in large numbers, but, as in Korea, if some of them were brave enough to fight for sexual liberation as well, their voices were soon drowned.

The colonial control over 'unruly' women's bodies extended into postcolonial times as well. According to Victorian morality the Devasasi, temple servants in South Asia, were no more than prostitutes. The practice had to disappear. Likewise the dance (nautch) girls came under strict control. These debates have resurfaced in postcolonial India and recently the dancing girls were even banned in Mumbai (Vasudevan, 2013).

In Indonesia the charismatic nationalist leader Sukarno produced a very influential feminist book, Sarinah, in which he extolled women as the second wing of the national Garuda. Indispendable in the struggle for national liberation from the Dutch, the men welcomed them as guerrilla fighters. Women formed their own fighting units (laskyar wanita) and acted as messengers, as the Korean courtisanes did (Wieringa, 2002). But after national liberation was won, they were supposed to go back to their traditional tasks: kitchen, bed and well (dapur, kasur, sumur). Men separated from their guerrilla wives in large numbers, preferring docile virgins to hardened fighters as wives. The heroic part women played in the war was quickly forgotten, also by its historians, so that Anderson, as cited above, speaks of the nation as a 'fraternity,' ignoring the aspirations and sufferings of the women who also fought for national liberation. The political arena was claimed by men and retroactively the guerrilla struggle was recast as being fought by men.

Even though early feminists such as Kartini (Dutch East Indies), Rokeya (Bengal) and many others, had spoken out clearly about their needs and aspirations—no polygyny, purdah, male (sexual) domination, but the right to education, to citizenship—and these women were honoured as exemplary women, they were not written into the canon of nationalist politics (Jayawardena, 1986; Rokeya, 1988; Wieringa, 2006) Theirs was the women's realm, the domestic sphere, the home, or their own women's movements which the male nationalist actors would like to separate from the public sphere in which their own heroism was acted out (see eg Chatterjee, 1999). Menon, writing about the horrors of Partition and the difficult struggle to (re) produce a legitimate nation state, stressed that women's sexuality formed the center of debates around national duty, honor, identity and citizenship in a secular and democratic India. The same political and military leaders who had been responsible for the massive sexual crimes against women sat around in convention rooms to define and restore moral order, and reinforce women's sexual docility.

4. Postcolonial Amnesia

The imagination of postcolonial nations is partly drawn upon their selectively remembered sexualized histories. Postcolonial amnesia implicates two imbricating, seemingly paradoxical processes. On the one hand this concerns an amnesia of particular sexual practices, politics and relations, specifically those related to women's sexual autonomy and same-sex practices in general (also of matriliny, women's economic and political power, but these are not discussed here). This amnesia has critical consequences, not only in relation to the hate crimes committed on individuals who live lives that challenge or destabilize the unstable borders of the heteronormative gender regimes that various postcolonial leaders engineer and cling to, but also on women and men that live such normalized lives (their 'normality' being dictated by the supposed abjection of the 'others,' Wieringa, 2015). On the other hand we witness striking continuities in the sexual politics of postcolonial rulers compared to their colonial predecessors. Postcolonial leaders, inheriting the patriarchal powers of their white predecessors, insist on a similar kind of controls on women and sexual minorities (Wieringa, 2009a).

So far research has mainly focussed on the racialization of society that sexualized colonial practices produced.[12] In postcolonial societies these moral sexual strategies are no longer used to mark racial boundaries, but to demarcate the powers of the ruling national elites. Thus class stratification, (though no longer based on race), women's subordination and heteronormativity are the lines of convergence. The wounded, emasculated, colonial men became the proud, virile successors of the formerly superior virile white masters. The differences between colonial and postcolonial regimes in the area of sexual politics are more of degree than of substance: the tropes are similar. If 'tradition' was seen (and constructed as) the site of 'moral decay' in colonial days, postcolonial 'tradition' is invested with nostalgia and reconfigured as a site of heteronormative 'normalcy,' while the West is seen as the site of perverse desires.

In this process critical modifications appeared. First of all the composition of the ruling elite changed. It were no longer white colonial men who dominated the scene, so that made race as a vehicle of differentiation less useful. Ethnicity or caste might remain though; in Indonesia certain ethnicities managed to get the upper hand. In India high castes retained their position. Both in Sri Lanka and in Pakistan suppression of ethnic and political minorities led to bloody civil wars and the creation of Bangladesh. Instead wealth and power became the critical axes around which gender and sexual politics were played out. The fictional heroes in the political theatre changed colour but not tactics. During the protracted and bloody shift of power they might even use the same discourse and metaphors—

12 See Sinha (1995) and Stoler (1995).

usually that of a patriarchal, omnipotent father, who knows best for his subalterns.[13] These parental metaphors are used to this day. In Indonesia President Suharto used to call himself the 'Father of Development.' The democratic turn in many Asian countries (Korea and Taiwan in 1987, Indonesia 1998, the economic opening up of China and Viet Nam) comes with a new imagination of citizenship which entails changes in the patriarchal family system. This does not necessarily lead to more equality between the sexes though (Chang, 2005).

So what about precolonial (or premodern in Asian countries that were never colonised) forms of gender and sexual diversity? The topic is broad. I will give only a few examples. Male beauty is traditionally admired in East Asia and has been associated with spiritual dimensions. In Japan from the fourteenth century onwards a literary genre developed, in which relations between monks and a temple acolyte were portrayed. The samurai caste also had strong pederastic ideals. Both in China (nanse) and in Japan (nanshoku) male-to-male love, literally male colours, was characterised by gender-, class-and age-stratified relations. These were expected to exist side by side with heterosexual relationships (Leupp, 1995). Same-sex relations among males were widely accepted through most of China's dynasties. Numerous Han emperors retained large harems of wives and concubines, while they also had sexual relations with attractive young men, as Hinsch (1990) recorded.

Evidence of East Asian women engaging in sexual relations with each other is scant as men dominated the world of letters and didn't readily record women's pursuits. Men's control in most parts of Asia over women's sexuality was strong. Women had little say in the choice of their marriage partners and were supposed to accept violence and infidelity.

While elite men were at liberty to penetrate women and men, women had no such licence. Female sexuality seemed to be more circumscribed than male-male relations. For women with same-sex desires who could

13 See also Clancy-Smith and Gouda (1998).

not adapt to their marriage, suicide and an ascetic religious life were the only routes open. In certain regions and groups women couples could hide behind the veil of friendship.[14]

In certain societies (male-bodied) people with same-sex behaviours or attractions, whether they were crossdressing or were transgendered, were accepted or even admired as successful members of society, for instance crossdressing priests or shamans such as in Mongolia, Korea, Vietnam and Burma. Bugis society in Sulawesi has a long tradition of transgender or intersex priests, called bissu, who are important intermediaries between the world of the gods and that of the humans. Crossdressing and transgendered (male-bodied) calalai and (female-bodied) calabai took on the roles of their adopted gender and married partners of the opposite gender (and the same sex) (Clarence-Smith, 2012; Davies, 2010) Transvestite elements were also prevalent in theatrical traditions, such as in Japan (Kabuki, Takarazuka), China (Peking opera), and Indonesia (ludruk). Historically in many parts of Asia romantic attachments between men and between women co-existed with heterosexual marriage and procreation, as Vanita and Kidwai (2000) document for India. Eunuchs played important roles in the Chinese, Korean and Moghul courts; some rose to great prominence particularly during the Ming dynasty. South Asia has a tradition of hijras, communities of intersex, emasculated or transgender male-bodied persons who used to play important roles in ceremonies. Present day hijra communities have lost much of their former religious prominence. Many are reduced to sex work and begging (see also Sulivan and Jackson, 2001).

The European general condemnation of homosexuality as immoral wickedness helped create a climate in which the earlier tolerance where it existed fast disappeared. Through colonial influence practices that were condemned in Europe but accepted in large parts in Asia became ridiculed. Homosexuality was seen as another proof of Oriental moral degeneracy.

14 See Peletz (2009) and Wieringa, Blackwood and Bhaiya (2007) for references to precolonial or premodern gender diversity or forms of women's same-sex relations.

In China and Japan women's same-sex relations became an issue of public debate in the early twentieth century, associated with the rise of a feminist movement. The Chinese May Fourth movement was strongly influenced by the European modern science of sexology, characterised by essentialism and biological determinism. This new science was eagerly accepted in never-colonized (by Western powers), modernizing nations such as Korea, Japan and Siam, while it was imposed on colonised countries such as Indonesia and South Asia (Choi, 2013; Frühstück, 2003; Sang, 2003). The dominance of the monogamous, heterosexually married couple is a modern phenomenon, in part related to the imperial domination of large parts of Asia in the 19th and 20th centuries and modernization. The infamous anti-sodomy laws of the British were imposed on all areas under their control. Postcolonial amnesia thus has the effect that in the process of inventing itself as a viable nation-state patriarchal, heterosexual reproductive relations are (re-)inscribed as normative, while women's autonomous sexual practices (whether heterosexual or same-sex) and same-sex practices in general are (re)constructed as marginal. Political and religious leaders join in mobilizing emotions to naturalize this fiction of the 'always-already' patriarchal, heterosexual nation.

5. Nation Building: Indonesia's Genocide

A striking though unknown example of the social and cultural engineering that goes into creating the myth of a 'stable nation' built upon women's docility is the New Order of Indonesia (1996-1998), led by General Suharto, who shoved aside Indonesia's first president, Sukarno, in a 'creeping coup,' from late 1965 till mid 1966 (Roosa, 2006; Wieringa, 2002, 2003). The campaign of sexual slander that brought him to power is one of the most wide ranging moral panics and waves of sexual hysteria in history. After a putsch of leftist colonels in which the six senior generals of the country were murdered at a nationalist training site for socialist girls, in the night of 30 September and 1 October 1965, General Suharto was the only surviving general of his generation. He engineered a mass media campaign in which the girls were said to have seduced (with the help of the erotic 'Flower Dance'), castrated and murdered the generals. 'Proof' of these allegations appeared in the army press, based on 'testimonies' elicited after heavy torture, and a film shot in prison.[15] Following this campaign the army trained and armed youth groups, mainly of Ansor, the youth wing of the Muslim mass organization NU (Nahdlatul Ulema), and of the Hindu nationalist right in Bali. The gangs murdered between 1 million (Amnesty) and 3 million (colonel Sarwo Edhie, the organizer of the campaign, father in law of the former president, Susilo Bambang Yudhoyono) socialist people. Nobody was ever brought to trial for this genocide, the mass graves remain unopened.[16]

This campaign not only terrorized the Indonesian population into obedience, it also discredited the women's mass organization Gerwani (Gerakan Wanita Indonesia , Indonesian women's organization) and in general associated women's political agency with sexual depravity, including lesbianism. Indonesian women activists still have to fight that image. Since then the only 'good' woman is someone who obeys her husband, attends to his sexual needs, looks after his children and cooks his food. Gone are the days when women were honoured for helping build the nation and shape its future. Now, in the Reformation era (after 1998, the fall of Suharto). One of the most difficult topics for them to address is sexual empowerment. This campaign of sexual slander which triggered the massacre of one million people and destroyed the up to that moment vibrant Indonesian women's movement is not only ignored in New Order propaganda but

15 The girls were arrested and released again several times, until they were definitely detained by the end of October 1965. Around that time they were forced to undress in prison. These shots were later used to 'prove' that naked girls had seduced the generals a month earlier. Watching this propaganda film was obligatory for school children.

16 A few years ago some graves in East Java were opened by relatives of the victims. However the state has never made any attempt to locate and open the mass graves systematically. As many bodies were thrown in the rivers the exact number of those slaughtered will probably never be known.

also generally ignored by male-stream scientists (Wieringa, 2011).

6. Sexual Citizenship

Women are not only the physical reproducers of the nation; they are also seen to be the guardians of its moral boundaries—through socialisation of their children particularly as the nation's honour is invested in issues surrounding women's bodies. But though heterosexual women have become citizens with full rights (though different citizens than men are) LGBTI people are considered less than citizens in their nation states (Wieringa, 2013). Homophobia is rife in many parts of Asia, and on the rise in many. Taiwan and Thailand are notable exceptions. Lesbian women and gay men are murdered, thrown out of their families, forcibly married to cross-sex partners, raped, denied access to school, fired from jobs or not even hired. They are denied the right to form a family, adopt children and get state housing. In many countries they don't have the right to assembly, free speech and privacy, all rights regularly accorded to heterosexual people. These rights are contained in international binding treaties and consensus documents which most Asian government have ratified or signed. A group of lawyers collected the most relevant international rights documents in relation to LGBTI people in the so called Yogyakarta Principles.[17] Homophobic violence is gendered with lesbians and gay men suffering different forms of violence or violations.

Since the late 1980s identity-based social movements have sprung up in many Asian countries. I will just give some examples of such communities of female-bodies persons. In Thailand as in other countries of South and Southeast Asia, a community of gender-stratified women's same-sex relations has developed. In Thailand the partners are known as toms (from

17 These 29 '*Principles on the Application of International Human Rights Law in relation to Sexual Orientation and Gender Identity*,' clarify the existing international human rights standards with which all States must comply. Available at: www.yogyakartaprinciples.org.

tomboy) who play the masculine roles, and their feminine girlfriends, dees (from lady, Sinnott, 2004). In Indonesia tomboys are also known in some large cities, such as Padang (tomboys), Makassar (hunters) and Jakarta. Indonesian terms are also used, such as cewek-cowok (female-male), or kantul-sentil (Blackwood, 2010; Wieringa, 2007b). In Hongkong, Malaysia and Taiwan (here just the letter T is used to denote the masculine partners, while the po, derived from the Chinese term for wife, are their feminine partners) similar cultures are described. While the masculine partners in these relationship are considered transgendered, the feminine partners are usually seen as normatively gendered. Not all female homosexual practices fall within this stratified pattern. Neither do these homosexual experiences result in all-encompassing modern identities, such as 'lesbian.' This hybridized terminology points to transnational influences. It must be stressed however that these patterns develop in local patriarchal contexts and have local histories.

Within same-sex communities there are different sub-cultures, such as the onabe in Japan (female-bodied transgendered hosts in bars at times performing sexual services) versus rezubian (Japanese lesbians) (Wieringa 2007a). In Shanghai we find the gender-stratified t-p, but also the non-classified bufeb, or lala (in Korea called iban). In Indonesia gender-stratified all-female couples exist side by side andro or non-label lesbians, or lesbi.

Communities of transgendered males (kothi in India, kathoey in Thailand, bakla in Philippines, pondan in Malaysia, waria in Indonesia) exist side by side with expanding groups of gay-identified men (Boellstorff, 2005; Neil and Neil, 1996). These categories are consistently redefined and challenged; there is increasing local engagement with global discourses. The expanding market for female and male homoerotic cultural productions since the 1990s coincides with a growth of gay and lesbian identity politics.

While LGBTI people are organizing themselves and IDAHO (International Day Against Homophobia) is regularly held in more and more

Asian countries (Nepal, Hong Kong, Taiwan, Malaysia, Indonesia), the rising fundamentalisms in the region pose new problems. The (May/June 2012) hullabaloo around the Asian tour of Lady Gaga is instructive. She is widely seen as supportive of GLBT rights. Conservative forces took such offense that her scheduled performance in Jakarta had to be cancelled. Perversions, Muslim hardliners seemed to imply should not be imported from the west, into our 'pure' Muslim-dominated Indonesia.

However, as indicated above, there is overwhelming evidence from all over Asia that same-sex relations ranging from short term attractions to life long relations have existed. Yet the myth that homosexuality is imported by 'foreigners' (whether they are Moghuls or westerners) is widespread.

While in Nepal and Tamil Nadu legislation is enacted that allows for MTF transgenders to procure an identity card stating they are transgender, in other countries such as in Indonesia and Malaysia a slow process of criminalisation of same-sex sexuality is going on, in spite of a small but vibrant gay and lesbian movement. Arguments used to support this process of criminalisation are that human rights are western (so eastern states are exceptions), that 'traditional culture' never accepted this (these nations are imagined as always-already fundamentalist Muslim) and that LGBT people are either or both a social evil (to be punished) and sick (to be rehabilitated or cured). The heteronormative 'self' of these nations is thus created as opposed to the vilified, non-Muslim, western-inspired, other.

7. Conclusion

Above I sketched three imbricating processes that work towards fabricating gendered ethnic and national identities. In the first place the convenient amnesia of identities and sexual practices by postcolonial leaders in an effort to construct the nation as an 'always-already' patriarchal and heteronormative entity. This form of postcolonial amnesia ensured the continuity of certain colonial policies and practices that denied women's power, and that ignored gender and sexual diversity. Secondly sexual panics, the moral hysteria focussed on women's presumed sexual conduct can play a critical role in forging national identity: in Indonesia it helped construct the masculinist, military New Order State led by General Suharto. The two above mentioned phenomena deal with exclusions—of politically active women, of people living non-heternormative lives, from the nation. The third process I discussed deals with inclusion: the struggle for equal rights and an end to homophobia of LGBTI people.

A nation is an imaginary construct which however is very real in the political, social and economic realities of those who belong to it. The underlying fantasies are usually hidden from view—once you try to define what is 'Korean,' 'Indian,' or 'Indonesian,' you enter into an ephemeral realm. Yet two issues are critical. First it is important to ensure that all those within its boundaries are heard in the process of (re)creating the nation. Both the voices of the courtisanes, ethnic or religious minorities, women in general and LGBTI people and all those others who do not conform to the normativity of ideal citizenship. And second that the rights of citizenship are shared by all inhabitants. Women's and sexual rights are universal and indivisible. Gender and sexual subordination should ultimately not be reproduced, but resolved in the utopian process that a nation formation is.

References

Alter, Joseph S. (2000), *Gandhi's Body: Sex, Diet, and the Politics of Nationalism*, Philadelphia: University of Pennsylvania Press.

Anderson, Benedict (1883), *Imagined Communities: Reflections on the Origin and Spread of Nationalism*, London: Verso.

Blackwood, Evelyn (2010), *Falling into the Lesbi World: Desire and Differ-*

ence in Indonesia, Honolulu: University of Hawai'i Press.

Boelstorff, Tom (2005), *The Gay Archipelago: Sexuality and Nation in Indonesia*, Princeton: Princeton University Press.

Brah, Avtar and Annie E. Coombes (eds.) (2000), *Hybridity and its Discontents: Politics, Science, Culture*, London and New York: Routledge.

Chang, Pilhwa (2005), "Talking about Sexuality," *Women's Experiences and Feminist Practices in South Korea*, Chang Pilhwa and Kim Eun-Shil (eds.), Seoul: Ewha Womans University Press: pp. 29-67.

Chatterjee, Partha (1999), "The Nation and Its Fragments: Colonial and Postcolonial Histories," *The Partha Chatterjee Omnibus*, New Delhi: Oxford University Press.

Choi, Hyaeweol (2013), *New Women in Colonial Korea: A Sourcebook*, London: Routledge.

Clancy-Smith, Julia and Frances Gouda (1998), "Introduction," *Domesticating the Empire: Race, Gender and Family Life in French and Dutch Colonialism*, Clancy-Smith, Julia and Frances Gouda (eds.), Charlottesville and London: University Press of Virginia: pp. 1-21.

Clarence-Smith, William G. (2012), "Same-sex Relations and Transgender Identities in Islamic Southeast Asia from the Fifteenth Century," *Sexual Diversity in Asia, C. 600-1950*, A. G. Reyes and William G. Clarence-Smith (eds.), London: Routledge: pp. 67-87.

Connell, R.W. (2005 2nd ed.), *Masculinities*, Berkeley: University of California Press.

Davies, Sharyn Graham (2010), *Gender Diversity in Indonesia: Sexuality, Islam and Queer Selves*, London: Routledge.

Edwards, Louise and Mina Roces (eds.) (2004), *Women's Suffrage in Asia: Gender, Nationalism and Democracy*, London and New York: Routledge.

Enloe, Cynthia (1990), *Bananas, Beaches and Bases: Making Feminist Sense of International Politics*, Berkeley: University of California Press.

Foucault, Michel (1975), *Discipline & Punish: The Birth of the Prison*, New York: Random House.

______ (1978), "Introduction," *The History of Sexuality*, Vol. I, New York:

Vintage Books.

Frühstück, Sabina (2003), *Colonizing Sex: Sexology and Social Control in Modern Japan*, Berkeley: University of California Press.

Garon, Sheldon (1997), *Molding Japanese Minds: The State in Everyday Life*, Princeton: Princeton University Press.

Hicks, George (1995), *The Comfort Women: Sex Slaves of the Japanese Imperial Forces*, London: Souvenir Press.

Hinsch, Brett (1990), *Passions of the Cut Sleeve: The Male-Homosexual Tradition in China*, Berkeley: University of California Press.

Hyam, Ronald (1990), *Empire and Sexuality*, Manchester: Manchester University Press.

Jaganathan, Pradeep and Qafri Ismail (1995), *Unmaking the Nation: The Politics of Identity and History in Modern Sri Lanka*, Colombo: Social Scientists Association.

Jayawardena, Kumari (1986), *Feminism and Nationalism in the Third World*, London: Zed Books.

Jayawardena, Kumari and Malathi de Alwis (1996), *Embodied Violence: Communalising Women's Sexuality in South Asia*, New Delhi: Kali for Women.

Kim, Elaine H. and Chungmoo Choi (1998), *Dangerous Women: Gender & Korean Nationalism*, New York: Routledge.

Leupp, Gary P. (1995), *Male Colors: The Construction of Homosexuality in Tokugawa Japan*, Berkeley: University of California Press.

McClintock, Anne (1995), *Imperial Leather: Race, Gender and Sexuality in the Colonial Conquest*, New York and London: Routledge.

Menon, Nivedita (ed.) (2007), *Sexualities*, New Delhi: Kali for Women.

Mosse, George L. (1985), *Nationalism and Sexuality: Middle-Class Morality and Sexual Norms in Modern Europe*, Madison: University of Wisconsin Press.

Neil, J. and C. Neil (1996), *Philippine Gay Culture: Binabae to Bakla, Silahis to MSM*, Hong Kong: Hong Kong University Press.

Peletz, Michael G. (2009), *Gender Pluralism: Muslim Southeast Asia since Early Modern Times*, New York: Routledge.

Puar, Jasbir K. (2007), *Terrorist Assemblages: Homonationalism in Queer Times*, Durham and London: Duke University Press.

Rokeya, Sakhawat Hossain (1988 [1905]), *Sultana's Dream*, New York: The Feminist Press.

Roosa, John (2006), *Pretext for Mass Murder: The September 30th Movement and Suharto's Coup d'état in Indonesia*, Madison: The University of Wisconsin Press.

Said, Edward W. (1978), *Orientalism: Western Constructions of the Orient*, London: Penguin.

Saigol, Rubina (2013), *The Pakistan Project: A Feminist Perspective on Nation and Identity*, New Delhi: Women Unlimited.

Sang, Tze-lan D. (2003), *The Emerging Lesbian: Female Same-Sex Desire in Modern China*, Chicago: University of Chicago Press.

Sangari, Kumkum and Sudesh Vaid (eds.) (1989), *Recasting Women: Essays in Colonial History*, New Delhi: Kali for Women.

Sarkar, Sumit and Tanika Sarkar (eds.) (2008), *Women and Social Reform in Modern India: A Reader*, Bloomington: Indian University Press.

Sarkar, Tanika and Urvashi Butalia (1995), *Women and Right-Wing Movements: Indian Experiences*, London: Zed Books.

Sinha, Mrinalini (1995), *Colonial Masculinity: The 'Manly Englishman' and the 'Effeminate Bengali' in the Late Nineteenth Century*, Manchester: Manchester University Press.

Sinnott, Megan J. (2004), *Toms and Dees: Transgender Identity and Female Same-Sex Relationships in Thailand*, Honolulu: University of Hawai'i Press.

Stoler, Ann Laura (1995), *Race and the Education of Desire: Foucault's History of Sexuality and the Colonial Order of Things*, Durham: Duke University Press.

Suiming, Pan (2005), *Sexuality in China*, Nakornpathom: Mahidol University.

Sullivan, Gerard and Peter A. Jackson (eds.) (2001), *Gay and Lesbian Asia: Culture, Identity, Community*, New York: Haworth Press.

Vanita, Ruth and Saleem Kidwai (eds.) (2000), *Same-Sex Love in India: Read-*

ings from Literature and History, New York: St Martin's Press.

Vasudevan, Nitya (2013), ""Public Women" and "Obscene" Body-Practice: An Exploration of Abolition Debates," *The Sexual History of the Global South: Sexual Politics in Africa, Asia and Latin America*, Saskia E. Wieringa and Horacio Sivori (eds.), London: Zed Books: 168-187.

West, Lois A. (ed.) (1997), *Feminist Nationalism*, New York: Routledge.

Wieringa, Saskia E. (1985), *The Perfumed Nightmare: Some Notes on the Indonesian Women's Movement*, Working paper, ISS, The Hague.

______(2002), *Sexual Politics in Indonesia*, London: Palgrave/McMillan Publishers.

______(2003), "The Birth of the New Order State in Indonesia: Sexual Politics and Nationalism," *Journal of Women's History*, Vol. 15 No. 1, Spring 2003: 70-92.

______ (2006), "First Wave Feminism, Nationalism and Colonialism: Aletta Jacobs, Begum Rokeya and Raden Adjeng Kartini: An Exploration into Transnationalism," *Protesting Patriarchy: Contextualising Rokeya*, Najma Chowdhury (ed.), Dhaka: University of Dhaka: 35-49.

______ (2007a), "Silence, Sex and the System: Women's Same Sex Practice in Japan," *Women's Sexualities and Masculinities in a Globalizing Asia*, Saskia Wieringa, Evelyn Blackwood and Abha Bhaiya (eds.), London: Palgrave: 23-47.

______ (2007b), "'If There is no Feeling…' The Dilemma Between Silence and Coming Out in a Working Class Butch/Fem Community in Jakarta," *Love and Globalisation: Transformations of Intimacy in the Contemporary World*, Mark B. Padilla, Jennifer S. Hirsch, Miguel Muñoz-Laboy, Robert E. Sember and Richard G. Parker (eds.), Nashville: Vanderbilt University Press: 70-93.

______ (2009a), "Postcolonial Amnesia: Sexual Moral Panics, Memory and Imperial Power," *Moral Panics, Sex Panics: Fear and the Fight over Sexual Rights*, Gilbert Herdt (ed.) New York: New York University Press: 205-234.

______ (2009b), "Women Resisting Creeping Islamic Fundamentalism in Indonesia," *Asian Journal of Women's Studies*, Vol. 15(4): 30-57.

______ (2010), "Emerging Sexualities in Asia, an Introduction to the Special Issue of the Journal of Gender," *Technology and Development*, 14(2): 127-141.

______ (2011b), "Sexual Slander and the 1965/6 Mass Killings in Indonesia: Political and Methodological Considerations," *Journal of Contemporary Asia Volume*, 41(4): 544-66.

______ (2012a), "Gender Variance in Southeast Asia: Discursive Contestations and Legal Implications," *The Future of Asian Feminisms: Confronting Fundamentalisms, Conflicts and Neo-Liberalism*, Nursyahbani Katjasungkana and Saskia E. Wieringa (eds.), Newcastle upon Thyme: Cambridge Scholars Publishing: 447-476.

______ (2012b), "Passionate Aesthetics and Symbolic Subversion: Heteronormativity in India and Indonesia," *Asian Studies Review*, 36(4), December: 515-530.

______ (2013), "Marriage Equality in Indonesia? Unruly Bodies, Subversive Partners and Legal Implications," *Equal Rights Review*, Vol. 10: 97-111.

______ (2015), *Heteronormativity, Passionate Aesthetics and Symbolic Subversion in Asia*, Eastbourne: Sussex Academic Press.

Wieringa, Saskia E., Evelyn Blackwood and Abha Bhaiya (eds.) (2007), *Women's Sexualities and Masculinities in a Globalizing Asia*, London: Palgrave.

Yuval-Davis, Nira and Floya Anthias (eds.) (1989), *Woman-Nation-State*, New York: St Martin's Press.

Chapter 8

Feminist Ethics of Reproduction and Women's Bodies

Jyotsna Agnihotri GUPTA

1. Introduction

The issue of biological reproduction has always been central to women's lives. In all cultures and ages women have sought ways and means either to prevent conception, get rid of an unwanted pregnancy, to voluntarily remain childfree, or to deal with involuntary childlessness. The twentieth century saw the development and use of various scientific and medical technologies to intervene in the process of biological reproduction, and in principle to extend our reproductive options. With the development of the contraceptive pill in the early 1950s, and later other contraceptive methods, fertility management through modern technology became more efficient and reliable. Then came sophisticated technologies such as ultrasound for pregnancy management, followed by technologies for assisting conception. The technological management and control of fertility and infertility and pregnancy have steadily increased.

We now live in a world where science and technology shape the global economy and everyday culture, where new reproductive technologies are changing how we can reproduce, and have revolutionised the ways we engage with our bodies. Reproductive technologies offer contradictory possibilities. The contraceptive pill provided the possibility for increased self-determination, but further developments in contraceptive technologies also made it possible for the State, medical service providers, etc., to use the technologies for other ends, such as population control. Since the second feminist wave in the 1960s, women's control over their own fertility has been identified as crucial to women's emancipation. The women's movement and reproductive technology opened up possibilities for some women to shape their lives and make active choices for themselves. Efforts to control women's reproduction by others have been counteracted by women's efforts towards reproductive freedom. As technological advances take place within a profit-oriented economic system, health care has become an enormous industry and with it the possibility of increased control over individuals by medical scientists, pharmaceutical companies, religious institutions, and the State.

The structure of the article is as follows: First, I will define certain feminist bioethical principles which form the conceptual framework for my analysis of reproductive technologies. Then, I will sketch briefly the technological developments that have taken place in the field of human reproduction since the latter half of the twentieth century. Thereafter, taking the example of prenatal testing for sex selection in the Indian context, I will consider the consequences of these technologies for society in general and for women in particular. I will conclude by outlining the challenges these developments pose, while keeping in mind feminist bioethical principles, for feminist discourse and solidarity in a transnational perspective.

2. Conceptual Framework

2.1 Autonomy, Self-Determination and the Right to Choose

Autonomy is to be understood as having control or power over one's own life and one's own body in relation to others, in particular males and with regard to the structures of society. In this definition, autonomy is seen as a goal for individual women to strive for, but at the same time it has a collective aspect as the struggle is not only against individual men but against societal structures, thus working towards a collective goal of an ideal (egalitarian) society, so that an individual's autonomy is not at the expense of others. Also the question of individual and collective autonomy requires consideration—are the two compatible or are they irreconcilable and even antagonistic? Another interpretation, and the one more common among US (liberal) feminists, is one that identifies autonomy with 'self-determination,' with the 'right (of the individual) to choose.' In this interpretation the autonomy of the individual is central, although it may express women's collective interests, as it happened in the 1960s and 1970s within the women's movement for the right to contraception and abortion. On the other hand, the individual aspect of autonomy, while it may further individual desires, instead of bringing women together, it may even form an obstacle to feminist solidarity and the achievement of feminist goals, as will be demonstrated later in this essay with the example of sex-selection.

It is significant that in some definitions of autonomy the ability of the individual to withdraw from the power exercised by others is emphasised. This implies an understanding of how power works and the sources it draws upon so as to understand the conditions that are necessary to allow women the ability to withdraw from power exercised by others. This is another important aspect of autonomy in the field of biological reproduction. Concretely, this means women's control over their own bodies and reproductive capacities, including women's ability to resist control by others in this respect, and the role of new reproductive technologies in that.

2.2 Informed Consent

Informed consent is the universal gold standard of good ethical medical and research practice. By 'informed' we mean that in clinical practice pregnant women/couples must be fully informed about the nature of medical procedures and the interventions made in women's/men's bodies, their inherent risks and benefits. In a research setting it implies that respondents/subjects whose bio-material is taken are informed about who is conducting the research, for what purpose, why bio-materials are being taken, how they will be used now and in the future, what the expected benefits and risks are to subjects and benefits to researchers or humankind in general.

By 'consent' we mean that tests and procedures are conducted with the permission of the individuals concerned, and that there is no obvious or covert pressure on individuals from the State, service provider, husband or other family member(s), employer, health insurers, researchers, community and community representatives, etc. Informed consent entails respect for individual autonomy and aims to protect the privacy and vulnerability of individuals to discrimination and exploitation.

2.3 Vulnerability

Vulnerability refers to the inability to withstand the effects of a hostile environment, to the susceptibility of a person, group, society, sex or system to physical or emotional injury or attack. Social vulnerability refers to a person's state of being liable to succumb to manipulation, persuasion, temptation etc. Often, due to their lower social position (also within the family hierarchy), lack of education and inadequate income, women are more vulnerable than men. Also, pregnancy is a state which makes women temporarily more vulnerable than at other times in their lives.

2.4 Bodily Integrity

Bodily integrity, otherwise known as physical or corporal integrity, is a concept that refers to the inviolability of the physical body. It is one of Martha Nussbaum's ten principal capabilities (capability approach). She defines bodily integrity as: "Being able to move freely from place to place; being able to be secure against violent assault, including sexual assault ...; having opportunities for sexual satisfaction and for choice in matters of reproduction" (1999: 41-42). Though bodily integrity (according to the capabilities approach) is accorded to every human being, women are more often affected by its violations. These include sexual assault, unwanted pregnancy, domestic abuse, and limited access to contraception and abortion.

2.5 Reproductive Justice

Reproductive justice is a concept linking reproductive health with social justice. The term emerged from the work of reproductive health organisations for women of colour in the United States in the 1990s. Proponents of the concept of reproductive justice aim to recognise that women's reproductive health is connected to and affected by conditions in their lives that are shaped by their socioeconomic status, human rights violations, race, sexuality, and nationality (Silliman et al., 2004: 4). They argue that women cannot have full control over their reproductive lives, unless issues such as socioeconomic disadvantage, racial discrimination, inequalities in wealth and power, and differential access to resources and services are addressed.[1]

The grassroots organisation Asian Communities for Reproductive

1 Ross, Loretta (May 2006). *Understanding Reproductive Justice*. SisterSong. Advocates for the rights of women of colour connected reproductive health with social justice to create the new term "reproductive justice" after returning from the 1994 International Conference on Population and Development in Cairo, Egypt. http//:www.LSRJ.org. Accessed on 12 December 2011.

Justice defines reproductive justice as follows: "We believe reproductive justice is the complete physical, mental, spiritual, political, economic, and social well-being of women and girls, and will be achieved when women and girls have the economic, social and political power and resources to make healthy decisions about our bodies, sexuality and reproduction for ourselves, our families, and our communities in all areas of our lives."[2] The reproductive justice framework utilises an intersectional analysis of women's experiences and focuses on changing the structural inequalities that affect women's reproductive health and their ability to control their reproductive lives. Women's bodies and lives are generally more affected than men's by reproductive decisions.

2.6 Gender Justice

Gender justice requires men and women be judged on the basis of their common humanness, while respecting the differences that they embody as gendered individuals without imputing inferiority to one or the other on that basis.

3. Technological Developments in Reproductive Technology

Reproduction nowadays is far from being a unified process. Reproductive technologies have fragmented the process of procreation, sometimes also involving multiple bodies. First, with the development of contraceptive technologies it became possible to have sex without reproduction; later, with the development of technologies such as artificial insemination and in-vitro fertilisation, it became possible to have reproduction without sex.

2 Asian Communities for Reproductive Justice 2005. A New Vision for Advancing our Movement for Reproductive Health, Reproductive Rights and Reproductive Justice. http//: www.LSRJ.org. Accessed on 12 December 2011.

Since the 1950s technological innovation in the field of reproduction is going on at a very rapid pace. Technologies designed to intervene in the process of human reproduction cover three areas: (1) for preventing conception and birth. These include contraceptives (hormonal pills, injectables and implants), sterilisation, as well as methods for pregnancy termination; (2) for assisting reproduction. Technologies for this range from artificial insemination which can be very 'low-tech' requiring little or no medical intervention to variations of in-vitro fertilisation, synonymous with 'high-tech' medicine involving very sophisticated medical, surgical and laboratory procedures; (3) for genetic purposes and for pre-natal and pre-implantation diagnosis (including sex-detection and sex-(pre-)selection). Technologies in this field aim at improving the health and genetic characteristics of foetuses and of new-borns—with the search for, as some say, 'the perfect child.'

I will analyse some of the developments in the application of these technologies, in particular the technologies for sex (pre-)selection to consider their consequences for society in general and for women in particular. For this purpose, I will make use of some of the concepts in feminist ethics as defined above.

3.1 Preventing Conception and Birth

For males the only available contraceptive technology is the condom, or as a terminal method—sterilisation. Although, many people may know of the condom as a method, it is hardly mentioned by doctors when discussing contraception with their patients; this reinforces the idea that contraception is a woman's responsibility. For females, on the other hand a variety of methods are available: (i) methods for spacing or delaying birth (such as the condom, diaphragm, etc., hormonal methods including the oral pill, injectables and implants and intra-uterine devices; (ii) terminal methods—sterilisation by various means and methods; and (iii) methods for pregnancy termination (morning-after pill, abortion).

Contraceptives must enable people to exert greater control over their fertility (birth control). Women's desire and right to control their fertility is often thwarted by husbands/sexual partners, family, community, religious leaders or the State. This is done either by disallowing access to contraceptive technologies and services, or by forcing certain long-acting, provider-dependent contraceptive methods for compulsory contraception or sterilisation with the goal of population control by reducing births. Contraceptives were not invented by reproductive scientists to provide women with more autonomy over their bodies or their lives, although, in ideal circumstances that could be an important effect. Many interests have become enmeshed in the development, propagation and availability, or in other cases denial or restricted access, to means of contraception and abortion. These include economic, political and religious interests. The history of the development and use of the contraceptive pill, and the struggle for the right to legal and safe abortion are illustrative in this regard. There are enough examples to illustrate how these rights can be granted or curbed by leaders of organised religions as well as by different political regimes even within one country over a period of time, and for different groups within one country in either anti-natalist or pro-natalist contexts.

3.2 Assisting Reproduction

Technologies used for assisting reproduction range from simple or low technologies, such as artificial insemination to high-tech options, such as in-vitro fertilisation (IVF) in all its variations. While earlier IVF was meant to be a solution mainly for heterosexual women who could not conceive due to blocked tubes, now with the aid of this technology women without uteruses, or no eggs of their own, women past their reproductive years, infertile or sub-fertile men as well as lesbian women and gay men can have their own genetic children. The possibility to freeze and store sperm, eggs and embryos has opened up opportunities for new applications. In this sense, IVF and related technologies serve as the basis for far-reaching research and applications.

In most countries artificial insemination with donor sperm and IVF are not readily available to all women; lesbian women or single heterosexual women may be denied access. State legislation (generally reflecting public opinion), religious prescripts and medical specialists regulate access to these technologies. IVF can also be used within surrogacy, when a woman bears a child for someone else. There are variations within surrogacy. There is 'genetic' surrogacy and 'gestational' (full) surrogacy. In the first case, the classical model of surrogacy, a surrogate is inseminated with the sperm of the commissioning father. In this case her own eggs are used and she also provides her uterus. In the latter, she receives an embryo containing the genetic material of the commissioning couple or a donor and she rents her uterus.

A growing number of infertile couples and other individuals desiring children are seeking to fulfil their desire for parenthood transnationally through the use of donor gametes and a surrogate. Egg donation and surrogacy have since then become commercialised. Commercial egg donation and surrogacy in the globalised fertility market is a thriving global business, a business that operates within global relations that are characterised by stark economic inequalities and diverse and inadequate regulation and governance (Gupta, 2012a, 2012b). Poor women from developing countries and from the underclass in the developed world are reproducing for the world market and for the more privileged classes in their own countries, as well as (sometimes unwittingly) providing the raw material for stem-cell research and cloning (Gupta, 2011). Many reproductive-service providers use the feminist language of self-determination, agency, and empowerment to justify women's decision to undertake commercial egg donation and surrogacy. However, what may be understood under autonomy is itself controversial. A large number of Indian women are extremely vulnerable due to low educational levels, poverty, marginalisation in labour and job markets, and also patriarchal social and family structures. I think these terms are misused and misplaced in the Indian context. They only serve to aid and abet the power of neo-liberalism and free market capitalism (Gupta, 2012a, 45-46).

IVF is at the basis of a number of other techniques; it opens the door to a host of other procedures, such as pre-implantation diagnosis of an embryo for genetic disorders and sex-selection, use of embryonic and foetal tissue for research on stem cells and human cloning. Women are primarily involved because it is women's bodies which provide the eggs and it is their bodies which are needed to carry genetically manipulated embryos to term. Technological developments in the field of assisted reproduction have far-reaching implications for society.

3.3 Pre-Natal Testing and Pre-Implantation Genetic Diagnosis

Since the 1980s there is an increasing proliferation of technologies for prenatal testing (PNT) for the management of pregnancy, and to ensure foetal health and welfare. Besides prenatal testing, within IVF there is also the possibility for pre-implantation genetic diagnosis (PGD) of the embryo to detect congenital abnormalities, that are seen as a major cause of perinatal, neo-natal and infant deaths, and abnormalities and diseases which surface later in life.

Prenatal genetic diagnosis (PGD) or embryo screening is particularly useful in detecting autosomal gene disorders (not applicable for multifactoral disorders). It is considered a particularly interesting alternative for a select group of individuals and couples, for instance: (a) those who consider themselves at high risk of begetting a(nother) child with a serious genetic disorder; (b) women who have repeatedly miscarried; (c) those who are in principle against abortion but find PGD acceptable; (d) those who want to avoid going through (repeated) abortions were they to learn about the disorder only after conception through PNT.

Couples who seek PGD are normally fertile, yet the woman has to go through the risky IVF procedure to make use of the technique. Through PGD they can start a pregnancy with the knowledge that the future offspring does not have the disorder. The success of this method, however, depends on the success rate of IVF. Scientists have tried to create the impression that IVF-PGD will become a common procedure, that every embryo can be tested before being replaced in the uterus, and only the 'perfect' ones replaced; also that this will be the preferred method of starting a pregnancy in the future. However, it is an illusion to think that in practice this will be possible for all pregnancies.

In most of the countries of the global North prenatal testing is increasingly offered routinely to pregnant women to avoid giving birth to offspring with genetic or other disorders, mainly by aborting the affected foetus. Values ascribed to 'normal' and 'disabled' children prevalent in society play an important role. The pressure on women both to undergo tests and to opt for abortion in case an anomaly is detected is high. Once placed in the role of autonomous and responsible decision-makers, women are making very pragmatic decisions, although the information they possess is highly inadequate and incomplete and their life circumstances too constraining (Gupta, 2010). Women often face coercion from husbands and mothers-in-law in making reproductive choices regarding not only the number of children (quantity) but also the kind of children (quality) to be born (Gupta, 2000; Patel, T., 2007), thus making it more difficult to ensure their free and informed consent for use of genetic services.

In India and China, besides their medical use, the tests have been used primarily for sex-detection and sex (pre-)selection for social reasons, in order to avoid the birth of daughters, as there exists a strong preference for sons.

4. Discourses on Reproductive Technology

The development and use of reproductive technologies have thrown up gender issues, issues of a philosophical, ethical, political, economic, legal and eugenic nature as well as more general issues to do with the sociology of technology, and medical technology in particular. Some believe that technology is neutral and value-free and can be used or abused; the social and human meaning of a technology depends upon the type of use or application. Others, including feminist philosophers of science, contend that technology and the very paradigm of science in which it is embedded is value-loaded, having imbibed the values and prejudices of the ruling elite. The development and applications of reproductive technologies are creating contradictory possibilities for women. Such technologies while allowing the exercise of individual reproductive rights and offering 'choice' to some women have at the same time the potential to take away rights and choices for other women.

In the context of a world economy, technologies usually developed in the North, soon become internationalised. They take on a life of their own, especially when introduced in different socio-cultural contexts and when driven by motives of economic gain. They are often used for purposes other than originally intended and—particularly in a different socio-economic, cultural and political climate and a different health care infrastructure—have other implications. For instance, contraceptive technologies for individual fertility management and birth control are used by others to realise the goals of population control. Another example is that of pre-conceptional and pre-natal genetic diagnosis technologies, which were originally intended for detecting congenital abnormalities, being used to detect the sex of the foetus, followed by sex-selective abortion. The World Bank's 2012 World Development Report 'Gender Equality and Development' foregrounded sex selection as a major global issue perpetuating gender inequality. The report identified how complex social, behavioural, and technological factors have converged to skew sex ratios in various parts of Asia, Europe and North America.

I will now examine pre-conceptional and pre-natal diagnosis technologies in the context of India. I do this in order to understand the ideas about the roles of women and men from which they emanate, the politics of reproduction within which these technologies are used, the role of reproductive technology in reproducing gender relations, and the power relations implicit in their development and applications.

5. Pre-Conceptional and Pre-Natal Testing for Sex Selection

It is not only possible to detect but also to select/influence the sex of the future child with the use of reproductive technologies in this field. This can be done pre-conceptionally through sex selecting sperm to enhance chances of conceiving a child of the preferred sex at the pre-insemination stage (either for intra-uterine insemination, or within an IVF procedure), or by sex selecting the embryo after fertilisation within IVF). In India sex (pre-)selection is mostly done to ensure the birth of males. Another, more commonly used technique is pre-natal sex detection followed by abortion of female foetuses based solely on their gender (i.e. characteristics, abilities and expectations ascribed to female and male, defined as 'feminine' and 'masculine,' behavioural patterns and the sexual division of labour, roles and responsibilities and value defined by culture).

In India, prenatal testing technologies, such as ultrasound scanning, chorionic villi sampling (placenta screening), and amniocentesis (screening of amniotic fluid), have been advertised as 'boy/girl test' since the 1970s and are primarily used as such, and much less so for their medical purpose, i.e. for detecting genetic diseases and disorders in the foetus. In 1975, reports appeared of private gynaecologists from Amritsar (Punjab) and Bombay who were offering amniocentesis. The slogan 'Spend Rupees 500 now and save Rupees 50,000 later'—meaning, spend a paltry sum now on a sex detection test and, by comparison, save a huge amount later (presumably for dowry)—by a clinic in Amritsar was a call for sex selective abortion without explicitly saying so. The advertisement referred to daughters as a 'liability' to the family and a 'threat to the nation' and exhorted women to avail themselves of the services of the clinic to escape this danger (Mazumdar, 1994: 3). Cashing in on the demand for sex determination tests, partially also generated by the media reports, a doctor started his own genetic laboratory in New Delhi. All the leading newspapers carried the advertisement 'Normal Boy or Girl?' almost daily for several years. This marked the beginning of privatisation and commercialisation of prenatal diagnosis technology which has since grown into a thriving business of sex detection for the purpose of selective abortion of female foetuses in the quest for a male offspring.

In the 1980s private clinics providing prenatal diagnosis through amniocentesis and ultrasound scans mushroomed even in the remotest corners of India. Most people appeared to be completely unaware that the tests they know as 'sex tests' or 'Boy-Girl tests' were meant primarily to diagnose birth defects (Gupta, 2000). From the mid-1990s pre-conceptional sex selection techniques within assisted reproduction also proliferated. Public (government) hospitals do not provide sex detection and sex selection services for non-medical reasons; they are illegally provided only in the private healthcare sector. Although illegal, they are a major source of revenue for service providers forming the main driving force for the spread of these services. The proliferation of registered clinics offering ultrasound scans from 600 in 2000 to 41,182 (Sinha, 2011) in March 2011, as well as the increase in mobile services using portable ultrasound machines brought to a client's home in rural areas (for which no figures are available) and the use of agents to lure clients by medical practitioners since the 1990s, affirms this (George, 2009). The recent figures also demonstrate the failure of the Pre-natal Diagnostic Techniques Act (1994) enforced in 1996, and the revised Pre-conception and Pre-natal Diagnostic Techniques Act of 2003 to curb pre-implantation sex selection and sex determination.

The two main reasons for sex (pre-)selection are the population policy of the Indian government and the prevalence of son preference and daughter discrimination. The Indian government introduced the two-child norm, as part of the National Population Policy in 1992, which put down the "small family norm" as one of its goals for 2010. If couples are exhorted to have not more than two children, they want at least one or more sons, based on traditional ideas regarding higher value accorded to sons as compared to daughters. Initially, a girl child used to be accepted by most families as a first child, but later the family was less willing to accept a daughter until a son was born (Das Gupta and Visaria, 1997). Data indicate that the proportion of families aborting female foetuses even in the first pregnancy has increased (George and Dahiya, 1998). "Indications are that the problem may become further accentuated with the desire to limit family size imposed upon a society with male preference" (Ravindran, 1997: 32). Women are caught between the ideologies of population control (implying state control) and the ideology of motherhood (implying family control) and son preference. A large number of families in both rural and urban areas not only want smaller families, but also have a clear preference for a desired sex, birth order, and composition of children: two sons and a daughter (Sudha and Rajan, 1999). Due to coercive population control measures, in the name of family planning and welfare, the Total Fertility Rate (TFR) has come down to 2.5 in 2013, with wide variations between states and urban and rural areas.

Laws enacted by certain state governments in the late 1990 and 2000s that restrict the eligibility for candidates to stand for election in rural legislative bodies ('panchayats') to those with two or less children has severely affected the sex ratio. "Smaller families come at the expense of girls," says social activist Sabu George (Darnton, 2010).

Most doctors and health workers also believe that sex (pre-)selection technologies provide an effective method of family planning and are an important tool in the promotion of population control programmes in India. Sex selection is advocated as a method to obtain the desired 'family composition' and 'family balancing' when a family has one or more children of one sex and also wants a child of the opposite sex even in some countries of the global North. A woman is more likely to have abortions to achieve this so-called 'balanced' family—which among Indians has a clear sexist bias—than for medical or social reasons.

Studies, which used evidence from a variety of sources, reported that discrimination against girls had increased in India despite economic development and fertility and mortality decline. Sudha and Rajan (1999) argue that social and economic development worsened the situation of women in India and increased the preference for boys. The Green Revolution, which was ushered in by mechanised farming (marginalising female labour) and resulted in rising levels of prosperity and education in Punjab and Haryana, did not raise the status of women significantly. This notion is reflected in the increased masculinity of sex ratios, an indicator of the state of gender relations at birth, particularly in rural Punjab, Delhi, Haryana, Rajasthan, and Himachal Pradesh. These indicate a continuing practice of sex selective abortion, resurgent female infanticide, and persistent excess female child mortality, particularly in the 0-6 age group.

Often poverty and illiteracy are cited as the main reasons for gender bias against daughters in India; it is believed that economic development and education would help change these harmful attitudes. But studies demonstrating that it was in fact economically better-off and higher educated women and men who were keenly interested and willing to use these technologies for daughter elimination, contradict this notion (Shah and Taneja, 1991). These men and women considered themselves consumers who should be able to get the service they wanted as long as they could afford it. Women who already had one or more girls were more likely to seek testing and abortion afterwards. This was the case in rural and urban areas, irrespective of religion or state (Jha et al., 2006). Indians in the diaspora, in the UK and the US, in particular skilled professionals, also practice sex selection. Its "ready availability and legality in the United States increased the pressure and even obligation to use it."

The role of the family in reproductive decision-making processes in India seems to remain under-highlighted. In a traditional society the importance of children and sons, in particular within marriage, for both women and men should not be underestimated. Children strengthen the conjugal and kinship bonds and are crucial for achieving a satisfying identity, gaining status, and for present and future emotional and economic security and upward social mobility. In a patriarchal kinship structure a woman's status in the household is determined by her ability to produce male offspring so as to carry on her husband's lineage. Having sons provides status and security to a woman within the marital household; bearing only daughters may lead to abandonment and remarriage by the husband.

Traditionally, in most societies in South and Southeast Asia, boys are preferred over girls for economic, social and cultural reasons. A son is considered an asset, while a daughter is considered a liability. In patriarchal and patrilineal societies, like in India, sons carry on the family name as well as the craft, trade or profession; they help to maintain the family property; and they are expected to provide economic security and care for their parents in old age. In contrast, girls are considered to cost money for reasons of dowry payments and the giving of gifts to a married daughter and her conjugal family on various occasions throughout life. No payment is necessary for a son's marriage; in fact a son brings in a dowry with his bride.[3] The consumerist lifestyle encouraged with rising economic prosperity has led to more numerous and intensified dowry demands (Agnihotri I., 2003; Patel, 2007).

There are also other social and cultural reasons for not wanting daughters, such as the perceived danger to a daughter's chastity, which is a question of the family's honour, and the concern of getting her married before she is 'too old.' Among upper caste Hindus certain religious ceremonies and rituals may be performed only by males. According to the Hindu scriptures, sons are required to light the funeral pyre of their parents, releasing them from the trammels of this world and ensuring their souls' entry into heaven. With the birth of a son the father is released from his debt

3 The giving and receiving of dowry was banned in 1961 under the Dowry Prohibition Act of Parliament, which was further amended in 1984 and 1986. However, the practice has flourished, increased in magnitude, and instead of being given with goodwill as gifts by the parents it has turned into a financial transaction that is even considered a rightful demand on the part of the bridegroom and his family.

to his ancestors. Besides, it is often believed that 'having sons signifies masculinity' (Williamson, 1976).

Son preference is not confined to India alone. Cross-cultural studies by social scientists (cf. Parikh, 1989: 8 for references) show a marked bias in favour of sons. The birth of a boy (especially the first-born) is announced and received with more exhilaration than when it is 'only a girl.' Folklore and proverbs from various countries are evidence of this bias for sons. This is hardly surprising given the patriarchal nature of most societies. Modern science not only reflects this bias, but also provides the scientific tools to perpetuate it. Although some countries, like China and India, record female infanticide, the use of modern technologies for sex detection and selection exacerbates the situation. This leads to a further devaluation of girls.

Since 1994, 10 million female foetuses have been aborted in India with far-reaching demographic and social consequences (Jha et al., 2006). This is demonstrated by the declining and skewed male-female sex ratios, in particular child sex ratios. Analysis of data obtained from the Special Fertility and Mortality Survey undertaken in 1998 in 1.1 million households revealed that based on conservative assumptions there were 0.5 million missing female births a year. This demonstrates what Amartya Sen (1990) has called the phenomenon of 'missing females.' There are 100 million missing females worldwide, with China and India being responsible for 80 million, in total more than 35 million in India alone in 2001.

India has a low female-male sex ratio in contrast to most developed countries. In relation to 1,000 males this was 972 in 1901, 933 in 1981, and only 927 in 1991, with a marginal increase 933 to 1000 in 2001, and 940 to 1,000 in 2011 (Registrar General of India). In 1961, the (ages 0-6) child sex ratio in India was 976 girls to 1,000 boys, which fell to 927 girls to 1,000 boys by 2001. Also worrisome is the sharp decline in the under-6 sex ratio. The provisional results of the 2011 Census show that India's child sex-ratio has dipped to 914 girls from 927 per 1,000 boys recorded in the 2001 Census. Regional variations in sex-ratio are further evidence of the bias against girls.[4] This bias is particularly visible in states where female literacy is low (Agnihotri S.B., 1999, 2000; Sudha and Rajan, 1999) in certain states such as Punjab, Haryana, Himachal Pradesh and Delhi.[5]

In the 1980s there was a debate in the *Economic and Political Weekly* on the possible consequences of the falling sex ratio in India (Kumar, 1983a, 1983b; Dube, 1983a, 1983b; Jeffery and Jeffery, 1984). Some argued that the market forces of supply and demand would raise the value of women, while others contended that it would devalue women further. Recent figures show there is a surplus of males and a shortage of women, particularly of marriageable age (future brides). Men already face difficulty in finding a wife in states like Delhi, Punjab and Haryana where the sex ratios are highly skewed in favour of boys.

Demographic consequences of sex (pre-)selection have far-reaching social consequences. Sex (pre-)selection leads to a surplus of males, and in the long-run a shortage of women of marriageable age. Between 2015 and 2030 in China 25 million men will have no hope of finding a wife. A "marriage squeeze" is already well under way in China and India (World Bank, 2012). In India, there is already a shortage of brides in the states of Punjab and Haryana. More girls are dropping out of school and more girls are being married at a younger age, resulting in increased mortality as a result of early child bearing. There is an increase in rape and violence against girls/women, abduction and trafficking of girls/women across state borders and inter-community trafficking, and kidnapping and sale of much desired boys. Also, wife sharing between brothers (forced polyandry) is reported.

There is a growing number of men with no prospects of marriage in societies where marriage is regarded as virtually universal and social status

4 Missing: Mapping the adverse child sex ratio in India, Office of the Registrar-General and Census Commissioner, India, Ministry of Health and Family Welfare and United Nations Population Fund, New Delhi, November 2003.

5 "Female foeticide rampant in Delhi," *The Times of India*, New Delhi, 15 July 2005.

and acceptance depend, in large part, on being married and creating a new family. According to some, this will lead to greater anti-social behaviour and ultimately present a threat to the security of society (Hesketh and Xing, 2006). Scarcity of women leads to a situation in which rich, skilled and educated men will marry, but poor, unskilled and illiterate men will not. A permanent subclass of bare branches from the lowest socio-economic classes is created. Conservative estimates of the number of young adult bare branches in India are about 28 million, i.e.12-15 per cent of the young adult male population. In general this is likely to lead to an increase in aggression and organised crime, and drug and alcohol abuse (Hudson and Den Boer, 2004). Some studies go even further and argue that a surplus of unmarried men, called 'bare branches' because they are branches of the family tree that will never bear fruit will lead to geopolitical instability and has security implications for countries (Hvistendahl, 2011), arguments which I find rather far-fetched.

6. Challenges for Feminist Discourse and Ethical Principles

Parents/women now have the power to choose the sex of their children. But, as technology answers prayers, it also raises some troubling questions. Modern science not only reflects the cultural gender bias against females but provides the scientific tools to perpetuate it. Although interest in sex selection is not new, use of modern technologies for sex detection and (pre)selection make the interventions more precise, so much so that the right of the girl to be born is threatened and in turn leads to a further devaluation of women (Gupta, 2000). Pre-conceptional and pre-natal sex selection in favour of males, abortion of female foetuses, and female infanticide are various practices that form a continuum and which result in the elimination of females in India.

It is difficult to untangle the direct and indirect pressures of patriarchal family structures and values in a society where gender relations are largely unequal and contribute to the vulnerability of women. What is known, however, is that women have very little negotiating power within the family, both in their natal family and even more so in relation to husbands and in-laws. Women may join in perpetuating these practices, believing them to be a form of protection for their children and themselves (reducing their vulnerability), and exercising some sort of autonomy or agency. Reproductive decision-making, including opting for sons instead of daughters, occurs under difficult circumstances and is seldom an expression of a woman's right to choose. In this setting, technology serves to reinforce patriarchal biases, not to change social relations.

Sex selection is legal in most of the world, and it is practiced also in Western countries. There is fertility tourism from the United Kingdom to the United States for sex selection, because PGD, which can be used for sex selection, is prohibited in the UK, except when it is used to screen for genetic diseases, while the laws in the US are more relaxed in this matter (Fishburn, 2009).

Sex (pre-)selection technologies have elicited contrary responses and have even divided feminists. While some acknowledge that sex selection is wrong, they consider it to be unavoidable in the Indian social set-up. A majority of providers of sex selection technologies argue that they are offering a humane service to women who do not want any more daughters and others allegedly hold that they offer it for reasons of 'a woman's right to choose' (Malpani, 1998, and personal communication, 2001). In their opinion it is an expression of reproductive rights, initiated and pursued by women, and is a sign of female empowerment that allows couples to make well-informed family planning decisions, prevents occurrences of unintended pregnancy and abortion, and minimises intimate partner violence and/or child neglect. Also, sex selective abortion is often considered the lesser of two evils, the other being female infanticide (Macklin, 1999). It is argued that if abortion is legal, a democratic state should not interfere in a woman's or couple's decision to abort a female foetus. In contrast, women's health and rights activists argue that in the absence of medical indications sex selection leads to invasive medical interventions. They also question whether women can truly express free choice under pressure from family and community. "What is interesting to note is how increasingly procreative liberty linked arguments permeate medical discourse, ascribing to individuals (particularly women) an independent moral value and decision-making power detached from any relational context—familial, community or social" (Mallik, 1999).

Sex (pre-)selection is big business. These technologies are provided only in the private health care sector in India. Although illegal, they are a major source of revenue for service providers and this is one of the main driving forces for the proliferation of sex selection technologies. Legal measures taken by the state[6] have not proved effective enough to curb the practice. Also, the risks of other testing technologies in future cannot be underestimated. As certain state governments have imposed a ban on sex detection through ultrasound machines, people are now buying sex determination kits online from China and the US. Experiments are on with non-invasive prenatal testing through screening foetal cells in maternal blood (FCMB) and detection of foetal cells and foetal DNA circulating in maternal blood—performed in the first trimester also known as non-invasive pre-natal testing (NIPT) in early pregnancy. The introduction of these new technologies coupled with entrenched cultural attitudes according a higher value to sons above daughters, and the return of coercive population control policies could increase sex-selective abortions further.

In sum, those who are in favour of sex detection and selection do so mainly on the grounds that it offers a 'solution' to the 'population problem' of India; that abortion is a woman's right; and that it is an individual's and couple's right to choose the sex of one's child. Those who oppose the practice and demand state intervention in terms of legislation and its enforcement do so on various counts such as arguing that the practice con-

6 Pre-natal sex selection is illegal under PNDT (Regulation and Prevention of Misuse) Act 1994 and pre-natal and pre-conceptional sex selection are illegal under PNDT (Regulation and Prevention of Misuse) Amendment Act 2002.

stitutes gender discrimination; that it harms women's health, and that it violates women's dignity and human rights, the reasons for which lie not in the x-chromosome which determines biological sex, but in the cultural meaning given to it, i.e. gender (Gupta, 2011). Applied in a social, political and economic context of inequality, exclusion and discrimination reproductive technologies replicate or exacerbate existing inequality, and create new forms of inequality. In this way, while they may further the individual interests of a few women, they violate several feminist ethical principles, in particular the principles of reproductive justice and gender justice. They are contrary to the strategic gender interests of all women, and form an obstacle to feminist solidarity and the achievement of collective feminist goals.

References

Agnihotri, I. (2003), "The Expanding Dimensions of Dowry," *Indian Journal of Gender Studies*, 10(2): pp. 307-319.

Agnihotri, S.B. (1999), "Inferring Gender Bias from Mortality Data: A discussion note," *Journal of Development Studies,* 35(4): pp. 175-200.

______(2000), *Sex Ratio Patterns in the Indian Population: A Fresh Exploration*, New Delhi: Sage.

Darnovsky, M. (2011), "Selecting for Sons: Indian Women in the US," *Biopolitical Times*, 27 April 2011.

Darnton, K. (2010), "A Gender Deficit that Could Haunt Us for Decades," *The Deccan Herald*, 4 September 2010.

Das Gupta, M. and L. Visaria (1996), "Son Preference and Excess Female Mortality in India's Demographic Transition," *Sex Preference for Children and Gender discrimination in Asia*, Research Monograph 96. 02, Seoul: Korean Institute for Health and Social Affairs and United Nations Population Fund.

Dube, L. (1983a), "Misadventures in Amniocentesis," *Economic and Political Weekly*, 18(8): pp. 279-80.

______ (1983b), "Amniocentesis Debate Continued," *Economic and Political Weekly*, 18(38), pp. 1663-65.

Fishburn, A. (2009), "US Clinic Offers British Couples the Chance to Choose the Sex of Their Child," *The Times*, 22 August 2009.

George, S. (2009), "Sex Selection as Genocide," *Undoing Our Future: A Report on the Status of the Young Child in India*, New Delhi: Forum for Crèche and Child Care Services, pp. 41-59.

George, S. M. and Dahiya, R. S. (1998), "Female Foeticide in Rural Haryana," *Economic and Political Weekly,* 33(32): pp. 2191-98.

Gupta, J. A. (2000), *New Reproductive Technologies, Women's Health and Autonomy: Freedom or Dependency?*, New Delhi: Sage.

______ (2010), "Exploring Indian Women's Reproductive Decision-making Regarding Prenatal Testing," *Culture, Health and Sexuality*, 12 (2), pp. 191-204.

______ (2011), "Unwanted Daughters: Discrimination and Elimination of the Girl Child in India," *Tijdschrift voor Genderstudies,* 14 (3): pp. 42-57.

______ (2012a), "Reproductive Biocrossings: Indian Egg Donors and Surrogates in the Globalized Fertility Market," *International Journal of Feminist Approaches to Bioethics*, 5 (1), pp. 25-51.

______ (2012b), "Parenthood in the era of Reproductive Outsourcing and Global Assemblages," *Asian Journal of Women's Studies*, 18 (1): pp. 7-29.

Hesketh, T. and Xing, Z. W. (2006), "Abnormal Sex Ratios in Human Populations: Causes and Consequences," Proceedings of the National Academy of Sciences of the United States of America, 103(36): pp. 13271-75.

Hudson, V. M. & Boer, A. M. den (2004), *Bare Branches: The Security Implications of Asia's Surplus Male Population.* (BCSIA Studies in International Security), John F. Kennedy School of Government, Cambridge, Mass.: Harvard University.

Hvistendahl, M. (2011), *Unnatural Selection: Choosing Boys Over Girls and the Consequences of a World Full of Men.*

Jeffery, R. & Jeffery, P. (1984), "Female Infanticide and Amniocentesis," *Social Science and Medicine*, 19(11): pp. 1207-12.

Jha, P., Kumar, R., Vasa, P. et al. (2006), "Low Male-to-Female Sex Ratio of Children Born in India: National Survey of 1.1 million Households," *The Lancet*, January 9, 2006, published online.

Kumar, D. (1983a), "Male Utopias or Nightmares?," *Economic and Political Weekly*, 18(3): pp. 61-64.

______ (1983b), "Amniocentesis Again," *Economic and Political Weekly*, 18(24): pp. 1075-76.

Macklin, R. (1999), *Against Relativism: Cultural Diversity and the Search for Ethical Universals in Medicine*, Oxford: Oxford University Press.

Mallik, R. (1999), *Pre-Natal Victimisation of the Female Lifeworld: Analysis of Discourses on Sex Determination Test and Sex Selective Abortion in India*, M.A. Thesis, The Hague: Institute of Social Studies.

Malpani, A. (1998), "Sex Selection by IVF: The Freedom to Choose," *Issues in Medical Ethics*, 6(2): 54.

Mazumdar, V. (1994), *Amniocentesis and Sex Selection*, Occasional Paper 21, New Delhi: Centre for Women's Development Studies.

Nussbaum, Martha C. (1999), *Sex and Social Justice*, Oxford: OUP.

Parikh, M. (1989), "The Challenge of Sex Selection: Controversy over Amniocentesis Tests in India," *Women and Politics*, Women's Studies Department, University of Arizona.

Patel, T. (ed.) (2007), *Sex-Selective Abortion in India: Gender, Society and New Reproductive Technologies*, New Delhi: Sage.

Ravindran, T. K. S. (1997), *Health Implications of Sex Discrimination in Childhood: Unravelling the Complexities*, Geneva: World Health Organization.

Sen, A. (1990), "More than 100 million Women are Missing," *The New York Review of Books*, 37(20), 20 December 1990.

Shah, A. and Taneja, S. (1991), "What Do Males and Females of Delhi City Think about Female Foeticide," *The Journal of Family Welfare*, 37(2): 28-39.

Silliman, J., Fried, M. G., Ross, L. & Gutiérrez, E. R. (2004), *Undivided*

Rights: Women of Color Organize for Reproductive Justice, Boston: South End Press.

Sinha, K. (2011), "Govt Gives More Teeth to Law against Sex Tests," *The Times of India*, 3 June 2011.

Sudha, S. and Rajan, S. I. (1999), "Female Demographic Disadvantage in India 1981-1991: Sex Selective Abortions and Female Infanticide," *Development and Change*, 30 (3): pp. 585-618.

Williamson, N. E. (1976), *Sons or Daughters? A Cross-Cultural Survey of Parental Preferences*, Beverley Hills, CA: Sage Publications.

World Bank (2011), *Gender Equality and Development*, World Development Report 2012, Washington D.C.: World Bank.

Chapter 9

Women's Movements and NGOs in Asia

Mala KHULLAR

When individuals or groups within civil society work together to advance a broad common set of interests, and these interests become a significant force in shaping the direction of society, the outcomes of such a process are often called social movements. These can be thought of as broad societal initiatives organized around a particular issue, trend or priority. Civil society organizations and academic institutions may generally be part of such initiatives and often assume the leadership in these, while state and society comprise the so-called establishment that such movements address and seek to change.

Sometimes civil society groups (including academia) are seen as apolitical rather than truly political, but they often comprise the first building blocks for effecting change and articulating people's voice. Equality, democratic principles and genuine political participation may be part of their objectives and modus operandi. The existence of such groups has been perceived as essential in many contexts and they operate in different ways. I will not try to enumerate these here, but shall try to dwell on the inevitable need for civil society participation for all movements, in particular women's movements. Civil society groups are the ones that represent voices of people; their emergence may be spontaneous to start with as they articulate opinions and viewpoints of people at grassroots levels. In time, these formations may grow and coalesce to form larger movements, associations and even professional groups that seek to address specific issues on the one hand and mediate between the state and people at large on the other. The impetus for movements, however, has also been seen as external, being due to outside or non-indigenous forces, but must be connected to local needs and perceptions in order to become sustainable and relevant in any given context.

Commonalities in the way certain issues were dealt with in the nineteenth and early twentieth centuries across different regions illustrate the kinds of developments that were underway via the burgeoning processes of imperialism and nationalism in several parts of Asia and Africa. Articulations by national movements therefore often spoke about challenging the external imperial or colonial powers on the one hand and the ruling feudal and religious structures and traditions that were entrenched within. As part of this, nationalist reformers made appeals regarding the cultural identities of their respective countries in order to promote self-government and for reforms in their traditional social structures via educational and scientific advance. Pertaining to women, for example, formal education for girls and women was introduced in countries such as Turkey, Sri Lanka or India and illustrates the growing need in different milieus for educated wives and mothers in the nineteenth and early twentieth centuries. Accordingly, in Turkey "They wanted their daughters to have serious Occidental and Oriental education, as befitted the future spouses of important men" (Minai, 1981: 49), while in India "Education would not turn the women away from their familial roles, but improve their efficiency as wives and mothers …" (Mazumdar, 1976: 49-50).

1. Feminist Movements

Women's movements in the Asian region demonstrate a range of varied experience. Their political activism has generated a wealth of new experiences and information while spawning new perspectives and knowledge on women. What are these movements? Have these been externally sponsored processes or are they spontaneous and indigenous formations that have emerged from peoples'—especially women's—associations or organizations? What are the engines of such movements? In many cases, the role of civil society groups—organizations or associations—has been vital in carrying forward the aims of women's movements. Such groups may be NGOs or associations that have formed spontaneously around certain issues. These include people's organizations and political formations that also need to be defined as actors and participants in people's movements. Moreover, they would sometimes have close links with some arms of the state with attempts to enhance and articulate feminist ideologies, while at the same time combating others, either within the state apparatus or in society at large.

If we trace the history of women's movements, we often see the use of the "wave approach." For instance, in the case of India, Gandhi and Shah (1992) identified phases or "waves" in the emergence of women's movements. Similarly, in Korea we see the wave formulation in the work of Kim Seung Kyung and Kyounghee Kim (2011). In the West we see the wave approach as well and generally three broad waves have been identified in some of the European and American women's movements through their histories (Humm, 1992). Other observers have either looked at the role of state and non-state agents in the growth and development of women's movements. For instance, the emergence of feminism in China in fact has been understood as catalyzed by the state, rather than NGOs in its initial avatar, wherein equality for women was subsumed within the broader agenda of the Cultural Revolution and state sponsored equality for all. It is only more recently that top-down official feminism has given way to a more grassroots driven understanding of how civil society needs to (articulate spontaneous voices) at the ground level rather than be driven by a top down agenda formulated in contexts that are far removed from local situations. In other words, movements need a space of their own in order to arrive at objectives in their native contexts. Feminism is still grappling with this in the Chinese context, regarding which we are seeing insightful analyses in recent years, say of the All China Women's Federation (ACWF), an umbrella body that has focused on virtually all matters pertaining to women in China since the 1940s (Liu, 2011; Cai, 2013).

2. Agenda Setting

It has often been alleged that feminism in many parts of Asia is imitative of western and 'foreign' political and social currents and has no bearing with local milieu. The traditionalist viewpoint therefore attempts to reject feminism as an external or foreign transplant, but this has been countered by studies on the rise of feminist ideologies in different parts of the world. For example, Kumari Jayawardena (1982) has argued that feminism was not imposed on developing or Third World countries by the West. The experiences discussed by her in her Feminism and Nationalism in the Third World include those of Japan, China, Egypt, and India. Movements for women's emancipation and feminist struggles that emerged in Asia and elsewhere thus need to be viewed in the light of the resistance that grew, on the one hand, against imperialism and foreign domination and, on the other, against local feudal structures and religious and traditional patriarchies. These are well illustrated in varying contexts, as seen in a few different Asian contexts. At the same time it may be worth emphasizing that feminist ideas had found expression before the western or European influences could do so in Asia. Women's writings that represent early expressions of feminism from different contexts of this period share many common elements illustrate some interesting instances. One such example is from India, of "Sultana's Dream" by Rokeya S. Hossain, written in the early twentieth century (Tharu and Lalitha, 1991 Vol. 1) visualized role reversal in a utopia where men were confined and secluded while women occupied positions of power and are allowed free access to public spaces. A similar piece was written by Li Ruzhen in 1825 in China in her novel "Flowers in the Mirror," reversing sex roles wherein men wore dresses, had their feet bound and were ruled by women who alone were educated and held official positions. Later this novel was considered to be the first declaration of women's rights (Croll, 1980: 38).

"Indigenizing feminism" or creating new feminisms is an expression that has been used by some scholars as they attempt to locate local experiences within a global and transnational scenario (Mazumdar, 2001; Roces, 2010). In the Asian context some observers have used the term "indigenizing" to describe the process whereby feminism has found a place in different national and regional spaces of Asia. For instance, Mina Roces (2010) suggests that feminism as a concept has its roots in western philosophical and political debates and then has been transmitted to its Asian counterparts; therefore she concludes that "Indeed, because Asian feminist theories developed partly as a rethinking of the applicability of Western feminism in local contexts, it might be possible to argue that Asian feminisms were transnationally produced" (6) or that "Indigenization often involved a rethinking of a Western idea" (8). Roces' argument seems a bit simplistic here and on the one hand begs the question regarding whether feminisms in the West were produced in a unique way and, on the other, were feminisms anywhere born in a context all of their own making without any external or "non-indigenous" inputs? Further, it tends to ignore the many and varied struggles for equality undertaken by women in their own local worlds, which were virtually unknown to most academic and policy pundits, thanks to a gender blindness that was neither Asian nor western but virtually universal.

The term "indigenizing" may imply a certain observation about the origin and development of ideas as if they must come from the outside and have to be turned into native ones by being embraced locally. While there have always been spontaneous and local feminist groups and individuals who have sought to create change in women's status in most contexts—national, personal or otherwise—rather than bring in or be inspired by external events and forces. For example, seeking the right to work or education by combating traditions that were inimical to women's lives and rights. Many of these factors in a sense did and continue to provide the impetus for women's movements and studies as they have emerged in different contexts. There are many stories about how individuals and groups of women struggled against social and familial pressures to work or gain an education—from here at Ewha in Seoul to right across Asia and elsewhere—and found allies for their struggles both in their local and wider global contexts. For example, in China during the early phase of the women's movement, while feminist principles were considered to be secondary to those of nationalism, both for the Chinese Communist Party (CCP) and the Guomindang, women's contribution to the war effort led to an increase in group consciousness. Feminist voices did emerge as well, for instance, in areas such as Fujian women organized an effective protest demanding equal opportunities for work when the provincial government dismissed all female employees in August 1938 in the name of cost-cutting. Right from the twenties onwards, there were debates regarding the role of women in China, whether they should be good wives and mothers, rather than contributing to the war effort, entering the work force or gaining rights as individuals (Pan, 1997).

While the interaction of local knowledge and external perspectives is a matter of considerable and ongoing debate in many circles, it is sometimes suggested in analyses of Asia and Africa that women's movements have emerged as a result of western intervention or influence, conveying a top down approach to the understanding of how feminist ideas have permeated different regions of the so-called non-West, even if it mildly accepts the influence of Asian regional feminisms on "transnational feminisms," which more often than not appear to be conflated with western feminisms.

In contrast, Vina Mazumdar describes how she and the other members of the Committee for the Status of Women in India (CSWI) set out to undertake field research on women from diverse groups and different regions in 1974. Mazumdar also used the term "indigenizing," but in a somewhat different manner. She described how the CSWI heard over ten thousand women from diverse rural, urban, class and caste groups in India over a year. This enlightened them on how much work and burden is borne by women, without their having any corresponding rights. She described this as an experience that "… shattered our *arrogance of learning*" (2001: 141), which led to new perspectives, following a major questioning of existing frameworks of social science. Thereby, a process of 'indigenizing' or the formation of new perspectives influenced by local realities took place in the social sciences. Maitreyee Chaudhuri too used the concept of indigenizing to speak of the uneasy relationship between Indian feminism and the charge that this was an outcome of western influence. However, the local-global link in feminist theory—as in many others—has been a difficult one, tied up with nationalist rhetoric. The charge of the western 'other' has plagued many social science perspectives and disciplines, including women's studies. For instance, in Korea Kim Eun-Shil notes that the "the discourse of Korean feminism has spawned the notion that Korean women have a different cultural outlook and values distinguishable from the cultural subjectivity characteristic to Western or American women in particular" (Kim Eun-Shil, 2005: 30). She also questions the essential and cultural uniqueness of women that is often seen to be natural and essential as part of the nationalist agenda of defining women as symbols of the nation in Korea or elsewhere, even in the views of several Korean feminists. The idea of the modern being equated with the western has been a matter of concern and reflection in many discussions regarding women's studies and maybe others as well: thus in the case of the development of women's studies in Korea Kim observes that "When women's studies was introduced into Korean universities, it was also considered to be modern and Western …" (2004: 50). However, now a global rather than a western impetus from without may be more appropriate to understand the transnational influence of modern democratic principles of gender equality as they have interacted with local feminisms, even before the term feminism had gained currency.

Thus the rise of feminism in Asia and elsewhere has occurred over several years and unevenly between the 1920s and the 2000s and in many contexts has addressed somewhat similar issues. The agenda of women's organizations, which were civil society groups of a kind, in many cases included the "soft" issues of family and charity, widely regarded as appropriate for women's concern. From these they went on to move into advocacy on political issues, moving closer to being encompassed in what were predominantly concerns for reform and not necessarily to do only with women. Suffrage movements, national movements, combating social evils of early marriage, health, FGM, foot-binding, plight of widows, education for women, paid employment/ work, and so on were some of the things that are easily identified as issues for their attention. Civil society groups—along with government bodies and international organizations—have increasingly challenged the power and scope of traditional political institutions within the state. They lobby national and international agencies to interpret development policies in accordance with the yardsticks of equality and gender parity. Civil society has expanded in many Asian countries, while it is still to acquire major influence in others. But along with such development trends, peoples' organizations have become real arenas for citizens' participation, providing a space that can either generate or nurture democratic values of gender equality, among others. The growth of women's movements and women's or gender studies in Asia have thus taken place over the last three to four decades, starting in the late seventies in some countries and as recently as the late 1990s or early 2000s in others.

3. Country Experience: India

I will look at the case of India in a little more detail as this is the one I know best and then see if there is scope for comparative insight. The first phase of the Indian social reform movements, which more or less spanned the length of a century in the first wave of modernization from the 1850s to the 1940s saw men responding to colonialism, seeking to assert their identities. The main focus at the time was on mobilizing change in Indian society at large, which was widely perceived as riven by caste differences and other kinds of inequalities, including gender disparity. This was a period during which campaigns for societal reform were undertaken and issues relating to women were tackled within the broader agenda for change. On the one hand, Indian men were preoccupied with western ideas seeking to emulate, assimilate or reject these and on the other hand, they wished to incorporate revivalist elements by reasserting and reinforcing a cultural identity that was distinct from that of the British rulers, as part of the nationalist agenda. In a sense, this also represents reaction to outside intervention in changing and modernizing situations. Alongside, the male indigenous elite were successful in acquiring wealth and skills that enabled them to take advantage of newly emerging opportunities thrown up by the socioeconomic changes that were underway at the time.

The broad sweep of change that was generated by the social reform movements led to the rise of a westernized male elite—men who sought to imitate their British masters and to be their social equals. In time, this created significant disparities between men and women of this class as the latter were were slow to 'progress' in the same way. Subsequently, it became clear that these gaps needed to be bridged and education for women became the major tool for doing so. This was a means of not only modernizing women but also enhancing the image of India as a modern and civilized society whose women were to be made presentable in colonial society and suitable companions for the men of the new Indian bourgeoisie. This provided a significant impetus for women's education, which was visualized as a way of creating appropriate wives for the men of this class of the newly westernized elite.

As improving the lot of women was a major goal, social activists sought reform through legislation and legal reforms, which were preceded by the creation of a climate conducive to such changes. Opinion was mobilized against many traditional practices such as caste, women's seclusion and other practices such as sati by a range of organizations. This process, generated within the reform movements that emerged within a colonial context, was not always a progressive one that improved things for women. In fact, some of the educational outcomes derived from these resulted in the promotion of newer norms of femininity that derived from Victorian models and strengthened women's socialization for inequality within the middle class. In turn, these added to the growth, rather than the decline, of institutions such as dowry and norms based on gender inequality, caste, community and religion. For instance, in the mid-seventies the Committee on the Status of Women in India (CSWI) noted "... that the majority of women are still very far from enjoying the rights and opportunities guaranteed to them by the Constitution" (CSWI 1974: 101). However, during the reform phase the women were considered to be recipients of social reform and welfare by the colonial government and the early reformers, were predominantly drawn from the upper and middle classes. This may have been so partly because women were inducted into organizations by accommodating to their separateness and also by drawing on lessons from the past, actual or imputed. Sarojini Naidu, in particular, used ideas about the supposed political roles of women in ancient India to insist that purdah or veiling need not prevent women from performing their civic duties. These organizations first addressed themselves to the charitable and development goals of uplift and improving the lot of women from poorer and backward groups, also arising out of the broad agenda for modernization. However, many of these women's groups donned a political mantle as well and they became part of the freedom struggle against the British colonial state. For example, the All India Women's Conference, which went on to become one of the major organizations of women that took part in the freedom struggle, suggested separate and different education for women, which would include social work for which they were said to have a special calling. Women would then not be breaking with tradition, but following in the footsteps of those who had supposedly lived in the "radiant far-off yesterdays of our history." Women's organizations therefore gained support precisely because they were supportive of traditionally given "separate worlds" and accommodated norms and practices of seclusion (Basu and Ray, 1990; Papanek and Minault, 1982; Forbes, 1982).

In the twenty-five to thirty years following independence in 1947 some attempts were made to improve the status of women in India, key among these being the constitutional guarantees for equality. However, the promise of gender equality, inherited from and evolving out of the preceding period of the national struggle, was not fulfilled and there was a "regression from some of the norms developed during the Freedom Movement" (CSWI 1974: 101). The critical consciousness gained during the freedom struggle—as well as women's access to a political public arena provided by it—was lost to a great extent. Programs for women undertaken by the state and others ? including women's organizations, focused considerably on women's welfare and their maternal roles. These efforts were coordinated by a government body (Central Social Welfare Board, formed in 1953), which funded activities of voluntary organizations that worked in the fields of social welfare under which gender issues were subsumed. Therefore, important questions relating to women were either ignored or included within wider concerns for economic growth, poverty alleviation, and so on (Government of India, 1985, 1995; Desai et al., 2003).

The nineteen seventies and eighties saw a renewal of concern for the status of women and the issue became significant for a range of actors including the State, policy makers, activists and academics across India and different Asian regions. In some cases it was the UN mandate given to governments of all member countries to critically assess the status of their women. In others it was part of a major exercise in action research, carried out by the specially appointed Committee on the Status of Women in India (CSWI) that included activists, academics and members of parliament as its members.

One of the major issues addressed by the contemporary Indian women's movement during the last three to four decades has been that of violence against women within the State, community, family and society. This brought considerable visibility to the movement as activists mounted campaigns for legal action and organized public protests and campaigns against rape, dowry, amniocentesis and sex selection, population control policies, political violence, and so on. Groups and organizations comprising the movement have employed a variety of approaches, depending on the situation at hand. Quite often they have joined hands with other kindred movements within the democratic space. Over time, some small gains have become visible, for example, laws on rape saw some changes. In India, the anti-dowry campaign of the 1980s led to increased awareness about the issue, particularly because it was taken up by the media in a big way. Sex-selective abortions and misuse of medical technologies became the focus of attention for women's groups in different parts of the country. Whether or not the particular campaigns have had success in terms of getting the State to respond to specific issues in a favorable manner has been a matter of considerable debate and analysis and remains a matter of ongoing debate (Kumar, 1993; Agnihotri and Mazumdar, 1995).

Some of the successes of the women's movement include the major headway made in both understanding and attending to issues pertaining to rural women, notwithstanding the criticism that the movement is a largely urban phenomenon. Grassroots organizations in different parts of the country spearheaded movements and campaigns in rural areas around issues of livelihood, literacy, alcoholism, the environment, reservation for women in local government and so on, proving that there is large-scale mobilization and action in rural areas. At the same time, the women's movement has come up against major barriers associated with the growth of right-wing politics in India as well as the persistence of gender norms, communal violence, and the strengthening of caste politics and religious ideologies/practice (Agnihotri and Mazumdar, 1995). Compounding these tendencies is the growth of patriarchal capitalism/globalism and the focus on the market that has been noted to affect women adversely. Well-articulated critiques of development directions reveal unequal costs and benefits to different sections of the population, including women (Krishnaraj, 2000).

In recent years the Indian State has responded in a variety of ways. State-sponsored initiatives also exemplify cooperation between movement activists and the government. The relationship between the two, however, tends to be ambivalent. While the State is generally held responsible for not protecting women from crime and political violence, women's groups have little choice but to address it in their advocacy work and quite often seek state intervention in order to further their short and long-term goals in the way of appropriate policy, legal change, funding and so on. The reverse also occurs, that is, government bodies seek the support of women's organizations, NGOs and think tanks for implementing their programs and examples are numerous in fields of education, rural development, health and so on.

The activist spirit generated by the women's movement had an important impact on academia. The University Grants Commission (UGC), an apex state body that determines policy and financial support to higher education in India first sought to incorporate women's studies in the National Educational Policy in 1985, by initially setting up four women's studies centres in universities in Kerala, Panjab, Delhi and Varanasi and in 1986 their number rose to 22. Today it is possible to say that the objectives of women's studies—to remove the invisibility of women in social science and policy and to highlight women-specific problems—have received some attention. Nonetheless, inequality, injustice and oppression remain well entrenched (Krishnaraj, 1988; Desai and Patel, 1989).

The purpose of women's studies was not just to generate information and analyses on women, but to stimulate change, to redefine conceptual frameworks of existing disciplines and to evolve a new discourse to accommodate the complexity of women's experiences. The University Grants Commission (UGC) accepted the need to introduce 'women' into the university curriculum. It also provided funding for activities such as seminars, workshops, research and the setting up of centres of women's studies in departments at the university level (Jain and Rajput, 2003). Furthermore, as Neera Desai and others have observed, the objectives of incorporating women's studies within the university system were both academic and social (Desai, 1986; Desai et al., 2003; Krishnaraj, 1988). The ultimate goal was to change prevailing attitudes, promote awareness about using women's potential to the fullest, oppose reactionary forces, revitalize university education, generate awareness about sexist attitudes among teachers, update university curricula by incorporating the new perspective and studies, promote collaboration between disciplines; produce new and organic knowledge through fieldwork, and contribute to the Indian experience through practice and research.

The dominant view thus was that women's studies had a dual role—of discourse as well as movement—and was to emerge out of both action and research and thus enrich various disciplines by providing new perspectives and changes in women's reality. It was seen to give context to knowledge in the process of understanding reality and effecting change (Krishnaraj, 1988; Desai et al., 2003). At one point Upendra Baxi, a well-known legal expert and academic, cautioned against turning women's studies into a "master" social science in India and reiterated the importance of maintaining it as an 'emancipative human science' or for the creation of knowledge through action. He emphasized it as an 'insurrectionary science' animated by clear ideological militancy which will link production and accumulation of knowledge pertaining to women's exploitation and ongoing struggles (Baxi, 1987). Other observers viewed women's studies in a leadership role for women's empowerment and pointed to its emergence as a sign of maturity in the social sciences that would lead to the development of innovative methodologies in teaching, research and action (IAWS, 1995). The interesting and sometimes not always convivial cooperation between the activist and academic streams of the women's movement in India has also been an important feature. This however, represents the democratic political space that is inhabited by activists, in particular women's groups.

4. Feminist State or State Feminism?

Broadly, I would say that the experience of India and some other countries in Asia has also brought the role of women's organizations—as civil society groups—on to the agenda of feminist politics. The issue of official feminism has yet again become significant, although it has been around for a long time. In some cases groups started with state sponsored feminism and sought to make it more civil society-centric, via NGO agenda building, for example, Ng and Ng (2002) spoke of "state feminism" in the case of Hong Kong, using a definition and tool for measuring state feminism provided by Stetson and Mazur (1995) wherein government structures undertake to further the status and rights of women. The Equal Opportunities Commission (EOC) and anti-discrimination laws that have become part of state efforts for gender equality are assessed, but they conclude that Hong Kong did not fulfill all the conditions and is not even a "semi-feminist state." Lenore Lyons too points to the ambivalence of feminists in Singapore in the organization AWARE that is often understood to be synonymous with the feminist movement in the country, while discussing the ever-present state and its "over-determinist role" (Lyons, 2004: 173).

The "gendered modernization project" in Korea was seen to undermine the place of women in many ways such as the ability to seek loans or any sort of state sponsored support in rural and urban contexts. The resistance to such a state framework is discussed by Cho Oakla (2005) as one that initially led to resistance by some women who broke away from their families, leading to a situation where men in rural areas found it difficult to find brides. The feminist movement in Korea, however, is seen to have evolved as part of the modernization process of the late 19th Century and of wider trends in the nationalist movement, the labor movement and the Christian women's movement. However, in the 1980s it became part of the broader social reform movement, when it started to form into what has been called the 'progressive' women's movement and represented a range of different perspectives and purposes (Cho Joo-hyun, 2005).

The direction and extent of change that states or governments can undertake towards obtaining gender equality is clearly bogged down by their multiple agendas, requiring the support and intervention of social groups in wider society. This again indicates that the impetus of change cannot come from agents of the state or in a top down manner. This is fairly obvious at one level, but needs reiteration in the present context where sometimes the state is seen as all-powerful and the only establishment that needs to be addressed.

5. Feminist Research and Publishing

As feminist scholars and activists, we continue in our studies through varied channels and one that has abiding importance is that of feminist research and publishing. Feminist writing in Asia has received a lot of attention over the last 40 years or more, along with the emergence of women's movements and women's studies in different regions of the world. The concern regarding feminist publishing and the challenge Women's Studies publishing has responded to during this time has been virtually ubiquitous in the many different contexts of feminist publications. This does not mean that women did not write before, but that the earlier environment had not been hospitable to publishing on women's issues. The increase in the writing of women's studies has gone hand-in-hand with a change in the social milieu that made it acceptable—and today maybe lucrative as well—for women's studies researchers to have their work published. For instance, Urvashi Butalia (1998) noted the surprise expressed by people at the "sudden" emergence of so much writing by women in India in the 1980s and 1990s. This, however, did not mean that women did not write, but that the earlier environment had not been hospitable to research or publications on women's issues. The increase in women's writing therefore went hand-in-hand with a change in the social milieu that made it acceptable for women writers to have their work published. Similarly, in the context of Uganda, Goretti Kyomuhendo (2003) noted that there were virtually no women's voices to be heard within the literary scene of the country until the 1990s, more specifically 1996, when FEMRITE, an association of women writers, was established. This again took place in a context of increasing public debate in civil society, along with the growth of the women's movement, the teaching of gender studies and the inclusion of women's and gender issues in politics, policymaking and the work of NGOs.

Feminist publishers have clearly played a role in altering the culture of publishing and providing a space for writing on feminist issues. For instance the Feminist Press and Virago were set up in the seventies in the US and the UK respectively in order to do precisely the same thing, i.e., provide a means for feminist writers to find visibility in a print culture that was earlier controlled by mainstream (male) publishers that were not receptive to their work (Howe, 1995; Wilkinson, n.d.). Similarly, Kali for Women started in India in the mid-eighties with the aim of giving voice to feminist writing in a field dominated by mainstream publishers who were not interested in women's issues as such. In addition, they saw themselves as chroniclers of the movement and aimed at reversing the flow of knowledge and direct it from South to North and East to West rather than the other way around (Butalia, 1998; Menon, 2000).

Academic publishing has always had its gatekeepers, as Dorothy Smith (1978) pointed out. The yardsticks of academic acceptability and marketability have all too often provided the parameters of what is considered to be worthy of publication. Editors of journals have also been included in the category of those who set the standards, i.e., as gatekeepers who play a significant role in the "politics of the printed word," for they determine what is published and rejected (Spender, 1981). Accordingly, Dale Spender also noted the limited representation of feminist scholars among academics who decided on what constituted "scholarly excellence" in the world of academic publication and argued for the need to have a larger number of feminists included in the community of experts as its gatekeepers. More recently, it is seen that feminist publications have not only acquired a significant niche, but with greater acceptability, hostility regarding women's issues has been on the rise, in addition to uncertainty about the future in the face of media and corporate commercial interests that not only try to appropriate and manipulate feminist agendas (Chaudhuri, 2000; Lee Young-ja, 2000). In a sense, our publication of the *Asian Journal of Women's Studies* at Ewha Womans University too has required us to act as gatekeepers, sometimes rather reluctantly, of what we understand is appropriate knowledge for dissemination in the sphere of feminist scholarship, more specifically in women's studies from and on Asian concerns (Khullar, 2005).

6. The Future

If a meaningful understanding is to be sought on the different paths that feminisms have followed across different regions, it is important both to identify their local formations or avatars, along with transnational feminism that is an external catalyst, albeit an important one as feminism seeks to become anchored not only to national agendas, but to truly global ones. As we continue with our movements, research and publication, it seems important nevertheless to keep the spirit of activism alive in women's studies, if it is going to address gender issues in scenarios that are local, global and/or both. The concern for addressing the state and other social institutions in order to effect change for women remains significant in Asia, and today this has often to do with the high-jacking of the feminist agenda by state or market institutions and political forces that may be national, regional or global, all for purposes that may not be entirely what we had bargained for. At the same time, we are also looking at the need to grow in tandem with and sustaining women's studies as a movement that addresses issues of importance for both research and activism. How we do this is difficult in the face of political, professional and market demands and remains a challenge.

In any event, whether or not the impetus has come from within national contexts or from outside, what we see today across Asia is a plethora of research, policy initiatives and practice that is clearly feminist insofar as it seeks equality for women in different respects. However, the local-global opposition in feminist theory—as in many others—has been a difficult one. On the one hand this is linked to what has been pointed out as 'the idea of Asia' that has been on the rise since the 1980s (John, 2005), while on the other, it is important to focus on the challenging commonalities among Asian women and their struggles. The western 'other' has both plagued and rallied the discourse of women's studies in Asia and it may eventually be irrelevant if we were to see the scope of women's studies as global, universal or at least pan-Asian, as represented in different perspectives of both the women's movements and women's studies. A global rather than a western impetus from without may thus be more appropriate to define the transnational influence of modern democratic principles of gender equality in interaction with local and Asian feminisms.

References

Agnihotri, Indu and Vina Mazumdar (1995), "Changing Terms of Political Discourse: Women's Movement in India, 1970s–1990s," *Economic and*

Political Weekly, July 22: pp. 1869-1878.

Banerjee, Narayan (1985), "Women, Participation and Development: A Case Study from West Bengal," Occasional Paper No. 5, New Delhi: Centre for Women's Development Studies.

Baxi, Upendra (1987), "Towards the Liberation of Women's Studies," *ICSSR Newsletter*, 18(5), October–December.

Butalia, Urvashi (1998), "Miles Covered, Miles to Go," *The Fiftieth Milestone: A Feminine Critique*, Shanta Sarbjeet Singh and Jyoti Sabharwal (eds.), New Delhi: Sterling: pp. 225-238.

Cai, Yiping (2013), "Re-vitalize, Re-strategize and Re-politicize the Chinese Women's Movement in the New Era," *Asian Journal of Women's Studies*, 19(1).

Chanana, Karuna (1988), "Social Change or Social Reform: The Education of Women in Pre-independence India," *Socialisation, Education and Women: Explorations in Gender Identity,* Karuna Chanana (ed.), New Delhi: Nehru Memorial Museum and Library and Orient Longman.

Chaudhuri, Maitrayee (2000), "'Feminism' in Print Media," *Indian Journal of Gender Studies*, 7(2): pp. 263-287.

Cho, Joo-hyun (2005), "The Politics of Gender Identity: The Women's Movement in Korea in the 1980s and 1990s," *Women's Experiences and Feminist Practices in South Korea*, Chang Pilwha and Kim Eun-Shil (eds.), Seoul: Ewha Womans University Press.

Cho, Oakla (2005), "Modernization Experiences of Urban and Rural Low-income Korean Women," *Women's Experiences and Feminist Practices in South Korea*, Chang Pilwha and Kim Eun-Shil (eds.), Seoul: Ewha Womans University Press.

Croll, Elisabeth (1978), *Feminism and Socialism in China*, London: Routledge.

CSWI (Committee for the Status of Women in India) (1974), *Towards Equality*, Report of the CSWI, New Delhi: Government of India.

Desai, Neera, Vina Mazumdar and Kamalini Bhansali (2003), "From Women's Education to Women's Studies: The Long Struggle for Legitimacy,"

Narratives from the Women's Studies Family, Devaki Jain and Pam Rajput (eds.), New Delhi: Sage Publications: pp. 44-80.

Forbes, Geraldine (1979), "The Women's Movement in India: Traditional Symbols and New Roles," *Social Movements in India*, M. S. A. Rao (ed.), Columbia: South Asia Books: pp. 149-165.

______ (1982), "From Purdah to Politics: The Social Feminism of the All-India Women's Organizations," *Separate Worlds: Studies of Purdah in South Asia*, Hanna Papanek and Gail Minault (eds.), New Delhi: Chanakya Publications.

Gandhi, Nandita and Nandita Shah (1992), *Issues at Stake*, New Delhi: Kali for Women.

Government of India (1985), *Women in India: A Country Paper*, Delhi: Department of Women and Child Development, Ministry of Social Welfare.

______ (1995), *Country Report*, Fourth World Conference on Women, Beijing: Department of Women and Child Development, Ministry of Human Resource Development.

Howe, Florence (1995), "Feminist Publishing," *International Book Publishing: An Encyclopedia*, Fitzroy Dearborn.

Humm, Maggie (ed.) (1992), *Modern Feminisms*, New York: Columbia University Press.

IAWS (Indian Association of Women's Studies) (1995), "Looking Forward, Looking Back," Report of the IAWS Conference, Jaipur.

John, Mary (2005), "Women's Studies in India and the Question of Asia: Some Reflections," *Asian Journal of Women's Studies*, 11(2): pp. 41-66.

Kasturi, Leela (1998), "Greater Political Representation for Women: The Case of India," *Asian Journal of Women's Studies*, 4(1).

Khullar, Mala (1997), "Emergence of the Women's Movement in India," *Asian Journal of Women's Studies*, 3(2): pp. 94-129.

______ (2005), "Asian Journal of Women's Studies: Ten Years and Beyond," *Asian Journal of Women's Studies*, 11(4).

______ (ed.) (2006), *Writing the Women's Movement*, New Delhi and Seoul: Zubaan and Asian Center for Women's Studies.

Kim, Eun-Shil (2005), "Republic of Korea," *Women's/Gender Studies in Asia-Pacific*, UNESCO, Regional Unit for Social and Human Sciences in Asia and the Pacific, Bangkok, pp. 49-77.

______ (2005), "Women and Discourses of Nationalism: Critical Readings of Culture, Power and Subject," *Women's Experiences and Feminist Practices in South Korea*, Chang Pilwha and Kim Eun-Shil (eds.), Seoul: Ewha Womans University Press.

Kim, Kyounghee and Seung-kyung Kim (2011), "Gender Mainstreaming and the Institutionalization of the Women's Movement in South Korea," *Women's Studies International Forum*, Volume 34, Issue 5, September-October 2011, pp. 390-400.

Kumar, Radha (1993), *The History of Doing: An Illustrated Account of Movements for Women's Rights and Feminism in India*, New Delhi: Kali for Women.

Kyomuhendo, Goretti (2003), "FEMRITE and the Politics of Literature in Uganda," *Feminist Africa*, 2.

Liu, Xiaoqing (2011), "From Larva to Butterfly: Sophia in Ding Ling's *Miss Sophia's Diary* and Coco in Wei Hui's *Shanghai Baby*," 17(4).

Lyons, Lenore (2004), *A State of Ambivalence: The Feminist Movement in Singapore*, Leiden and Boston: Brill.

Mazumdar, Vina (1972), *Education and Social Change: Three Studies in Nineteenth Century Bengal*, Shimla: Indian Institute of Advanced Studies.

______ (1982), "From Purdah to Politics: The Social Feminism of the All India Women's Organizations," *Separate Worlds: Studies of Purdah in South Asia*, Hanna Papanek and Gail Minault (eds.), Delhi: Chanakya Publications: pp. 219-245.

______ (1990), "The Social Reform Movement in India: From Ranade to Nehru," *From Purdah to Modernity*, B.R. Nanda (ed.), New Delhi: Radiant: pp. 41-66.

______ (2001), "Whose Past, Whose History, Whose Tradition? Indigenizing Women's Studies in India," *Asian Journal of Women's Studies*, 7(1): pp. 133-153.

Menon, Ritu (2000), "Dismantling the Master's House," *Indian Journal of Gender Studies*, 7(2): pp. 289-301.

Minai, Naila (1981), *Women in Islam: Tradition and Transition in the Middle East*, New York: Seaview Books.

Ng, Catherine W. and Evelyn G. H. Ng (2002), "The Concept of State Feminism and the Case for Hong Kong, *Asian Journal of Women's Studies,* 8(1): pp. 7-37.

Pan, Yihong (1997), "Feminism and Nationalism in China's War of Resistance against Japan," *The International History Review*, 19(l): February: pp. 115-130.

Papanek and Minault (eds.) (1982), *Separate Worlds: Studies of Purdah in South Asia*, New Delhi: Chanakya Publications.

Rose, Kalima (1992), *Where Women are Leaders: The SEWA Movement in India*, New Delhi: Vistaar Publications.

Smith, Dorothy (1978), "A Peculiar Eclipsing: Women's Exclusion from Man's Culture," *Women's Studies International Quarterly*, 1(4): pp. 281-96.

Spender, Dale (1981), "The Gatekeepers: A Feminist Critique of Academic Publishing," *Doing Feminist Research*, Helen Roberts (ed.), London: Routledge.

Yaziji, Michael and Jonathan Doh (2009), *Understanding NGOs*, Cambridge University Press.

Chapter 10

Korean Feminist NGOs' Strategies for the Empowerment of Women and Social Change:

Focusing on the Anti-Sexual Violence Movement[1]

LEE Mikyoung

1. Introduction

Women's status in the Korean government, schools, and companies has been elevated rapidly in recent years. Such change is attributable not only to government efforts but also to the actions of nongovernmental organizations (NGOs) which can be considered as the "heart of a society." The changes were possible thanks to the growth of the civil society that went through democratization movements against the authoritarian military regime, student movements, and labor movements during the 1980s, and feminists' passion for social change. In particular, liberal feminist NGOs carried out various projects for gender equality, human rights, environment, health, and peaceful unification of Korea. As a result, laws such as Framework Act on Women's Development (1985), Act on Equal Employment of Men and Women (1987), and acts to prevent violence against

1 This article was originally published on "Peace and Culture" (Vol. 5 No. 1, March 2013) of Joint Research Institute for International Peace and Culture of Aoyama Gakuin University. Also it was presented at the International Symposium: Empowering Women for Globalizing Asia held at Aoyama Gakuin University on January 26th, 2013.

women (1994, 1997, 2004), as well as many institutions were established, while hojuje, the patriarchal family system, was abolished in 2005. In other words, Korea's laws and institutions which had been feudalistic on women's rights except for the political suffrage guaranteed in the constitution are now gradually changing. However, as more people believe that women's rights issues are more or less resolved, a backlash is surfacing as well.[2]

Violence against women is a topic that has been the focus of many women's movements, laws, and policies. Movements to counter violence against women began with the projects of women's rights organizations to help survivors of sexual violence, and became the basis for introduction of legal measures including the Act on the Punishment of Sexual Crimes and Protection of Victims Thereof (Hereafter "Special Act on Sexual Violence"). Nowadays, the government and the National Assembly are busy proposing new laws and policies whenever child sexual abuse cases come under the spotlight of the media and stir up society. Recently, sexual violence was removed from the category of offense subject to complaint as women's organizations have demanded for the past 20 years.

Still, according to a nationwide survey of 1,000 women, violence against women and safety is the biggest factor that causes anxiety among women along with employment insecurity[3] (Korean Women's Association United, 2012). Such a reality implies that while many issues regarding violence against women that women's organizations have been pushing for improvements on have been addressed by laws, they were not able to change the patriarchal social order that remains the fundamental reason for such violence.

Furthermore, as support measures for survivors of violence against

2 The Lee Myung Bak administration tried to abolish the Ministry of Gender Equality and Family with its inauguration in 2008, but failed due to strong opposition of civil and women's movements. Moreover, the quota system for female teachers in elementary schools is changed into equal employment system. Also, abortion, which had practically been condoned, is now strictly cracked down and punished due to the low birth rate. Such changes illustrate the backlash.

3 Korean Women's Association United (2012), *Project Anxiety Relief 2012: Women Voters Talk about the Anxiety of Korea* (Sourcebook).

women are becoming more established, unexpected obstacles such as the excessive instruction and supervision of the government are surfacing. Meanwhile, the survivors of sexual violence are changing as well. While they were close to the stereotypical passive image of the victims in the past, they are now raising their voice in various ways. In addition, the socio-cultural environment and the forms and values of family are rapidly changing. Due to significantly different contexts when compared to that of 20 to 30 years ago, discussions on sexual violence should undergo transformations.

This study observes feminist NGOs' strategies to empower women and bring social change, focusing on the anti-sexual violence movement. The study used relevant statistics and research reports from year 1990 to 2010. As for the specific strategies of the NGOs for social change, Korea Sexual Violence Relief Center (KSVRC)'s projects were analyzed based on the 22 years of NGO experience the author has. The study begins with the following questions. First, what is the socio-cultural, economic, and legal status of Korean women like? Second, what strategies were adopted by the Korean feminist NGOs to empower women and bring social change, especially in the anti-sexual violence movements? Third, how did such strategies influence women's rights and damage restoration? And finally, what are the remaining challenges and the prospects for future?

2. Overview of Anti-Sexual Violence Laws and Institutions

<Table 1> indicates that the number of reported sexual violence cases was 3,919 in 1992 and 19,393 in 2010. While it may appear that the statistics imply that sexual violence cases have increased in overall frequency by about 5 times, there is no data to prove that.

Because of daily media reports on sexual violence cases, some express concerns that sexual violence occurs more frequently these days. However, it is more reasonable to conclude that we now hear more about cases that have always existed but have not been revealed to the public or spoken of. Victims are now changing their mind set and becoming more proactive in reporting and responding to such unfortunate cases. Meanwhile, a survey conducted by approximately 200 sexual violence counseling centers (MOGEF, 2012) shows that counseling on sexual violence is done around 60,000 times annually. Considering that it takes great courage for most sexual violence survivors to seek counseling, it is likely that the actual number of sexual violence cases is much higher.

Table 10.1. Reported Sexual Violence Cases[4] (Unit: Number of cases)

	1992	2001	2002	2004	2006	2008	2010
Total	3,919	10,446	9,435	11,105	13,573	15,094	19,939

Source: Legal Research and Training Institute (2012), 「2011 White Paper on Crime」.

Meanwhile, only around 43% of sexual violence cases were prosecuted since 2008. The prosecution rate is low because the victim's experience is not taken into consideration accurately in deciding the damages from a sexual violence case. Many studies have found the reality that the concepts of justice and objectivity that the relevant laws pursue are discriminative against women.[5] For example, due to the relevant officers' lack of human rights sensitivity and understanding, additional damages occur during the criminal justice process.

2.1 Anti-Sexual Violence Laws and the Rights of Victims

In Korea, sexual violence is punished under Chapter 32 of the Criminal Act titled Crimes Concerning Rape and Infamous Conduct. There are also

4 The original title of the table was <Sexual Violence Cases>. However, it was changed to <Reported Sexual Violence Cases> because the actual number of cases occurred cannot be estimated accurately, and because the statistics estimated the number of reported cases.

5 Kook, Cho (2003), *Gender Bias of the Criminal Code*, Seoul, Korea: Pakyoungsa.

various other legislations such as the Special Act on Sexual Violence, and the Act on the Protection of Children and Juveniles from Sexual Abuse. The relevant acts can be categorized as follows: acts on the criminal justice process, acts on the punishment of, monitoring and control over perpetrators, acts on the protection of and compensation for the victims, and others.

In 1991, women's rights organizations pointed out that there were too many limitations in preventing and responding to sexual violence under Chapter 32 of the Criminal Act because it categorized it as a "crime against chastity." They created the "Committee for Enactment of Special Act on Sexual Violence" and began activities to push for new laws. Women's organizations wrote a bill and filed a petition for legislation at the National Assembly level. As the Presidential and the general elections drew near, political parties actively tabled the bill for the Special Act on Sexual Violence. The Act was legislated upon in January of 1994, and has been revised 15 times since. It was later divided into two separate acts, one concerning the punishment of offenders and the other on the protection of victims. The Special Act consisted of general provisions, special provisions on the punishments and the punishment procedure for sexual violence crimes, regulation on sexual violence counseling centers, and penal provisions. To be more specific, it stipulated the responsibilities of the central and local governments in preventing the crimes and protecting the victims, the categorization of sexual violence and its punishments, special cases of filing complaints against sexual violence crimes, regulations on the investigation and subsequent trials of sexual violence crimes, and the protection of victims through counseling centers, protection agencies, and medical centers.

In 1999, the Act on Prohibiting Gender Discrimination and the Remedies which banned sexual harassment at work places, as well as the Act on Equal Employment of Men and Women was revised.[6] In 2000, the Act

6 Stipulations on sexual harassment were later moved to the National Human Rights

on the Protection of Children and Juveniles from Sexual Abuse was enforced thus mandating that the profiles of sex criminals against children be revealed to public and that their employment be restricted. The Child Welfare Act was introduced in the same year as well. In 2007, the Act on the Electronic Monitoring Et Cetera of Special Criminal Offenders (the so-called "Electronic Anklet Act") was introduced and in 2010, the Act on Drug Treatments for Sexual Urge of Sex Offenders (the so-called "Chemical Castration Act") was introduced to strengthen punishment, monitoring, and control over the offenders. For the protection of and compensation to the victims, the Act on Special Cases Concerning Expedition Et Cetera of Legal Proceedings, the Crime Victim Protection Act, the Crime Victim Protection Fund Act and others were put into place.

The legal rights of sexual violence victims can be summarized as follows.[7] First, the current law guarantees the victims' right to protection. The Crime Victim Protection Act stipulates the victim's right to human dignity and privacy (Article 2). It also mandates that the central and the local government protect such rights for the victims (Article 9). In the case of sexual violence victims, they have the right to apply for a closed trial (Article 27, Act on Special Cases Concerning Sexual Violence). Under the same law (Article 21), victims also have the right to safety measures and protection from any sort of publication. Moreover, related public officers and workers of counseling or protection facilities are banned from disclosing the identity and privacy of the victims (Article 22, Act on Special Cases Concerning Sexual Violence & Article 30, Sexual Violence Victim Protection Act).

Second, Article 27 Clause 5 of the Constitution and the Criminal Procedure Act (Article 294-2) stipulates the victim's right to make statements, one of the most fundamental rights of the participation process. After a

---

Commission Act and the Equal Employment Opportunity and Work-family Balance Assistance Act.

7 Koichi, Miyazawa (1999), Lee, Ho-joong (2006), Chang, Pilhwa et al. (2012), Chung, Do-hee (2009), Han, In-seop (1994), Wolhuter, Lorraine, Olley, Neil and Denham, David (2009).

revision of the Criminal Procedure Act in 2007, the victims are allowed to apply to be questioned as a witness in trial to exercise their constitutional right in making statements. In other words, victims now have the right to testify at the court not only under the direct order of court, application by prosecutor, or the evidence denial of the defendant or his/her lawyer, but also at their own request. By exercising such rights, the victim can now testify to the level of damage and offer other opinions on the case. However, the victim's right to make statements as a witness is limited in content to only those related to the damages of the crime. Victims do not yet have the right to talk about the secondary damages caused in the criminal justice process, the release of the offender or the weight of offense, and examination of parole.[8] In addition, the current law stipulates the victims' right to receive information concerning the criminal justice process as a part of their right in participation to the process. The Criminal Procedure Act mandates a public prosecutor to notify the victims about their indicted case upon application (Article 259-2). It also stipulates that a complaint about the proceedings of the case should be in writing (Articles 56, 258, and 259). The victims are also allowed to inspect and copy the litigation record (Article 294-4).

Third, as a compensation for the damages, victims can claim medical aid according to the Sexual Violence Victim Protection Act. If a victim of sexual violence suffered grievous bodily harm or disabilities stemming from the crime, they can receive relief funds in accordance with the Crime Victim Protection Act. They can also request compensation to the defendant in the criminal justice process. Such rights to compensation are limited to medical service fees. While the victims have the right to apply for compensation, the court can dismiss the application if it is deemed to substantially delay or interrupt the trial process. In such cases, the victims are not allowed to appeal (Article 30, 32 of the Act on Special Cases Con-

8 Lee, Mikyoung (2012), *The Rights of Sexual Violence Victims Viewed through the Lens of Secondary Victimization* (Doctoral dissertation, Ewha Womans University, Seoul, Korea), pp. 43.

cerning Expedition Etc. of Legal Proceedings), meaning that the victims' right to compensation is limited. Often the stark reality is that some victims have no choice but to drop their charges and settle with the offender even though they want the offender to be brought to some type of justice if such compensation costs are involved.

The enactment movement gave a name to the previously hidden problems of sexual violence and made it a social issue. Moreover, it revealed how the existing legal system which had long been considered objective and neutral are actually male-dominant and ignorant of women's experiences and voices. The significance of the movements lies in the fact that the voices of women were finally taken seriously and reflected.

2.2 Support Measures for Victims

The number of sexual violence counseling centers and protection facilities rose from only one in 1994 to around 200 currently nationwide. Fifteen special centers against child sexual abuse run on government commission called "Sunflower Centers," sixteen one-stop support centers which do both investigation and medical treatments, and many other kinds of care centers have been established.

Since 2000, medical subsidy is provided to the victims of sexual violence through a nationwide network of counseling centers. Most women who suffered from such crimes need long term medical treatments for the aftereffects. Thus streamlined paperwork and efficient management of the medical subsidy (up to five million KRW per person) providing system would help many victims, as they require support and care. In case of the domestic violence victims, the scope of exemption for the right to indemnity of medical bills should be expanded and made to be more practical.

Legal aid for sexual violence victims is currently provided by several organizations under the arrangement of MOGEF. Victims can receive legal aid for both civil and criminal court cases if they prepare a confirmation document for counseling from the counseling or protection centers designated in the Special Act on Sexual Violence, a written diagnosis for injuries from sexual violence requiring two or more weeks of hospitalization, a copy of the written complaint, and the filing receipt for the complaint. The aid is one million won or less for each case.

3. Advocacy Strategies for Social Change: Focusing on the Case of Korea Sexual Violence Relief Center

3.1 Empowerment Strategies for Survivors beyond Counseling Support

Most sexual violence centers provide telephone counseling, face to face counseling and on-line counseling. Statistics indicate that over 200 centers nationwide deal with about 60,000 to 70,000 sexual violence counseling cases per year. They offer psychological support, legal and medical assistance, and shelters. At times, they provide group counseling and family counseling, and when deemed necessary, art therapy, music therapy, dance therapy and other forms of assistance.

In recent years, various empowerment programs that go beyond traditional counseling have been employed for survivors. In 2003, women's movement organizations opened the "speaking out day" programs. On the predetermined day, 10 to 50 survivors speak out about their experiences in front of 200 to 300 people. The audience gives support and encouragement to the survivors. In the beginning, the program was run on a pre-registration basis out of concern for the privacy of the survivors. However, in recent years, this once-a-year program has been held in various forms for example, as a small concert at a college sports ground, a pop concert, or a "complaints choral festival."

In addition, on the last Wednesday evening of each month, around 20 survivors meet at a café for a kind of healing session where they talk about their suffering and how they overcame their problems. Self-defense training is given not only to young girls, but for all survivors, and this is one of the important aspects of the empowerment programs. It is extremely heartening to observe recent survivors aggressively letting their demands be known and seeing such demands met. This change of attitude in survivors is especially prevalent among young college students. They no longer think sexual violence means a loss of virginal purity or a source of lifelong regret and torment. Instead, they view sexual violence as an infringement upon sexual autonomy, and wish to exercise their rights as survivors with confidence.

3.2 Education, Research and Campaign Strategies for a New Sexuality Culture

The activities of women's movement organizations are composed of two components, counseling and sexuality culture movement. Recently, more emphasis has been placed on the latter as it is a preventive approach and a more fundamental solution to sexual violence. Various creative programs have been formed for the sexuality culture movement. For example, whenever a major case occurs, activists would organize flash-mobs at subway stations in attempt to drive out sexual harassment, or organize performances and press conferences in front of courts where decisions for major cases are to be delivered, as well as on-line discussions, campaigns etc. Recently, SNS emerged as one of the main means of communications among Internet users.

Since 2004, an event called 'Take Back the Night' is held once a year on the first Friday night of July. Its aim is to promote the awareness of women's rights to travel around as they please, even during night hours without the threat of any form of violence. A fancy dress parade was once held where an activist dressed as a delinquent girl. This parade caused a heated confrontation between the activists and an old man, who yelled that "this is how you make yourselves more likely to be sexually abused" at the aforementioned delinquent girl. The event's purpose was to be a demonstration demanding the government to guarantee the safety of nighttime walks, as well as being a festival for women to enjoy nighttime freedom of moment. In addition, the "Slut Walk" is an event held in Korea since 2011 that began in Canada when a police officer declared that women should avoid "dressing like sluts" to be safe from sexual violence.

Large concerts are another means of powerful anti-sexual violence awareness, mainly by fund-raising, but also as a means for communication with the larger public. Research is also an important part of the anti-sexual violence movement. The definition of sexual violence, the current status of the problem, and methods with which to eradicate sexual violence problems are the major research topics. In particular, research on the relationship between youth sexuality culture and sexual violence, sexual violence status in the military, legal practitioners' including judges, public prosecutors and defense lawyers awareness of gender equality, and their attitudes toward sexual violence produced very important outcomes.

In Korea, sexual violence prevention education at schools and the work place has been made mandatory by law. Nationwide counseling centers offer various education programs at schools and work places.

3.3 Students and Citizens' Participation through Various Volunteering and Membership Programs

Many volunteers take part in the anti-sexual violence movement. There are some trained volunteers who are in charge of counseling activities. These volunteers consist mainly of housewives and graduate students. Along with them, there are many college students who volunteer in assisting with paperwork.

Some college students with such volunteering experience later on choose to become women's movement activists. Other student volunteers even after graduation continue helping various organizations for individual events and invite people around them to become members of women's organizations. In particular, many housewife volunteers confessed that they were able to think of themselves as independent women because of such activities. This volunteer-centered nature in Korea differs greatly from their Australian rape crisis centers counterparts, who avoid using volunteers on the principle that all work must be fairly compensated.

3.4 Requests to Create or Amend Laws, Policy Monitoring, Reviewing, Suggesting and Lobbying

One of the most significant achievements of women's organizations has to do with the role that they play in when it comes to establishing new laws and regulations. Korea had very few legislations on sexual violence except in criminal law until about 20 years ago, but that has since changed rapidly. The Special Act on Sexual Violence was enacted in 1994, the Domestic Violence Prevention Act in 1997, the Sexual Harassment Prevention Act in 1999,[9] the Special Act on Sexual Protection of Adolescents in 2000, and the Prostitution Prevention Act in 2003. The MOGEF, Ministry of Justice, and Ministry of Health and Welfare have corresponding offices and departments that deal exclusively with sexual violence issues.

However, Korea's laws regarding sexual violence still contain a number of limitations. Marital rape is not regarded as an offence. It is regarded as an offence only when it involves physical violence and threats. To remedy this, the Korea Sexual Violence Relief Center (KSVRC) ran a two-year project called "Challenging the Supreme Court Precedence," which critically reviewed problematic Supreme Court precedents regarding sexual violence cases, and sent the reviews to judges and prosecutors across the country each month.

In addition, a number of anti-sexual violence organizations have been proposing new bills by giving presentations to the National Assembly's Legislation and Judiciary Committee, attending the national audit to give

9 The Joint Task Force for Sexual Harassment Case on the Teaching Assistants of Seoul National University (2001). White Paper on the Sexual Harassment Case on the Teaching Assistants of Seoul National University (Vol. 1).

presentations upon the Parliament members' request, and presenting their opinions through media channels. Other strategies involve holding street campaigns, forums, and press conferences.

From time to time, the organizations present their opinion on government policies to a range of governmental committees. Some people are skeptical about the effectiveness of such activities, as the role of the committees are often limited to a symbolic one. That being said, it is now mandatory for all Korean governmental committees to have at least 30% of their staff be female, and it seems to be a kind of trend for the committees to have NGO's under them. Some also question how effective the committees are based on the fact that they simply monitor the already-made government policies and regulations. However, the importance of these activities should not be ignored considering that the organizations are able to obtain up-to-date information and they can advocate on behalf of the victims through these activities.

3.5 Networking and Expansion of Coalition with Women's Rights Movements and Civil Movements

Around 180 counseling centers are working closely together under the auspice of the Korean Association of Sexual Violence Relief Center. They mainly review and monitor government policies, while acting jointly on some major agendas. For example, the "Citizen Surveillance Group for the Investigation and Trial Process of Sexual Violence Cases" was organized to monitor secondary damage to victims that could be inflicted by the police or legal professionals. This watchdog group also awards prizes such as the "Stepping Stone for Women's Rights" and exposes injustices through the "Obstacle of the Year" award at their annual general meeting.

However, because the 180 groups were established for different purposes, not all of them have a feminist point of view, and they are very different in size and character. Conflicts arise from time to time because of these different points of view. Unfortunately, these conflicts are expected to get worse in the future, possibly becoming a hot potato in the anti-sexual violence movement in Korea.

International networking is not going relatively smooth due to language barrier issues. Recently, however, efforts have been made to make progress as the Korean Association of Sexual Violence Relief Center has arranged a string of visits to related organizations in the USA, Japan, and Taiwan, and also invited experts to give speeches at seminars. In 2005, we organized a session called "World's Anti-Sexual Violence Movement" at the World Women's Studies Conference in order to share information and movement strategies with activists from other countries, including Australia, the UK, and Myanmar. Korean organizations also take part in online international signature gathering campaigns in order to help address major issues. Such online and offline international networking projects should be promoted more actively.

3.6 Review of the Media's Role and Strategic Use of the Media

The media has often walked hand in hand with the anti-sexual violence movement, but at other times distanced itself from the issue, causing somewhat of a tension. The media helped raise public awareness nationwide by giving huge publicity to several startling cases. One of them is an incident that occurred in 1991 where a sexual violence victim murdered the man who had raped her 21 years ago, screaming in court that she had killed a beast not a human. Another case that was at the center of media's attention is when a college student's boyfriend murdered her stepfather because the stepfather had been constantly raping her for 13 years. The active role the media played regarding these issues helped make sexual violence an important social issue and successfully drew substantial public attention. At the time, as many as 56 groups came together to organize a joint committee to counter sexual violence. Every time a trial took place, more than 300 students and citizens came to watch, while tens of thousands of people signed petitions, and major newspapers competitively covered these cases on their front pages.

On the other hand, the media have limitations as they tend to primarily focus on provocative issues such as serial rape or child rape, rather than sensitive issues like date rape, which can be highly controversial in society. Another problem that is being constantly pointed out is about how journalism violates the privacy of victims. Other problems include down-playing the seriousness of rape cases by calling a rapist who raped a housewife in front of her whole family simply a mere "family destroyer," or making light of cases by saying that a serial rapist had merely acted like a dog. Whenever these issues arise, women's activist groups come together to respond swiftly. From time to time, activists appear on TV shows or news to talk about sexual violence issues in order to further raise public awareness.

4. Key Issues of Anti-Sexual Violence Laws, Policies, Movements and the Remaining Challenges

4.1 Narrowing the Gap between the Legal Provisions and Their Actual Implementation

Victims of sexual violence can now bring along a confidant to investigations and trials. They can testify to exclusive investigators and courts dedicated to sexual violence in a closed trial or through teleconferences. Moreover, the revealing of their identity or privacy is strictly prohibited by law. Counseling centers are established to support the victims, and free legal and media aids are provided. Still, about 25% of the sexual violence complaints are about the secondary damages the victims suffer during the criminal justice process.[10] This implies that the legislation on victims'

10 According to the 2008-2009 survey of KSVRC, 25% of all complaints were on the unjust secondary damages and the pains caused by them. KSVRC (2011), *Reversing Sexual Violence*, Seoul, Korea: Imagine.

rights is not being implemented properly. The following two points further discuss the problems.

4.1.1 Loopholes in the Exclusive Bodies for Sexual Violence: Expertise and Human Rights Sensitivity Needed

The Special Act on Sexual Violence requires that sexual violence cases be dealt with by investigators, prosecutors, and courts that are designated exclusively for sexual violence. However, the exclusive officials change every one or two years because of the rotating system. Under such a system, it is impossible for any of the officials to build expertise in sexual violence cases. In fact, police officers, prosecutors, and judges are relocated to different departments every two years, and their jobs as exclusive personnel for sexual violence cases are passed on to their replacements. Under such a system, it is difficult for the exclusive officers to acquire expertise and a clear understanding of the goals of the system. Therefore, the most ideal case would be to introduce a new system in which the officials are allowed to stay in the sexual violence division for more than 10 years so that they can mature as true experts. When the relevant officers become experts in sexual violence cases, the offenders are more likely to be punished heavily for their crimes.

4.1.2 Abortion after Sexual Violence

Abortion is legally allowed for women who become pregnant as a result of rape.[11] Still, many rape victims claim that it is difficult for them to have a safe and timely abortion (KSVRC, 2010). Some have no choice but to keep the baby because they missed the proper timing to have abortion. In that sense, women who become pregnant after rape not only suffer from the rage, confusion, and pain from rape itself, but also from other physical and psychological damages.

11 While the Criminal Act (Article 269) bans abortion, the Mother and Child Health Act (Article 14) allows abortion in the case of eugenic or genetic handicaps, pregnancy severely damaging the mother's health, or pregnancy from rape or quasi-rape.

There have been no specific studies or statistics on how many unwanted pregnancies occur as a direct consequence of rape, and what problems the victims face in the abortion process. Also, discussions that prove rape was the fundamental reason for the above-mentioned problems have been progressing at an extremely slow rate. There are no specific policies addressing this issue. Unfortunate cases of unwanted pregnancy from rape are only conveyed to the public through the sexual violence counseling centers or the "Sunflower Centers."

Although abortion is a crime according to the current Criminal Act, it was not strongly enforced until more recently. However, due to the falling birth rate, the Korean government has begun actively pursuing policies promoting birth. In 2010, the government announced the Comprehensive Prevention Plan against Illegal Abortion, and began a crackdown on abortion. On top of that, there are concerns over pregnant women faking rape to receive an abortion,[12] making it even more difficult for rape victims to rightfully terminate their pregnancy.

4.2 Overcoming the Slow Changes in Social Stigma

Until recently, the benefits and protection of laws against sexual violence focused on women's chastity. Chastity was strongly emphasized in a patriarchal society, forcing women to keep their sexual virginity until giving birth to a son who will carry on a family line.[13] In fact, until 1995, the chapter on sexual violence in the Criminal Act was titled "Crimes Against Chastity."[14] That means that sexual violence was considered as a crime that harms a woman's exclusivity to one man under the concept of monogamy, rather than a crime against a woman's sexual dignity or nobility. In

12 Mothers Write 'Rape' as Reason of Abortion for Fake Legitimacy. (Sep 24, 2011). *Kukminilbo.*

13 Chang (Yun), P. (1999), *Women, Body, Sex*. Seoul, Korea: Alternative Culture Press.

14 MacKinnon, C. (2001[1989]), Rape: On Coercion and Consent. In K. Conboy, N. Medina & S. Stanbury (eds.), *Writing on the Body: Female Embodiment and Feminist Theory* (A. Cho, Trans.), Seoul, Korea: Hanul Publishing Company.

other words, women's chastity was considered as part of men's honor and asset, not as a right of a woman.[15]

As a result, punishment for offenders has been done under the notion that they destroyed the chastity of women, which was a tool to maintain the patriarchal system. Under such a social system, if a woman files a complaint of sexual violence, it would imply fault as a woman. Fortunately, the title of Criminal Act Chapter 32 was revised to Crimes Concerning Rape and Infamous Conduct as a result of strong criticism of women activists who declared that it is discriminative against women and that it infringed upon women's rights. Still, many studies have pointed out that the social stigma regarding women's chastity has not changed much.

Moreover, there are cynical, skeptical and even critical views going against the victims for "inducing" sexual violence, which tends to cause secondary damage on victims that are often even more severe than the initial damage. Referring to sexual violence as a "murder of soul," or having an unwarranted view of sympathy towards victims as if they are underprivileged people who suffered their whole life does not help the victims' healing process. While legal measures and institutions against sexual violence were introduced within a relatively short period of time, changes in social perception have been slow, resulting in it being the biggest obstacle and challenge for Korea.

4.3 From Strengthening Punishment to Increasing Punishment Rate

In recent years, the assessment standards for the punishment of sex offenders have been raised, and various new policies have been introduced such as electronic bracelets, sex offender DNA banks, medical treatments for sex drive, and detailed registries of sexual offenders. It may seem as

15 Lerner, G. (2004[1986]), *The Creation of Patriarchy* (S. Kang, Trans.), Seoul, Korea: Dangdae.

though such strong measures would prevent recidivism by offenders and make the society safer. However, it is worth mentioning how many sex offenders are actually ordered to wear electronic bracelets. Only 7.6% of sexual violence victims file complaints, and only 43% of those cases are prosecuted. Among the prosecuted, less than 50% are found guilty in the first instance. That means that only one or two out of 100 offenders actually end up wearing an electronic bracelet. Thus, it is problematic to think that the electronic bracelet in itself can reduce recidivism significantly. Indeed, electronic bracelets can only provide proof of whether the offender was present at a crime scene. There are no reliable international studies on the effectiveness of electronic bracelets in preventing sexual crimes by past offenders. In addition, considering that many sexual crimes take place at the homes of victims or offenders, it is problematic to say that the bracelets will reduce sexual violence.

Legal measures simply focusing on punishment are based on the false pretense that sexual violence issues can be resolved by basically isolating and excluding offenders from society. Such beliefs place all the blame for sexual crime on the offenders only, and proceed to ignore problems such as loopholes in the policies or the relevant officials' lack of awareness. Ultimately, that makes it impossible to take a holistic approach to the issue of sexual violence.

4.4 From Protecting the Victims to Securing Their Rights

Victims are generally considered to be subject to protection in Korean society. Such viewpoints can be observed in the titles of the numerous legislations on the rights of victims such as the Act on the Prevention of Sexual Crimes and Protection of Victims Thereof. Protection certainly is one of the important rights of the victims. However, it is a passive and limiting concept which does not take into account the general position and the independent status of the victims. In the victims' point of view, protection is closer to a gesture of consideration than a natural execution of their rights.

In that sense, the term protection does not include various rights that the victims deserve.

Furthermore, despite popular belief, sexual violence victims are not powerless, miserable people who live in agony for their whole life. First of all, they are proactive people who can voice out about what they have been through, and ask for changes and help against unfair treatment from the authorities. Nonetheless, media often portray sexual violence as "a lifelong damage," "a deep scar that is difficult to heal," or "the murder of soul," making the victims look more passive and powerless. Such tendencies can be referred to as the "politics of victimization" which implies that the victims need others to interpret their experience for them since they have become completely powerless and unable to comprehend the experience.

4.5 Securing More Stable and Sufficient Funding to Support Victims

Funding is the necessary foundation for implementing legislations and policies on violence against women. There is a need to accurately estimate how much of the government budget is being used for countering sexual violence. This estimation should not be limited to the projects of the Gender Equality and Family Ministry, but should also include those of the Ministries of Justice, Health and Welfare, and the National Police Agency. Understanding the budget is essential for planning future projects and deciding their capacity, but not enough research and discussion is taking place.

4.6 Taking the Policies beyond Sexual Violence on Children

Sexual violence against children is a clearly a heinous sexual crime that would infuriate most people. However, if too much of the attention, laws, and policies are focused solely on this secular subject, date rape, spousal rape and other rape cases would be neglected, thus ignoring the true nature of sexual violence. According to a 2011 report by the MOGEF, among the total 33,749 counseling cases by sexual violence counseling centers, 47.2% were about violence against adults between the ages of 19 and 60. In a survey on 19 protection facilities for sexual violence victims, 48.2% of the total 266 victims at the facilities were over 20 years old, making them the largest group. However, while sexual violence against children stirs up society, adult sexual violence victims constantly receive skepticism. Some sexual violence victims are unfairly sued and punished on charges of making false accusations or defamation. Therefore, the attention, policies, and budget must be not only for children victims, but for all sexual violence victims as well.

4.7 From Supporting to Empowering the Victims

All anti-sexual violence movements, laws, and institutions have their foundation on the struggles and the extraordinary courage of the victims who faced inappropriate social stigma. In some extreme cases, victims killed themselves or their offenders in attempt to be heard. Many others filed complaints about their undeserved sufferings, rage, and pain from their experience to the police, or talked to their friends, family, boss, or counselors. On the "Speaking Out Days" hosted by women's organizations, many survivors share their hardships and experiences of overcoming them in front of an audience. The event is now becoming a forum for healing and activism. Through such activities, victims can find new perspectives about their unfortunate experiences, reconfirm that what they went through was not their fault, and gain new strength to face the world. Self-defense training is also one of the important measures for empowerment.

The "Take Back the Night" is an event that is being held globally to demand women's right to move around freely at nighttime without worries of violence. It is both a protest against the government asking it to guarantee women the right to move around freely at nighttime as well as a festival for women. Moreover, women's organizations have successfully led a campaign to ban the nationwide broadcasting of beauty pageants, which encourages the commercialization of sex. They are now leading the nationwide campaign against prostitution. Research in this field is an important pillar in reflecting upon the movement and making future projections.

4.8 From Instructing and Monitoring of NGOs by the Government to Building a Public-Private Partnership

Violence against women has a long history and deep roots. To eradicate it, all members of society must put forth effort and dedication. Above all, an equal and ubiquitous cooperation between the government and the civil organizations is needed. The government and all organizations helping the victims of violence against women must understand each other's role, play the role faithfully, and cooperate with each other.

To eradicate violence against women, the government must provide funding to movements targeting it, and run national level projects including campaigns. Civil organizations should help the women in need of help by utilizing the spontaneity, creativity, and independence of NGO's, and should also carefully monitor government policies.

While laws and institutions are being introduced, some raise concerns that the government is not developing a healthy partnership with the NGO's and is undermining their autonomy.[16] It was women's organizations and not the government that began helping sexual violence victims and first raised issues regarding sexual violence. In fact, that has been a global trend. As a result of enactment movements, some counseling centers now receive around 60 million won in subsidies from the government every year. However, the government uses the terms "monitoring"

16 Kim, Hyun-Jeong (2000), Chung, Kyung-ja (2002), Seo, Mi-ra (2002), Kim, Bo-yeon (2006), Shin, Sang-sook (2007), Kim, Hong Mi-ri (2008), Lee, Yoon-sang (2009), Lee, Mikoung (2012) were used as reference.

and "instructing" when describing the relationship with the organizations. Considering the double edged sword of institutionalization,[17] thorough discussion and reflection upon the future cooperation between the government and the organizations are required.

5. Conclusion

The laws and institutions on violence against women which have taken a firm grasp should now be implemented more actively to make the lives of women safer and freer. What is more urgent than the introduction of new laws is the implementation of the existing laws that were put in place after tough discussions. Above all, specific measures need to be devised to evaluate whether these relevant laws and institutions are actually protecting the rights of the victims favorably, whether such measures are preventing sexual violence in daily lives, and whether the measures are serving their originally intended goals. The implementation process must be carefully reviewed in great detail, from checking the awareness of the relevant officials to the execution of budget.

Also, the goals of the laws and policies on violence against women should be revised. To do so, fundamental questions should be re-addressed, including the denotation of sexual violence and why we as a society should be against it. Society should understand that sexual violence is not a personal problem. So that sexual violence survivors are not simply labeled as subjects of protection or skepticism and criticism, society should be informed, especially in light of the fact that Korea remains a structured patriarchal system. Also, the fact that most victims are women makes a gender-based approach to the issue natural. Sexual violence is not an incidental activity, but rather a human rights abuse by the more socially

17 Regarding institutionalization, Kim, Hyun-jeong (2000), Jung (2002), Seo, Mi-ra (2002), Kim, Bo-yeon (2006), Shin, Sang-sook (2007) were used as reference.

dominant male. Recognizing it makes us see the nature and the seriousness of sexual violence more clearly, as well as understand the problems that male or boy victims face, though small in number.

Such understandings have brought significant changes to the laws and institutions that resolve sexual violence issues, but almost no change to the daily lives of the general public. Reasons for such discrepancy should be investigated. The public's approach on sexual violence issue is still closer to providing dispensation rather than respecting the victims' human rights. That implies that the laws and institutions that focus on punishing the offenders have not contributed much to spreading the correct understanding of sexual violence. In conclusion, the focus of laws and policies must be shifted from protecting and helping the sexual violence survivors to guaranteeing their rights, empowering them, and changing the socio-cultural perception of sexual violence.

The anti-sexual violence movement of Korea is filled with countless heart-warming cases and stories. The extraordinary courage and wisdom of the survivors, the increasing participation of citizens, changes in government policies and laws, and people practicing small but significant changes in their everyday lives contribute to them. When compared to 20 years ago, there has been significant positive progress on sexual violence issues. We hope to see new and better strategies put in place in 10 to 20 years time. That will bring the world a step closer to becoming a place where human rights are more respected and citizens do not have to worry about sexual violence.

References

Chang Lim, D.H. (2012), "An Empirical Study on 'Criminal Settlements'," *Sexual Assault Cases: A Feminist Jurisprudential Approach*, Ph.D. dissertation, Seoul National University, Department of Law Graduate School,

Seoul, Korea.

Chang (Yun), P. (1999), *Women, Body, Sex*, Seoul, Korea: Alternative Culture Press.

Chang, P. H. et al. (2012), *Witness Protection and Support Measures for Women, Children, Disabled Victims of Sexual Violence*, Seoul, Korea: The Office of Court Administration, the Supreme Court.

Chung, D. H. (2009), Protection of Victim's Rights in Criminal Justice Process: Focusing on the Revised Criminal Procedure Act (Unpublished doctoral dissertation). Seoul National University, Graduate School of Law, Seoul, Korea.

Dunn, Jennifer (2010), "Survivor Movements Then and Now," *Judging Victims: Why We Stigmatize Survivors, and How They Reclaim Respect*, Boulder, Colo.: Lynne Rienner Pub.

Gender Equality and Family Committee, and the National Assembly (2012), *Gender Equality, Family, Youth, and Legislation* (Vol. 17).

Han, I. S. (1994), Special Act on Sexual Violence and the Protection of Victims: Problems and Ways for Improvement. *Victimology Studies* (Vol. 3), Seoul, Korea: Korean Association of Victimology.

Hwang, J. I. et al. (2011), *Ways to Prevent Sexual Violence and Recidivism and Improve Infrastructure for Victim Protection and Support*, Seoul, Korea: Gender Equality and Family Committee, the National Assembly.

Jung, Kyungja (2002), *Constitution and Maintenance of Feminist Practice: A Comparative Case Study of Sexual Assault Centers in Australia and Korea*, Ph.D. dissertation, Sydney: University of New South Wales (unpublished).

Kim, H. J. (2000), *The Relationship between a State and Women's Movement: Focusing on the Enactment Movements for Special Act on Sexual Violence and the Domestic Violence Prevention Act* (Unpublished master's thesis), Seoul: Ewha Womans University.

Koichi, Miyazawa (1999), *Introduction to Victimology*, translated by K. Chang, Seoul, Korea: Gilansa.

Kook, Cho (2003), *Gender Bias of the Criminal Code*, Seoul, Korea: Pakyoungsa.

Korean Women's Association United (2012), *Project Anxiety Relief 2012: Women Voters Talk about the Anxiety of Korea* (Sourcebook).

KSVRC (2011), *Reversing Sexual Violence*, Seoul, Korea: Imagine.

Lee, H. J. (2006), "Harmony of Legal Theory and Judiciary Practice; Criminal Procedure and Related Human Rights," *Hanyang Journal of Law* (19), Hanyang University, Department of Law.

Lee, Mikyoung (2012), *The Rights of Sexual Violence Victims Viewed through the Lens of Secondary Victimization*, Ph.D. dissertation, Ewha Womans University, Seoul, Korea.

Lerner, G. (2004 [1986]), *The Creation of Patriarchy*, translated by S. Kang, Seoul, Korea: Dangdae.

MacKinnon, C. (2001 [1989]), "Rape: On Coercion and Consent," *Writing on the Body: Female Embodiment and Feminist Theory*, K. Conboy, N. Medina, & S. Stanbury (eds.), translated by A. Cho, Seoul, Korea: Hanul Publishing Company.

Matthews, Nancy (1994), *A Confronting Rape: The Feminist Anti-Rape Movement and the State*, London: Routledge.

Ministry of Justice (2011), *2010 Women Statistics*.

Ministry of Public Administration and Security (2012), *The 2012 Public Administration and Security Statistics Yearbook*.

Mothers Write, "'Rape' as Reason of Abortion for Fake Legitimacy," *Kukminilbo*, Sep 24, 2011.

Shin, S. S. (2007), *The Institutionalization and Autonomy of Korean Anti-sexual Violence Movements*, Unpublished Ph.D. dissertation, Seoul National University Graduate School of Social Studies, Seoul, Korea.

The Joint Task Force for Sexual Harassment Case on the Teaching Assistants of Seoul National University (2001), *White Paper on the Sexual Harassment Case on the Teaching Assistants of Seoul National University* (Vol. 1).

Wolhuter, Lorraine, Olley, Neil and Denham, David (2009), "Victimisation," *Victimology: Victimisation and Victim's Rights*, London: Routledge-Cavendish.

Chapter 11

Surviving Hard Times:

The Women's Movement under the Conservative Administration in South Korea and Australia

Kyungja JUNG

Like the Australian women's movement of the 1970s, from the mid-1980s, the Korean women's movement exploded into action. From out of nowhere, seemingly, came a plethora of newspapers, journals, cultural groups, rape and domestic violence support services and other women-focused activities—right down to the humble food co-op. Despite the 15-year time difference, the Australian and Korean women's movements have seen women's studies graduates and feminist scholars become the creative force behind new women's organisations, the circulation of feminist discourses, the initial development of women's policy machinery and the emergence of femocrats. Both countries are internationally recognised for advanced and successful women's policies that were developed through close engagement with the state. There is little doubt that the women's movement's engagement with the state has produced significant advances in gender equality, including legislation and a range of programs in both countries that have seen a partial institutionalisation of feminist perspectives within state policy-making processes. However, during the conservative Howard government (1996-2007), the Australian women's movement markedly lost its policy gains and energy. The Korean women's movement had similar experiences when facing the conservative Lee government (2008-2013). Drawing on activists' accounts[1] in two countries, this chapter explores the challenges faced by the women's movement amid a hostile political context. It also explores how the women's movement might be reinvigorated. This chapter suggests the need for a critical assessment of the women's movement in a new context, including a re-examination of what constitutes the women's movement and how the success or failure of the women's movement can be measured. It also argues that the significance of activists in reconstructing and sustaining the women's movement ought to be recognised. This chapter contributes to the theorisation of women's movements, in particular, by exploring how the movement copes within the context of fading political opportunity, which has been rarely researched, and working to compare the trajectory of the women's movement in Australia and South Korea.

1. Australian Women's Movement under the Howard Government

Following the election of the Howard government in 1996, the women's movement lost many of its earlier achievements. There was overt hostility to feminist aspirations under the Howard administration. Ruth Phillips (2006) explains this as a 'double negative' (2006: 205), which she defines as neoliberalism and neo-conservatism. The Howard government was hostile to the forms of participatory governance that had given more opportunity to social movements, including the women's movement. Its strong conservatism was apparent in its conspicuous hostility to feminism and the goals of the women's movement (Phillips, 2006).

The broader political and economic context contributed to a downturn

1 Interviews with Australian activists and former femocrats had been conducted a several times in 1999, 2000 and 2004 and interviews with Korean activists had been undertaken in 2009.

in feminist influence and visibility. By the end of the 1980s, a restructured economy had shifted the political focus away from social justice considerations to a neoliberal, market-driven focus on individualism and a winding back of the welfare state (Bacchi, 1999). An activist who had worked for a feminist rape crisis centre from 1991-1994 recollected the change in the practice of the women's movement in Australia:

> We work within an accountable code that can be measured. We have health outcomes. We have performance indicators. We've got a government with certain expectations—the legacy of receiving funding for the centre is that we have to fit into a particular mould that adheres to the government's guidelines. I loathe using the word, but we are professionals now, which has both its good and bad points. You have to have some piece of paper, some qualification in a health-related or training field, and somehow that may remove you one step from the women who started the service (Cited in Hay, 1996: 126-7).

Women's movement organisations were labelled as non-government organisations, and began to be framed as 'special interest groups' under the increasingly dominant public choice rubric as implied by the account of an activist:

> We're often at a dangerous place of specialising too much, and see yourself [the rape crisis centre] as, you know, too different, and better than everyone else or something. I think that is dangerous, so I think we've got to be really careful not to do that. You know, we've come from a position of confidence because we know we do good work. But, we must come from a position of humanity and acknowledging that there is a lot of expertise out there with lots of other stakeholders (Interview).

The women's movement organisations became more service oriented and less political, further reducing the pressure on government to listen to the feminist voice and advice. The introduction of New Public Management techniques to reform and reduce the size of government led to a reduction of 'in-house policy expertise' including gender analysis expertise (Sawer, 2007). Inside government, 'femocrat' positions came to be filled by women with no background in the women's movement (Sawer, 1990). Meanwhile, feminists in government continued to grapple with their dual sense of accountability both to government and to an increasingly diversified women's movement. Over time, and by necessity, feminists tried to hold on to their gains and resist both a neoliberal onslaught and a neoconservative backlash against feminism itself. The result has been the almost total demise of a feminist presence in government (Maddison and Jung, 2008).

The Howard government also dismantled and demoted women's national machinery and women's units such as Women's Bureau across all portfolios at the federal level. In the first year of the Howard government, the budget of the Office of the Status of Women was cut by forty percent. In 2004, the Office for the Status of Women was demoted from the Department of Prime Minister and Cabinet to the Department of Family and Community Services (Sawer, 2007: 30). However, the decline of both Commonwealth and State policy structures and processes has been met with barely a whimper from feminists in the broader women's movement. The struggle for gender equality—once considered a 'permanent priority' in the national capital—began to be wound back (Maddison and Jung, 2008).

The Howard government refused to become a signatory to the Optional Protocol to the United Nations Convention to Eliminate All Forms of Discrimination Against Women (CEDAW). There was also a defunding of many women's organisations, in particular those that had been critical of government and/ or represented constituencies outside the mainstream by the federal Office for Status of Women. The funding for the women's organisations has been supported mostly for projects not for operation and the funding was also 'tied to competitive tendering for service provision with no scope for representational or advocacy work' (Sawer, 2007: 25).

There was also the successful mobilisation of the idea of 'post-feminism,' which promoted the notion that the women's movement was a thing of the past (Andrew and Maddison, 2010: 175). Howard viewed the social movement in general, including the women's movement, as 'outdated and represent[ing] nobody but an 'elite minority' (Sawer & Hindess, 2004, cited in Andrew and Maddison, 2010: 175). There was even the emergence of the men's rights movement from the mid-1990s, well supported by the Howard government (Sawer, 2007). Over the following years, the women's movement appeared to enter a period of abeyance, resulting in the loss of many gains from the previous period. Even under the subsequent Labor governments of Kevin Rudd (2007-2010) and Julia Gillard (2010-2013), the situation didn't greatly change. For instance, neither the Coalition (the Liberal Party in coalition with the National Party) nor the ALP (Australian Labor Party) appeared to produce a women's policy for the 2010 federal election or any overall plan for achieving gender equality. However, the ALP did eventually release a women's policy—one day before the election. One achievement of the Gillard government was Australia's first government scheme for paid parental leave. Since January 1, 2012, most working women have had access to up to 18 weeks of paid leave. The scheme sees primary carers, most of whom are women, paid the minimum wage by the government for that period, with the pay administered through their employers. Partners can take two weeks of leave at the same rate. Women and men earning more than $150,000 per year are not eligible for the scheme.

2. Institutionalised, Fragmented and NGOised Women's Movement

When Howard came to power, the women's movement was not at the peak of a wave of protest, but was already fragmented and lacking in energy (Andrew and Maddison, 2010: 175). To a certain extent, the women's movement may have shot itself in the foot by becoming overly dependent on government funding. As many scholars have pointed out, where the State has become the major source of funding for many feminist organisations, increased reliance on that funding may lead them to lose their critical edge (Alvarez, 1999, 2009; Maddison and Jung, 2008; Jung, 2013).

Even in the 1970s there were concerns that the relatively immature women's movement would be compromised if it rushed to accept government funding for its operation and programs in a favourable political opportunity structure. There was fear that the newly christened femocrats would be co-opted and serve to merely legitimise the 'irredeemably patriarchal' state without fundamentally changing it (Maddison and Jung, 2008).

The entry into government also led to the inevitable 'dilution' of feminism, particularly in its more radical forms, through the process of negotiation and compromise (Sawer, 1990: 252). The Australian women's movement clearly demonstrates the limitations faced by institutionalisation. As most women's movement organisations in Australia have relied mainly on state funding for their survival, the Australian women's movement has lost its bargaining power to negotiate with the state as indicated clearly in this interview with an activist:

> The New South Wales Department of Health is the only funding source that this centre has. That is a weakness because … they want to tell us what to do, how to run our agency. And we want to have some autonomy, obviously. … We have very little bargaining power (Interview).

Among the feminist activists in Australia who I interviewed, there was a degree of self-criticism, especially regarding failure to network and collaborate across the various women's organisations. The activists felt that in an unfavourable political climate, an alliance between feminist groups would have been necessary for the women's movement to resist the state, or at least negotiate with the state and other agencies such as funding bodies. As women's organisations became more and more specialised and fragmented, they tended to forget the root of the organisation and made insufficient effort to build alliances with other women's organisations as indicated in the account of an activist:

> I think that this centre's [the rape crisis centre] got a critical role to play in the women's movement. I mean it's got its root in the women's movement and we must never lose sight of our roots. ... But, in order to maintain that critical role, we have to constantly guard against becoming mainstream or becoming narrow. We have to keep broadening ourselves, and see what's happening, how we are working with what's happening out there. And I think that this service has been through phases where it has isolated itself ... it's being the expert and, not talking to anyone else, thinking we were the best ... So, we have to keep coming back to our roots, we have to keep connected. And also given the fact that the political climate is so anti-women and anti-migrants, anti-welfare, so economic rationalist. The only way we are going to combat that is if we unite and we collaborate, not just as the white women's movement, the Aboriginal women's movement, migrant women's movement, you know, disabled women's movement. So that the women's movement has got to stretch its boundaries, and that this service has got to keep trying to stretch that as well (Interview).

The Australia women's movement has also failed to recruit sufficient numbers of young women 'to ensure the continuance of a collective strong feminist movement (Bielski, 2005: 9). There has been much discussion about a generational schism in the movement, brought about by suggestions from older women that young women were not 'reach[ing] out for the torch' (Summers, 1994: 197, cited in Maddison and Jung, 2008) in the way that they had hoped. Although young women are still engaging in feminist activism on university campuses, in the community and in coalition with other movements, it isn't clear why they are not engaging more with the women's movement and why their feminist activism is not strong enough to be visible and influential.

3. Korean Women's Movement under the Lee Administration

The electoral victory of Lee Myung-bak in February 2008 opened up a new conservative era in Korean politics, effectively ending a decade of progressive rule and bringing crisis to the women's movement. Even before his inauguration, President Lee announced plans to downsize the Ministry of Gender Equality and Family (MOGEF) or merge it with the Ministry of Health and Welfare (MHW). The former, then known as the Ministry of Gender Equality, had been founded under the Kim Dae-jung administration in 2001 before expanding under the Roh Moo-hyun administration in 2004 to include childcare affairs. The establishment and subsequent enlargement of the MOGE/MOGEF provided women's movement leaders and activists an entry point into government. After strong protests from the women's movement and women's groups, the merger planned by the Lee Myung-bak administration did not happen, but the MOGEF was downsized, its budget halved, and childcare affairs were returned to the MHW. The context in which feminist organisations worked worsened and the political opportunities to pursue a feminist agenda narrowed. The state's coercive powers were enhanced in tandem with the erosion of feminist services and the women's movement.

In 2008, anti-US and anti-beef demonstrations further worsened the relationship between the women's movement and the government. South Korea had once been a big market for US beef, but imports had been suspended in 2003 after an outbreak of Bovine spongiform encephalopathy (BSE) (commonly known as "mad cow disease"). When the government decided to allow US beef imports to resume, hundreds of thousands of people took part in weeks of candlelit protests. Health fears became bound up with general discontent toward the government and protesters urged President Lee Myung-bak to resign. The demonstrations were reportedly the country's largest anti-government protests in its 20 years of democracy. However, the Lee government dismissed the protesters' demands and used force to repress them. The government claimed that fears around BSE were exaggerated and that political radicals and pro–North Korea leftists were actually behind the demonstrations. Still, the protests escalated into a mass political opposition movement.

The Lee government took hostile measures to control and monitor those progressive women's movement organisations and NGOs that took part in the anti-beef demonstrations. The measures included reducing or removing government funding, closing down services without due notice, and stricter and more frequent supervision of organisations by government officers. For many feminist organisations, mere survival became an urgent task (Kwon, 2011). Some organisations had to reduce the number of full-time paid activists, forcing those who wished to continue, to do so as volunteers. This was even the case for the KWAU (Korea Women's Association United), the umbrella organisation for the progressive women's movement, which faced a massive funding cut and lost its close ties with the government.

The rise of the new conservative government also contained and reduced the political spaces open to feminists by marginalising and delegitimising feminist agendas, femocrats, and feminist frameworks. Major progressive feminist organisations were pushed to the margins of political influence. Progressive women's movement organisations were less frequently invited to government advisory committees. Instead, the government turned to social welfare organisations and service providers as partners in the policy-making process. For instance, in the area of sexual violence, the government invited the National Federation of Sexual Violence Services and the National Federation of Shelters. Similarly, many feminist activists or scholars who worked in government departments, government funded institutes and women's centres lost their positions.

Femocrats were replaced with female politicians or female scholars who did not hold feminist perspectives or had little involvement with the women's movement.

The Lee government effectively silenced and marginalised feminist voices through intensified regulations and control of their activities. Another controversial move was the introduction of an electronic administrative system and national social welfare information system as part of its e-government program. Women's services were asked to input all their clients' details into this system, and some local governments threatened to cut funding if they did not comply. The providers of feminist services for victims of domestic violence, sexual abuse, and sex workers strongly criticised the measure. They were particularly concerned that by uploading the personal details of victims they could possibly put the women at risk.

The funding cuts to feminist organisations discussed above and the government's much closer scrutiny of their operations are not the only issues provoking outcries from the Korean women's movement. The feminist framework and gendered understanding of women's issues have been sidelined by government. For instance, the majority of funding for sexual violence issues has been allocated to sexual assault centres working on child sexual violence cases in hospitals and focuses on therapeutic and psychological treatment. The Lee government tended to approach sexual violence within a degendered and individualised framework and to erase structural analyses of sexual violence. While the protection of children is clearly very important, feminists are concerned that this focus might cause an increase in the policing of women, children, and the general public, and that there might be a danger of the state using the issue of sexual violence as a means of controlling and disciplining people (KSVRC, 2011: 153).

4. Ways of Reinvigorating the Women's Movement

The Korean and Australian experience reveals that the women's movement is constituted by a specific historical, political and social context. Australia's welfare state has been characterised by a social liberalism that depends on the state as a vast public utility. The state's duty has been to provide the greatest good for the greatest number. But feminist organisations have become almost solely reliant on that state funding, taking it for granted for a long time. In Korea, the negative consequence of institutionalisation became a concern to some feminist activists and scholars from the late 1990s; however, most women's movement organisations in Korea were busy delivering direct services for women and providing expert advice to government committees thanks to generous support from the state under the women-friendly Kim and Roh governments.

It would be very difficult for the movement to change its routine practice. It needs to reflect on and re-examine its practices, but is short of time and resources. It has been almost impossible for the women's movement to reflect on its aims, strategies and relationship with both the state and grassroots women, and then reflect on and reconstitute its practice in a new political climate as indicated in an interview with a Korean activist:

> We have been pressed for time these last few years although there was a strong suggestion of the need to reflect on our activities from a perspective of a bigger picture: the women's movement. We have been always driven by urgent matters and day-to-day activities, so left this serious business undiscussed (Interview).

5. Looking at the Women's Movement from the Inside

In 2011, some 180 feminist activists, scholars, and artists from across the nation came together to reinvigorate the women's movement and discuss solutions for its future. The conference was the first time in the history of the Korean women's movement that women's activists from all sectors and regions had got together. Participants ranged in age from their twenties to their eighties, and this enabled so-called 'old feminists' and 'young feminists' to attempt to understand each other's positions and differences. Among the participants were many activists who had been involved in the women's movement for several decades. Debates focused on the sustainability of the women's movement: the direction and vision of the women's movement, how to embrace differences of age, class, sexual orientation, marital status, experience, and their views on specific topics such as sex work within the women's movement and how activists can be retained by the women's movement and how the women's movement can mobilise more women and its members.

At the conference activists identified the challenges the progressive women's movement faces as a lack of enthusiasm about feminism and the women's movement among young women, and difficulty recruiting and mobilising activists and grass roots women. One young activist, in charge of publishing a feminist magazine at a university, told the conference: "It has been very hard to mobilise students, but I cannot blame them. I can fully understand the situation of female university students who are juggling part-time work and study to survive the times of high unemployment rates in Korea." She told the audience she often wondered why she became a feminist activist and how long she could continue to be one. Both young feminists and long standing feminists face a dilemma between their own survival and pursuit of their ideology and beliefs.

In a similar vein, interest in women's studies courses at universities has dwindled. Given that new feminist activists used to be mobilised from undergraduate and postgraduate women's studies courses, the decrease in the number of women's studies students and the lack of interest in gender issues among young university students threatens the sustainability of the women's movement. The representative from the KWAU, Mi-hyuk Kwon confirmed this, telling conference participants how difficult it has been over the last few years to recruit new activists for the movement.

Most women's movement organisations face a similar challenge. The recruitment problem is also linked to the worsening living conditions of

Korean youth, as demonstrated by a young activist's remarks. "Activists used to join and remain in the movement or organisations because they were committed to the social and political cause, rather than because of material incentives. The wages received by activists are still too low to financially support them. If they decide to work for a women's movement organisation, they must find a second job to survive. Despite this sacrifice, activists in the past were more willing to take the path of an activist life because it was more meaningful for them. Their commitments to and sacrifices for a cause were honoured and recognised by the society."

The conference also examined why young feminists had turned away from the women's movement. There is a widespread belief among young feminist activists that institutionalised women's movement organisations have turned into cheap social welfare agencies for the government or are being co-opted by the government. The young feminists dubbed the 'third wave of the Korean women's movement' or as 'new feminist groups' (Hur, 2011) want to keep their distance from the hierarchies and bureaucracy of the institutionalised movement, which they feel fails to reflect diverse women's voices and needs. As a result, from the 2000s many began to create their own groups or organisations. These are largely web- or membership-based and have been created mostly at universities in Seoul by the female activists involved in the social movement organisations of the late 1990s and/or the labour movement (Hur, 2011). These activists have been influenced by the women's studies programs offered by their respective universities, and their feminist perspectives have drawn from postmodernism, post-Marxism, and postcolonialism. They seem to prefer to organise activities on a small scale, in contrast to the practices of the existing women's movement. These new organisations have contributed to the creation and expansion of feminist cyber space, which has become a new site for the production and circulation of feminist discourses (Hur, 190–191) and has provided alternative ways for organising political action and public dialogue.

In Australia, the biggest feminist conference in 15 years was held in

Sydney in April 2010. Some 400 participants, aged from 12 to 84, and at least three pro-feminist men attended (Horin, 2010). The two-day conference was organised by a diverse collective of women who wanted to bring women together to discuss how to enliven and reignite the feminist movement in Australia. Each of the organisers was an activist and representatives from various organisations, including the Women's Electoral Lobby New South Wales, Amnesty International, the Feminist Bookshop, the AIDS Council of NSW (ACON), the Sydney University Students Representative Council and the Australian Services Union took part. The conference discussed and examined a range of issues including: What can feminism learn from indigenous women's knowledge? Why is feminism relevant for all of us? What sort of future can we create from this conference? There were over 30 workshops on issues such as women and education, mothering and maternal activism, sexism and sexuality in the media, feminist perspectives on pornography, women and poverty, female genital mutilation, domestic violence, women in prison, women and disability, and so on.

The conference also discussed at length the generational schism within the Australian feminist movement. It was clear that many young women resented being patronized and policed by the older generation of feminists. Rosa Campbell, one of the younger conference organisers, admitted the divide between the feminist generations: "we're told all the time we have raunchy pornographic sex, binge-drink, pole-dance and are not active feminists. We've taken all the choices the '70s feminists won and used them for our own oppression. We're ungrateful and rude." (cited in Horin, 2010)

Gabe Kavanagh, another organiser, contended that while feminism needed to be made more accessible to young women, many of them had already identified as feminists, but their work and politics were seldom recognised by more established feminists, and in many ways young women's activities were invisible to them. She also added that 'feminist ideals have remained somewhat consistent over time but our methods have changed considerably and this has produced a generational disconnect' (cited in Funnell, 2010). As Kavanagh suggested, if the Australian feminist movement is ever to expand, then new channels of communication need to be established to promote and consolidate understanding and respect between the various generations of feminists (Funnell, 2010). It is very clear that while the 70s and 80s women's movement fought for social and political change, today's young women think feminism is more about changing the culture (Horin, 2010).

6. Redefining the Women's Movement

Both the Korean and Australian women's movements were led to reconsider what the women's movement is (Sawer, 2010). For example, Karen Beckwith defines women's movements as 'those where women mobilise around a collective identity as women, develop women centred discourses and engage in gendered claims-making' (cited in Grey and Sawer, 2008: 5). Andrew and Maddison see the women's movement as 'a wide range of women's activities, including women's collective actions and individual actions and from women's organisations and women's policy machinery' (Andrew and Maddison, 2010). In Korea, the women's movement encompasses campaigns, mass protests and demonstrations, but also activities of women's movement organisations including rape crisis centres, domestic violence support services, feminist food-coops and various women's advocacy groups. In Australia, the terms "women's services" or "women's groups" or "women NGOs" are increasingly used.

It is questionable if women's policy machinery or any other women's policy structure, including femocrats, is part of the women's movement. Rather, the machinery and femocrats would be the outcomes that the women's movements have achieved through their vigorous campaigns. It has only been possible to have women's policy structures or femocrats inside government because of the women's movement. This broad definition of the women's movement, which includes women's policy machinery, threatens to overlook the transformative nature of the women's movement, namely being radical, transformative and feminist. Being radical has been seen as one of the core objectives of the women's movement. Ryan uses the term ideological purity as "a sincere application of feminist principles" to explain 'being radical' (1992: 157). Buecheler (cited in Staggenborg, 1995: 343) defines "radical" as "one whose ideology, goals and program pose a fundamental challenge to a particular system of power relations." Daherup explains 'being radical' as being outside the system (1986). She claims that all social movements are "marginal, and are neither part of routine politics nor part of the dominant ideology."

In addition, for the women's movement to be influential and effective, it must be collective and based on massive mobilisation or massive membership. The aim of the women's movement is to achieve social, political and cultural change. This change cannot be achieved through a few prominent, individual women's actions and struggles. The history of the women's movement worldwide tells us that it has been the very collective women's movement that has brought many changes in women's lives and status. In this situation, it is critical and urgent that women's movements define what constitutes "radical, feminist and transformative practice" (Reinelt, 1995: 91).

In the case of the Australian movement, not only has women's policy machinery been demoted and dismantled, but the women's movement has also changed in various ways under the conservative administration. Despite claims that the women's movement exists, albeit faint and uninfluential through submerged networks and community groups, the term "women's movement" can barely be found in academic discourse and the media. Instead, it has been replaced with the terms "women's services" or "community organisations." Major women's movement organisations, such as the Women's Electoral Lobby, could not continue their advocacy work after funding was withdrawn by the state. In a similar vein, the terms "women's activist" or "feminist activist" are nearly as obsolete as the terms "feminism" and the "women's movement." A few feminist academics and some feminist activists have strived to give renewed life to these terms, but it has not been sufficient to bring a new momentum and the terms remain old currency.

As Australian radical feminists in the 70s precisely predicted, too close an engagement with the state and too much reliance on government funding turned the women's movement into a group of women's services which often provided just that but at a cheaper cost for government. In this situation, grass-roots women who were supposed to be a central driving force of the women's movement became mere clients or service users. It became increasingly difficult to mobilise women for feminist causes. Even public demonstrations, such as International Women's Day and Reclaim the Night marches, attracted dwindling numbers from the late 1990s in Australia. A lack of support from women in general meant that the women's movement lost its influence. The power of the women's movement had come from the support of the people.

Visibility in the public sphere, such as the media, in the street and massive mobilisation, is one way of measuring the failure and success of the women's movement (Outshoorn, 2012). What has been missing in the debates on the decline and rise of the women's movement is how the activists, themselves, feel and think about the movement. Their accounts have been neglected to some extent in academic research. Mackay (2008: 18) has argued that research on the women's movement is under-theorised because research on the women's movement is often based on 'personal testimony, historical accounts and prescriptive analyses, often written by activists. According to Mackay (2008: 18), the aims of such accounts are to bear witness to what has happened and to inform future strategy, rather than contribute to systematic evaluation.' In my view, more research on the women's movement should be done by activists and their accounts should be taken into consideration when evaluating the success and failure of the women's movement (See Andrew, 2010). It is important to consider how activists feel about their movement, their passions and frustrations.

For instance, the Korean women's movement from the mid 1990s to the mid 2000s, under women-friendly governments could have been seen as extremely successful if activists' narratives were not taken into account. Although there were massive policy gains and the women's movement became visible and influential, ironically some activists began to question if the movement had taken the right direction and if they were doing so-called 'movement work' (Jung, 2013).

In both countries, it is evident that the role of activists is essential in reconstituting the women's movement in a shifting context. Activists play a vital role in shaping their practice by way of on-going discussions. And when the external environment, such as funding sources and the political situation, are fluctuating, feminist values may be undermined. So it will be the willingness and commitment of feminists that determines whether these forces can be withstood (Alter, 1998). Furthermore, the role of activists in interpreting their situation and making creative and conscious decisions must be an essential component of the reconceptualisation of feminist practice in relation to the shifts in internal and external environments.

7. Hope for Change

In both countries, change in political climate forced the women's movement to rethink its dependence on state money and necessitated a revisiting of favoured strategies such as the close engagement with the state. It is time to turn away from the state, and to develop a renewed focus on networks and alliances among women's movement organisations and cultural change. Activists in both countries see the crisis presented by hostile government as an opportunity and as 'opening up a new way of doing things':

> Where we are here now, it's a case of beginning the whole new phase of this organisation, you know. We've seen the end of it, where our struc-

> tures have been collapsed in the last couple [of] months … I guess it would be really good to ask us, how it's going in 12 months from now … I still see that we have, you know, entered into a new phase which is quite exciting and a new way of working which is quite exciting and a new structure which is exciting as well … I don't feel like there is no freedom … (Interview with an activist in Australia).

The Korean women's movement began to reclaim its movement nature by handling comprehensive women's rights issues, maintaining its advocacy role and avoiding becoming too specialised in women's services. In order to preserve its autonomy and political nature, the women's movement in Korea started a more careful selection of funding on the basis of ideological relevance and made an effort to mobilise more members.

In the case of Australia one activist succinctly summarised the situation and emphasised the urgent need to look for alternative sources of funding. She believed that the women's movement had reached the point where it had to re-examine its routine practice because the state had switched from a welfare state model to an economic rationalist state model:

> I think also that the women's movement has come to a point, where it can no longer rely on only government funding, it's got to look for private sources of funding to maintain its freedom. Because, as long as we depend on only government funding, they can dictate like they're doing at the moment and they've got community development. And we've got no leg to stand on, because we haven't got money from anywhere else except the Department. For sure, so, I think, the whole movement has to stop, really look at private funding, or fund raising. That was something that the feminists, 20 years ago or 15 years ago, were philosophically opposed to. Because they were coming from the position that in a welfare state, a government must take responsibility for social problems, and therefore, they must support services that people have the right to … It was totally unreasonable to expect women who survive sexual assault

> to go and raise money for their needs … But today, I think, it comes to a point where you've got to move from that, 'cause otherwise, we just, we won't be able to do what we want to (Interview with an activist in Australia).

Both countries also need to make further effort to keep the women's movement strong and autonomous. Many studies have indicated that the strength and independence of the women's movement is vital to the development of women's policy and its effective implementation (Kantola and Squires, 2012; Weldon and Htun, 2013). Weldon (2002: 1161) argues that 'it is not just the existence, but also the autonomy of women's groups that is important for their success in influencing policy.' An autonomous women's movement is an essential voice in the critique of government policies, improving the 'substantive' representation of women in the policy-making process. More significantly, it needs to be remembered that the success of the femocrat strategy depends upon the simultaneous existence of a strong and autonomous women's movement (Grey and Sawer, 2008).

Perhaps the focus for the new women's movements should not be on presenting a more coordinated national response in order to demand an adequate state response, but on attending to the grassroots including women from diverse backgrounds and with diverse issues. The belief in the collective power of women and the women's movement needs to be regained. The women's movement should strive to become more relevant to women regardless of their age, class, sexuality, occupation, cultural background, or whether they are able bodied or disabled.

This chapter concludes by raising the question, 'Does the women's movement still matter?' What is the significance of the women's movement in the current context? The women's movement should provide 'new ways of seeing, fresh modes of reflection and assessment' (Narayan, 1997: 33) about issues women encounter in their daily lives. The rapidly changing society, in a local and global context, needs critical investigation and in particular, requires a new feminist understanding and new movements.

The women's movement still needs to challenge a variety of important social institutions and practice from a feminist perspective. Finally, in order to accomplish these critical tasks, the women's movement needs self-criticism, self-reflection and openness to criticism by others. As reconfirmed in the 2010 Feminist conference 'while feminism is a movement marked by diversity and complexity, it is the commitment to examining the contradictions and nuances of argument found within feminism that makes for such a robust movement' (Funnell, 2010).

References

Alter, Catherine (1998), "Bureaucracy and Democracy in Organizations: Revisiting Feminist Organisations," *Private Action and the Public Good*, Walter W. Powell and Elisabeth S. Clemens (eds.), New Haven & London: Yale University Press: pp. 258-271.

Alvarez, Sonia E. (1999), "Advocating Feminism: The Latin American Feminist NGO 'Boom'," *International Feminist Journal of Politics,* 1(2): pp. 181-209.

______(2009), "Beyond NGO-ization?: Reflections from Latin America," *Development,* 52(2): pp. 175-184.

Andrew, Merrindahl (2010), "Women's Movement Institutionalization: The Need for New Approaches," *Politics & Gender,* 6(4): pp. 609-616.

Andrew, M & Maddison, S (2010), "Damaged but Determined: The Australian Women's Movement, 1996-2007," *Social Movement Studies,* Vol. 9 No. 2, pp. 171-185.

Bacchi, Carol (1999), "Rolling back the State? Feminism, Theory and Policy," *Women, Public Policy and the State*, Linda Hancock (ed.), Melbourne: Macmillan Education.

Bielski, Joan (2005), "Australian Feminism 2004: Gains, Losses, Countervailing Forces, Some Failure and Sobering Thoughts," *Social Alternatives,*

Vol. 24 No. 2: pp. 6-10.

Daherup, Drude (1986), *The New Women's Movement: Feminism and Political Power and the USA*, London: Sage.

Funnell, Nina (2010), "Who Says that Feminism is Dead?," *Sydney Morning Herald*, April 12, http://www.smh.com.au/federal-politics/political-opinion/who-says-feminism-is-dead-20100412-s3ei.html (accessed on September 5, 2013).

Gray, Sandra & Sawer, Marian (eds.) (2008), *Women's Movements: Flourishing or in Abeyance*, New York: Routledge.

Hay, Ashley (1996), "Rape Crisis: From Collectives to Bureaucracy," *DIY Feminism*, Bail Kathy (ed.), St Leonard: Allen & Unwin.

Horin, Adele (2010), "Women Gather for Burning Issues," *Sydney Morning Herald*, April 10, http://www.smh.com.au/national/women-gather-for-burning-issues--not-bras-20100409-ryu7.html (accessed on September 5, 2013).

Hur, Song-Woo (2011), "Mapping South Korean Women's Movements During and After Democratization: Shifting Identities," *East Asian Social Movements: Power, Protest, and Change in a Dynamic Region*, J. Broadbent and V. Brockman (eds.), Nonprofit and Civil Society Studies, Springer: pp. 181-203.

Jung, Kyungja (2013), *Practicing Feminism in South Korea: The Women's Movement against Sexual Violence*, London: Routledge.

Katonla, J & Squires, J. (2012), "From State Feminism to Market Feminism," *International Political Science Review,* September 2012, Vol. 33 No. 4: pp. 382-400.

KSVRC (ed.) (2011), *Rethinking Sexual Violence: Reflections on 20 years of KSVRC and its Vision*, Seoul: Imagine (in Korean).

Kwon, Mi-hyuk (2011), "In 2011, KWAU is not Well," *2011 Women's Conference: Exploring New Ways of Women's Movements*, Gender Network (ed.), Seoul: Gender Network: pp. 14-21 (in Korean).

Mackay, Fiona (2008), "The State of Women's Movement/s in Britain: Ambiguity, Complexity and Challenges from the Periphery," *Women's Move-*

ments: Flourishing or in Abeyance? Routledge, S. Grey and M. Sawer (eds.), Milton Park, Abingdon, Oxon: New York: pp. 17-32.

Maddison, Sarah & Jung, K. (2008), "Autonomy and Engagement: Women's Movements in Australia and South Korea," *Women's movements: flourishing or in Abeyance?*, S. Grey and M. Sawer (eds.), Routledge, Milton Park, Abingdon, Oxon; New York: pp. 33-48.

Narayan, Uma (1997), *Dislocating Cultures: Identities, Traditions, and Third-World Feminism*, New York and London: Routledge.

Outshoorn, J. (2012), "Assessing the Impact of Women's Movements," *Women's Studies International Forum*, 35: pp. 147-149.

Phillips, Ruth (2006), "Undoing an Activist Response: Feminism and the Australian Government's Domestic Violence Policy," *Critical Social Policy,* 26(1): pp.192-219.

Reinelt, Claire (1995), "Moving onto the Terrain of the State: The Battered Women's Movement and the Politics of Engagement," *Feminist Organisations: Harvest of the New Women's Movement*, Ferree and Martin (eds.), Philadelphia: Temple University Press.

Ryan, Barbara (1992), *Feminism and the Women's Movement: Dynamics of Change in Social Movement, Ideology and Activism*, New York: Routledge.

Sawer, Marian (1990), *Sisters in Suits: Women and Public Policy in Australia*, Sydney: Allen &Unwin.

______ (2007), "The Australia: The Fall of the Femocrat," *Changing State Feminism*, Joyce Outshoorn and Johanna Kantola (eds.), Houndmills, UK: Palgrave Macmillan.

______ (2010), "Premature Obituaries: How Can We Tell If the Women's Movement is over?," *Politics & Gender,* 6(4): pp. 602- 609.

Staggenborg, Suzanne (1995), "Can Feminist Organizations be Effective," *Feminist Organisations: Harvest of the New Women's Movement*, M. Marx Ferree and P. Yancey Martin (eds.), Philadelphia: Temple University Press.

Weldon, Laurel (2002), "Beyond Bodies: Institutional Sources of Representation for Women in Democratic Policymaking," *Journal of Politics,* 64 (4): pp. 1153-1174.

Weldon, S Laurel and Htun, Mala (2013), "Feminist Mobilisation and Progressive Policy Change: Why Governments Take Action to Combat Violence against Women," *Gender and Development,* 21: 2, pp. 231-247.

Chapter 12

Together and Apart:

Transnational Feminist Activism and Solidarity in Asia

Yonson AHN

1. Introduction: Crossing Borders

In 1992, I met a group of comfort women survivors for the first time. After that meeting, my quest to involve in the problem of the comfort women as an activist scholar began in Seoul, where some of the surviving former comfort women eked out a meagre living as attendants in park and workers in restaurants, food stalls, and other manual occupations. A few others have become active internationally in drawing the attention of the world to this forgotten chapter of WWII history. Motivated by my growing interest in the subject, I interviewed comfort women survivors, activists, Japanese WWII veterans, scholars, journalists and a diplomat in the post-war South Korea and Japan. My engagement with the survivors, the activists and the veterans as an "insider" and observer has given me an opportunity to review the campaign more reflectively. This article is based on my border-crossing experiences involving in the issue directly and indirectly. In particular, it deals with issues of transnationalism, women's activism, and solidarity based on the comfort women redress movement in South Korea and Japan.

Examples of transnational circulation of people, goods, services, capital, cultural practices and ideas have been rampant. This cross-border flow creates or reinforces a possibility for direct people-to-people contacts and social and political networks amongst the participants and communities on both sides of the borders. This flow has an impact on both women's activism and making of government gender policies as well. Shared issues affecting women and mutual understanding are integrated and attribute to the spreading out of transnational advocacy campaigns; for example, those dealing with human trafficking, sexual violence, women's health, and so on. Mutual solidarity has been built from embodied shared experiences in facing these issues. Some issues such as sex-trafficking might be more efficiently handled through cross-border cooperation.

As Thoma (2000) eloquently defines "transnational feminisms are those various comparative forms of feminist practices and alliances that oppose particular and global versions of economic and cultural hegemony and seek social change for women in different locations" (p. 30). Transnational alliances forged through cross-border activism challenge the elite-driven top-down form of cooperation for example between the developed and the developing countries. Vertical networks linking domestic activists to external supporters oppose in forming transnational alliances and pursue interactive ones. Furthermore, the scope of transnational women's networks and alliances are not necessarily limited within the boundedness of localities or the boundaries of the nation-state. These networks linking local and transnational feminisms not only oppose global hegemony but also attempt to overcome or oppose nationalist hegemony of their domestic space. In practicing transnational feminist activism, transnational ideas are to be transformed in local terms, and local ideas are reinterpreted in the transnational contexts rather than downgraded as a lack of mobility. In this way, local and transnational ideas could be sustained and could complement each other.

Financial independence could be one of the significant issues in transnational activism. This plays a role in challenging economic and cultural hegemony held by one part and maintaining autonomy in cross border activism. Local autonomous women's movements need to be considered as the significant sources of power. There might be a tension between addressing the interests of funders and those of local communities. In the case of the comfort women redress movement in South Korea and Japan, the importance of financial independence was addressed from the beginning of the campaign. Concerns have been raised about accepting funds from private donors in Japan amongst South Korean activists. This effort for financial independence could be seen to maintain balances between the activist groups in South Korea and Japan.

In what follows, transnational cooperation amongst the comfort women survivors, activists and supporters in particular, the Women's International War Crimes Tribunal in Tokyo in 2000 and transnational protests will be investigated. This will lead to exploring transnational linkages through activism creating new networks and strengthening old ones. In the succeeding part, more empirical details on the transnational/domestic interactions are provided in this study of transnational activism in the comfort women redress campaign. This looks at the impacts of transnational cooperation on the local and the global women's activism. The focus will be on tensions between the nationalizing logic of comfort women campaign and the de-nationalizing imperatives of transnational comfort women campaign. This is related to the questions of maneuvering and mediating between the national/local and the transnational spaces. Based on the existing experiences of cross-border women's activism, challenges and limitations of transnational feminism will be explored. Finally, the concept of sustainable transnational advocacy activism which pays attention to the existence of complexities in both difference and commonality will be put forward.

2. Transnational Cooperation

In the late 1960s and throughout the 1970s, a substantial number of Japanese men went on sex tours to Taiwan and South Korea. This sex tourism expanded to Southeast Asia, particularly the Philippines and Thailand.[1] In the late 1970s, the campaign against sex tourism by Japanese men in South Korea was raised by women activists in South Korea and Japan. It was out of this campaign that the comfort women issue later emerged, with the realisation that sex tourism had a more sinister historical antecedent in the context of Japan's colonial relationship with Korea. The comfort women campaign was galvanised in South Korea and Japan and later spread to the Philippines, Taiwan, China, Thailand, North Korea, and other parts of the Asia-Pacific region where most comfort women survivors reside. Testimonies of comfort women survivors have mobilised supports around the issue from the younger generations. Activist groups from various countries, such as Hankuk chŏngsindae munche tech'ek hyŏpŭihoe (the Korean Council for the Women Drafted for Sexual Slavery by Japan) (1990), Jûgunianfu Mondai Uri Yosong Network (Military "Comfort Women" Issue Network of We, Japanese Korean Women) (1991), The Task Force on Filipino Comfort Women (1992), Lila-Pilipina (1994), Taipei Women's Rescue Foundation, and Washington Coalition for "Comfort Women" Issues (1992), have worked together closely and promoted solidarity.

When the governments, particularly in South Korea, ignored and participated silencing the comfort women issue for a half century, domestic activists were forced to forge transnational links by shared values and appeal to international supporters including the UN. The links and alliances across national boundaries on the issue have been built up and expanded outside Asia to the USA, the EU, and Australia together with increasing public pressure to clear the issue in these countries. Transnational femi-

1 See Murata (1996) and Matsui (1987).

nist activism in redressing the comfort women issues emanated from non-state actors and has had substantial impacts on the domestic government level and the UN. Domestic and transnational activists have been able to forge strong transnational ties and have regularly called both the Japanese and South Korean governments to deal with the unresolved issues. One of the efficient strategies available to the transnational activists in Japan and South Korea was to bring this issue to the UN to pressurise both the Japanese and the Korean governments to get involved in this issue. Thanks to transnational advocacy activism to resolve the comfort women issues, the Parliaments in the Netherlands (2007), Canada (2007), the EU (2007), and the Philippines (2008) passed the comfort women resolution.

The comfort women campaign in South Korea has been led by the Korean Council for the Women Drafted for Military Sexual Slavery (hereafter the Korean Council). In this campaign, the comfort women episode is seen as a symbol for Korean victimization, and collective victimhood of Korean versus collective guilt of Japanese are the two main axes to construct the campaign. The nationalising of the comfort women issue clearly took place in the campaign in the 1990s, since the issue emerged in the beginning in the context of a legacy of Japan's colonial domination in Korea. Furthermore, the campaign has been regarded as a source of Korean unity against Japan and reconciliation between two Koreas after North and South Korean actors have cooperated in dealing with this issue.

The comfort women campaign in Japan led by Violence against Women in War-Network Japan (VAWW-NET Japan, 1998) has been focusing on issues of violence against women and a formation of internal and external alliance based on gender issues. The comfort women issue is placed on a continuum of sexual violence or discrimination against women in everyday life (Ueno, 1998; Yamazaki, 1995; Ôgoshi, 1997). As the shared experience of oppression of women, especially, in the practice of patriarchal norms of sexuality is recognised as a momentum for this campaign, Japanese women's groups have attempted to transcend cultural and geographic boundaries in relation to gender issues. Yamazaki (1995) addresses, "Beyond state boundaries, women need to create common understanding of each other's history (sic.)" (p. 54).

Attention has been drawn to the shared experiences between Japanese comfort women and the other, especially since the 2000 Women's Trial in Tokyo. The women's groups in Japan including VAWW-NET Japan have actively supported former comfort women's lawsuits against the Japanese government for damages and other compensation. The lawsuits were filed by Korean, Chinese, Taiwanese, Filipino, Indonesian, and Dutch former comfort women.

The Japanese activist groups have had to face severe attacks by their nationalist groups who are right-wingers against the comfort women redress campaign, while their Korean counterpart has been enjoying supports from their nationalist civic groups. Fujioka Nobukatsu (1997) and other neo-nationalists in Japan assert that raising the issue of comfort women is "a grand conspiracy for the destruction of Japan, in collaboration with foreign elements"(p. 78). The transnational alliances have been threatened by the neo-nationalists' blame for damaging the interests of the nation of Japan. On the domestic level, the Japanese women's activist groups have confronted local resistance by their neo-nationalist right-wingers against such transnational alliance.

Transnational advocacy activism has evolved as solidarity between Japan and South Korea. Dense interpersonal networks amongst Korean, Japanese and ethnic Koreans in Japan have been successfully developed. Japanese Koreans or the so-called Zainichi activists, who hold transnational identities, have been playing a crucial role in mediating and leading the comfort women activism in Japan. For them, the issues of the comfort women are connected to the minority issues of Koreans in Japan. The transnational networks and alliances of the activist groups have made some tangible progress. Thanks to the experiences of international solidarity around the issue, the Women's International War Crimes Tribunal was staged in Tokyo in 2000 in order to draw international attention to Japan's refusal to take responsibility for its past. Various women's NGOs across

Asia organized the civic Tribunal on behalf of former comfort women. Sixty-four survivors from nine countries and areas in the Asia-Pacific region took part in the trial. Hundreds of legal experts, academics, human rights activists, journalists and politicians from around the world such as from North and South Koreas, China, Taiwan, the Philippines, Indonesia, the Netherlands, Malaysia and East Timor, attended.

Rallies against the Japanese government, known as the "Wednesday demonstration," have been held on a weekly basis since January 1992 in front of the Japanese embassy in Seoul, Korea. The survivors, activists, and supporters including students have been attending these demonstrations to show their solidarity and support for calls for justice. What has been demanded in the rallies are a formal apology and reparation from the Japanese government for the surviving victims and punishment of the "perpetrators." A campaign for education of the Japanese public concerning the colonial government's wrongdoings has been urged. Solidarity across borders has been witnessed in these transnational protests: the participants of the Wednesday rallies in Seoul are diverse in terms of age, nationality, sex and religion. Several global solidarity demonstrations have been held by women's groups in different locations. On March 15, 2006, the 700th Wednesday demonstration held in 17 cities including Seoul, Pusan, Masan, Tokyo, Kyoto, Osaka, Nagoya, Fukuoka, Kobe, Okinawa, Taipei, Berlin, New York, London, Hague, Canberra, and Basel. The Wednesday rallies marked the 1000th Demonstration on December 14, 2011. At this 1000th rallies, the Peace Monument "Pyŏnghwa-girl," a statue of comfort woman was erected in front of the Japanese Embassy in Seoul. The Korean Council has recently been working on a project to erect the same statue which was erected in Seoul in 2011, all around the world. The second one was installed in Glendale in the USA in July 2013. A plan has been made to erect another Peace Statue in Singapore.[2] The solidarity

2 Korean Council Weekly News Letter, No. 2013-02, January 7–13, 2013, https://www.womenandwar.net/contents/board/normal/normalView.nx?page_str_menu=2301&action_flag=&search_field=&search_word=&page_no=1&bbs_seq=11991&passwd

demonstrations marking the 1000th Wednesday were globally undertaken with participants from 60 cities in 20 different countries. This global solidarity demonstration is a platform not only for seeking apology and reparation from the Japanese government, but also for the elimination of violence against women and the promotion of women's human rights and peace.

Moreover, transnational linkages through civic activism have been expanded and strengthened through media, art, cultural events, and religious institutions. Novels, plays, photo exhibitions and documentary films on comfort women were released and shown globally. They have contributed to expanding the web of interactive transnational links, connecting diverse activists and supporters with the survivors across borders, and facilitating supports.

Rather than hierarchical relations and hegemony held by one party, inclusive, participatory and horizontal relations can be found in the transnational alliances in the comfort women redress movement between South Korean and Japanese civil groups.

3. Tensions

Not surprisingly, it has not always been a comfortable alliance on common grounds between the Korean and Japanese groups. Differences and tensions amongst survivors and activists have emerged over time. The tension emerging between the Korean groups and some Japanese groups in the end of 1990s was related to a controversy over the "Asian Women's Fund (AWF)"[3] for the Asian comfort women survivors. There was an intensive controversy over recipient of the AWF in the late 1990s. The fund was established by private donations from the Japanese public in Japan in

3 For details about the "Asian Women's Fund" for Women, See "The Comfort Women, the Asian Women's Fund and the Digital Museum" by Wada Haruki, *The Asia-Pacific Journal: Japan Focus*, February 1, 2008, http://www.japanfocus.org/-Wada-Haruki/2653

1995 and offered medical expenses for the survivors plus a one-time payment of around U.S. 20,000 dollars with a letter of apology issued by the Prime Minister of Japan. The majority of Korean survivors and the Korean activists refused the fund and asked for reparation and apologies directly by the state of Japan to the individual women. Those who accepted the AWF's offer were severely criticised in 1997 by the Korean Council activists and other survivors who were in line with the Korean activists. The fund was not seen as state redress by the Korean Council activists and supporters since it was primarily based on private donation from the Japanese public. The recipients of the Fund were excluded from a list of beneficiaries for financial support from the South Korean government. This caused splits and mistrust not only between the recipients and the activists in South Korea but also between the Korean groups and some Japanese groups. Some Japanese activists raised questions to their Korean counterparts whether the interests and wellbeing of the aging, ailing and destitute survivors were sufficiently considered in declining the AWF. Eventually, through the tension and controversy, the interests and wellbeing of the survivors have been more taken into consideration in the campaign.

When the Women's International War Crimes Tribunal was staged in Tokyo in 2000, some volatile aspects of the coalition work emerged in the process of the preparation for the Tribunal. Tensions between the Korean delegates and their Japanese counterparts were raised over some issues, such as whether or not the "perpetrators" particularly the Japanese Emperor should be prosecuted, where the venue for the Tribunal would be, and where to keep the written judgment. Korean nationalist scholars and activists contested that the distinct historical background of colonial Korea and the unique characteristics of the Japanese Imperial Forces have not been considered in the Trial (Yang, 2002; Hankuk chŏngsindae munche tech'ek hyŏpŭihoe, 2001; Shim, 2001). This is a tension between the nationalizing logic of comfort women campaign and the de-nationalizing imperatives of transnational comfort women campaign. Sticking to the nationalist approach in Korea has been a potential source of tension to transnational advocacy activism.

An impediment to transnational coalition building in the comfort women redress campaign stems from a sense of hierarchy of victimhood claimed by some Korean survivors and activists. The Korean victims who formed the most numbers of the comfort women are referred to as having suffered more severely than their Japanese counterparts and having being exploited for a longer period of time at comfort stations than their other Asian counterparts who were confined and raped during the Asia-Pacific War. In particular, rather different approaches have been disclosed in viewing Japanese comfort women between the Korean Council activists and survivors and their Japanese counterparts. The Korean groups differentiate the Japanese comfort women from those who come from other Asian countries, since they are accused of patriotic motivation in devoting themselves to their nation and their previous status as prostitutes. This self-defined hierarchy of victimhood does not translate well across borders, and has been an impediment to transnational coalition building. Nevertheless, a sense of shared experiences beyond nationalist affiliation as a victim of sexual violence by the Japanese forces during the war has worked as the catalysts for the foundations of transnational activism. In other words, it has been this sense of shared past experiences as victims of sexual violence that these tensions could be mediated.

4. Between the Local and Transnational Spaces

This part of the paper looks at the transnational and local/domestic interactions in the comfort women redress movement. The interactions including cooperation and tensions have emerged amongst transnational activists, state governments, and local survivors and supporters. Through the interactive transnational alliance, women's groups in different nations have been sharing the goal to combat violence against women externally, and also attempted to maintain a unified domestic narrative and possibly a unitary subject in order to organize the inner space of the nation, and to mobilize the population and generate the popular support for the campaign. This has been seen in the case of the comfort women movement in South Korea and Japan. The South Korean activists have accommodated their post-war nationalist animosity against Japan. They have stayed in line with other nationalist activism which deals with unresolved colonial legacies such as issues of forced and labour collaborators, and maintain a unified nationalist approach in which the comfort women issues are interpreted as suffering and humiliation of the nation. "Shaming strategies" towards the Japanese government has been employed in order to build coalitions with other civic groups and to promote supports from citizens in Korea. This strategy has been successful to organize the national inner space of Korea. But for the Japanese counterparts, only using "shaming strategies and moral persuasion" (Schmitz, 2010: 7198) is insufficient or sometimes inadequate to promote supports in Japan's inner space. The Japanese activists have appealed to their public with the issues of violence against women including sexual violence around the US military bases in Japan, and the anti-war peace movement.

From the intensive transnational cooperation for the 2000 Tokyo Women's Tribunal where cooperation and tensions were discussed, more efforts have been made in maneuvering and mediating between the national and the transnational spaces by both the South Korean and the Japanese activists. In order to build coalitions at home, domestic activists needed to maneuver their strategies in accordance with ideas prevalent amongst transnational activists in Asia. Strategic bargaining and persuasion have been employed (Schmitz, 2006, p.7). Towards external coalitions, domestic activists strive, on one hand, to represent local needs and causes to the external coalition's audience and on the other hand, to accommodate a shared women's issue. Demand of an apology and reparation to the comfort women survivors by the Korean civic groups present the survivors' needs and interests. At the same time, addressing the comfort women issue in the context of gender-based violence, human rights and anti-war campaigns accommodate globally shared issues and allow both the transnational and local spaces to be interconnected yet autonomous.

In the process of linking domestic and transnational spaces, the relationships between the activists and the survivors need to be reflectively reviewed.

As Ignatieff (2001) convincingly points out, activists have to learn how to give local populations a greater voice in defining the content of campaigns (p. 10) and in developing strategies of long-term social change, including redirecting and strengthening state capacity to effectively protect and advance human rights. In order to accommodate the local women's voice, the women should be considered as active agents of change rather than helpless victims of oppressive patriarchal practices. Interactive horizontal partnership between activists and survivors "as equal partners in a joint struggle for the expansion of rights and freedoms around the world" (Schmitz, 2006, p.3) need to be pursued for cross-border activism.

To resolve the comfort women issue, the following questions need to be paid attention in the transnational campaign:

- whether or not the survivors' voices are heard in defining the content of the campaign,
- whether or not they are mobilised for political purpose against the Japanese government and,
- whether or not their agency and interests are substantially represented in developing strategies of the campaign.

5. Towards Sustainable Transnational Feminist Activism

In post-war Korea and Japan, both societies maintained silence over the issue of comfort women for half a century until the comfort women campaign launched in 1990. Clearly, the Japanese government had no interest in exposure. But neither Korea nor other nations whose citizens had been subjected to such harsh treatment made any attempt to bring this issue to the forefront until non-governmental organisations in South Korea and Japan made it public at the beginning of the 1990s. Even after the launching of the redress campaign, both governments did not react sufficiently. In post-war Korea and Japan, the politics of not talking about and forgetting the past has been enacted. Issues over Japanese colonial history and the war including that of the comfort women have often been deemed as "matters of the past," which implies that it would not be appropriated at present by most of pro-Japanese military governments in South Korea before 1990.[4]

Meanwhile, Schmitz (2010) eloquently points out that when a government ignores social and political demands emanating from its own society, domestic activists are forced to appeal to international supporters. Transnational links which started between South Korea and Japan stretched to other parts of Asia, America and Europe, and the issue has been brought to the UN. Through transnational cooperation in dealing with the issue, remarkable domestic and transnational success of the redress movement has been achieved.

An increasing international consciousness on sexual violence in armed conflicts especially since the late 1990s contributed to the expansion of the transnational linkages. Not only the cross border networks have been expanding, but also the issues dealt with have been broadened as a consequence of transnational activism in the comfort women campaign. Not only issues of anti-Japanese government but also gender issues, such as violence against women and patriarchal indigenous social mores have been addressed by the Korean Council. A transnational memory of the comfort women put their experiences as sexual violence against women in war rather than a national humiliation in nationalist memory politics in Korea. Practices and projects of transnational activism in dealing with the comfort women issue contributed to a resistance against patriarchal na-

4 The last military government in Korea was replaced by civilian administration in 1993.

tionalisms and multiple and overlapping indigenous oppressions against women. These transnational efforts also contributed to a reflective review of nationalist narratives on the comfort women, and to awareness raising of an insidious gender hierarchy and paradigm, which persisted in the nationalist narratives in South Korea.

Practice of transnational activism has reinforced gender issue in the comfort women campaign in local campaign. Since the 2000 Women's Tribunal, more attention has been paid on the broader gender issues, such as women's rights and war. Transnational collaborative commitment has been made around the issues of peace, human rights, violence especially gender-based sexual violence in war and in peace and discrimination against women. A problem around military sexual violence around US military bases in Asia has been raised as well. The cross-border activism through the comfort women issue led to the shift from reactive to preventive transnational strategies. Initially, the comfort Women movement started as a reaction of the Japanese government refusing its responsibility in 1990, but the scale and scope of the movement expanded to the issue of violence against women and human rights for women.

Through continuous cross-border cooperation, the relationship between the activists and the survivors has been reviewed, and more attention has been paid to attend the survivors' interests in defining the content of the campaign. The agendas of the civic groups are not only political issues but also the agendas of supporting survivors with regard to financial support, physical and emotional health and memory politics such as establishing the War and Women's Human Rights Museums opened in the Independence Park opened in Seoul on the 5th of May, 2012.

Sustaining interactive transnational networks is an essential task to continue and develop cross-border activism. Plurality of experiences and agendas of each actor has surfaced through the cross border cooperation in addressing the comfort women issues. Further complexities could exist within the nation along the line of gender, and diversity among women along the line of nation as well. Male dominated nationalist civic groups in

South Korea seem to view this issue as an unresolved colonial legacy and focusing on anti-Japanese strategies, while the women's groups attempt to broaden the issue related to human rights and peace. Not all women's groups in Japan would support addressing the comfort women issue. Furthermore, there might be an assumption that raising the gender question could cause a split within the civic groups, and raising nation-related questions could weaken the very foundations of transnational alliance amongst women's groups. What needs to be considered in this complexity is to recognise the nation as gendered, and gender as articulating a specific ethnic or national identity. To build a sustainable transnational feminist activism, it is worth acknowledging and working out the existence of the complexities in both difference and commonality of actors, rather than emphasising one at the expense of the other in particular, in dealing with the multiple power differentials that exist among actors. In order to ensure a sustainable transnational feminist activism, one needs to maintain an ongoing dialogue and efforts to reflect and reconfigure solidarity within and outside the boundaries of nation and to keep the balance between local and transnational spaces through collaboration across borders.

References

Fujioka, Nobukatsu (1997), *Jigyaku shikan no byôri*, Tokyo: Bungei Shunjû.

Hankuk chŏngsindae munche tech'ek hyŏpŭihoe 2000 nyŏn Ilbonkun sŏngnoye chŏnpŏm yŏsŏng kukche pŏpchŏng hankuk wiwŏnhoe (2001), *2000 nyŏn Ilbonkun sŏngnoye chŏnpŏm yŏsŏng kukche pŏpchŏng pogosŏ*, Seoul: Hankuk chŏngsindae munche tech'k hyŏpŭihoe.

Ignatieff, M. (2001), *Human Rights as Politics and Idolatry*, Princeton: Princeton University Press.

Matsui, Yayori (1987), *Women's Asia*, London: Zed.

Murata, Noriko (1996), "The Trafficking of Women," *Voices From the Japa-*

nese Women's Movement, *AMPO-Japan Asia Quarterly Review*, New York and London: M. E. Sharpe.

Ôgoshi, Aiko (1997), "Feminismu no tachiba kara seidorei wo kankaeru," *Wadashiwa Ianfu Dewanai: Nihon no Shiryaku to Seidorei*, Osaka: Toho shuppan.

Schmitz, Hans Peter (2006), *Transnational Mobilization and Domestic Regime Change: Africa in Comparative Perspective*, Basingstoke: Palgrave Macmillan.

______ (2010), "Transnational Human Rights Networks: Significance and Challenges," *The International Studies Encyclopaedia*, Vol. XI, Robert A. Denmark (ed.), Wiley-Blackwell, pp. 7189-7208.

Shim, Younghee (2001), "Ch'amkwanki: 2000 nyŏn pŏpchŏng ŭn ajikto kkŭnnachi anakta," *Yŏsŏng kwa Sahoe,* Vol.13: pp. 145-162.

Thoma, Pamela (2000), "Cultural Autobiography, Testimonial, and Asian American Transnational Feminist Coalition in the 'Comfort Women of World War II' Conference," *Frontiers: A Journal of Women Studies,* Vol. 21 No. 1/2, Asian American Women, pp. 29-54.

Ueno, Chizuko (1998), *Nationalisumu to Genda: Engendering Nationalisumu*, Tokyo: Seidosha.

Yamazaki, Hiromi (1995), "Military Sexual Slavery and the Women's Movement," *AMPO Japan-Asia Quarterly Review*, Vol. 25 No. 4/ Vol. 26 No. 1, pp. 49-54.

Yang, Migang (2002), "2000 nyŏn Ilbonkun sŏngnoye chŏnpŏm kukche pŏpchŏng ŭn urieke muŏsŭl nankyŏnnŭnka?: Yŏsŏng ŭi Yŏoksa rŭl mamdŭlŏ kanŭn ilbonkun wianbu munche hekyŏl undongkwa 2000 nyŏn pŏpchŏng," *Sidae wa minchung*, Vol. 7, pp 310-340.

About the Contributors

CHANG Pilwha, Ph.D. is a Professor Emeritus in the Department of Women's Studies, Ewha Womans University. She is the Editor in Chief of the *Asian Journal of Women's Studies* and has served as Director of Asian Center for Women's Studies, Korean Women's Institute, Ewha Institute for Leadership Development and Dean of Graduate School of Ewha Womans University. She also served as President of the Korean Association of Women's Studies and Asian Association of Women's Studies. Her publication include *Women, Body and Sexuality* (1999) and co-edited books *My Feminism Recipe* (2015), *Our Voices: Asian Feminism and Women's Activism* (2015), *Women's Experiences and Feminist Practices in South Korea* (2005), *Gender Division of Labor in Korea* (1994).

LEE Sang Wha, Ph.D. is a Professor Emeritus in the Department of Philosophy, College of Liberal Arts, Ewha Womans University. She received her Ph.D. in social philosophy from the Eberhard-Karls-University Tuebingen in West Germany. Her special areas are feminist philosophy, philosophy of culture and social philosophy. Her recent work has focused on theories relating to feminism and globalization, Asian Women's Studies, Ecofeminism and philosophy of Difference/Becoming. She has served as Director of Korean Women's Institute, President of the Korean Association of Feminist Philosophy, President of the Korean Association of Women's Studies, and co-representative of Korean Women's Environment Network. She has published many articles, including "Local Community and Feminist Alternative Values in the Age of Globalization," "The Reception of Feminisms and Change in Philosophy in Korea," "Feminism and Politics of Difference" and so on.

KIM Eun-Shil, Ph.D. is a Professor in the Department of Women's Studies and currently the Director of Korean Women's Institute and Asian Center for Women's Studies at Ewha Womans University. She has been one of co-editors in the *Asian Journal of Women's Studies* for many years and has been involved in developing the intellectual community of feminist scholars in Asia since 1995. She worked as the secretary general when the Asian Center for Women's Studies at Ewha organized the Interdisciplinary Congress on Women in 2005. She has done research in the field of women's bodies, sexuality, nationalism, globalization and migration, feminist knowledge production and post-development issues. She published many articles including "The Discourse of Nationalism and Gender," "The Cultural Logic of the Korean Modernization Project and its Gender Politics," "Itaewon as an Alien Space Within the Nation-State and a Place in the Globalization Era," "The Postcolonial Politics of Food: Creating 'Locality' through Local Knowledge," etc. She also published several books in Korean including *Women's Bodies*, *The Cultural Politics of Bodies*, (co-authored) *Fascism Within Us*, (co-authored) *Locational Feminisms in the Age of Globalization*, (co-authored) *Noh Muhyun Government's Experiments: Unfinished Reform*, etc.

HARA Hiroko, Ph.D. is a Professor, Graduate School, Josai International University; Professor Emeritus, Ochanomizu University, in Japan. She has served as the Advisor of Japan Women's Watch, Advisor of Asia Pacific Women's Watch, and Member of Science Council of Japan.

DU Fangqin, Ph.D. is a Professor at the Institute of Gender and Social Development Studies, Tianjin Normal University, China. She has served as Vice president, board of directors of Chinese Women's Research Society. Her research and teaching areas include Chinese ancient women's/gender history, women's development and empowerment, and women's and gender studies. She published many books including, *The Transformation of Concept Women in China, The Discovery of Women's History in China, Engendering in Chinese History and Culture, The Native Exploration to the Women's Studies and Women's History, Poverty and Gender: Women's Development and Empowerment, Women and Gender in Chinese History, Quietly and Profundity Change: The Case of Zhoushan Village.*

LEE Myoung Sun, Ph.D. is a special professor at the Asian Center for Women's Studies, Ewha Womans University, Seoul, Korea. She is in charge of the Ewha Global Empowerment Program, which is a two-week course for Asian-African women activists. After receiving her Ph.D. in Women's Studies from Ewha Womans University in 2003, she has pursued her interest in sexuality by doing research on the construction of sexuality in Korean culture, sexual violence, sexuality education, women's policy etc. Besides her career as a researcher, she has had practical experiences in the government and women NGOs. From 2003-2005, she worked as Director of the Seoul Resource Center for Young Women, a government institution helping young girls involved in prostitution. She was also a founding member of the Korea Sexual Violence Relief Center, of which she is currently a committee member.

Saskia E. WIERINGA, Ph.D. is an honorary professor at the University of Amsterdam, holding the Chair on Women's Same-Sex Relations Crossculturally. From 2005 till 2012 she was the Director of Aletta, Institute for Women's History in Amsterdam. She is also the co-founder and presently secretary of the Kartini Asia Network. She has a long experience of activism in both the women's and third world solidarity movements. Since the late 1970s she has done research on women's movements, sexual politics and same-sex relations in many parts of the world, particularly in Indonesia. She wrote and (co-)edited more than 30 books and over 200 articles including *Women's Sexualities and Masculinities in a Globalizing Asia* (2007), *The Future of Asian Feminisms* (2012), and *Sexual Politics in the Global South* (2013). Presently she is the

Chair of the Foundation IPT 1965, dealing with the Indonesian genocide after October 1965.

Jyotsna Agnihotri GUPTA, Ph.D. is an Assistant Professor (Emerita) and senior research fellow in 'Gender and Diversity' at the University of Humanistic Studies in Utrecht, the Netherlands. She has taught at the University of Delhi, several Dutch universities, including Leiden University and Maastricht University. She has given guest lectures at various universities in Europe and Asia. She has also worked as a freelance trainer and consultant on gender issues for the Royal Tropical Institute (KIT) in Amsterdam, WHO Geneva and the International Commission of Jurists, Geneva. She has served as a member on various boards, including the Feminist Association of Bioethics, national and international advisory committees and expert panels. She is the author of *New Reproductive Technologies, Women's Health and Autonomy: Freedom or Dependency?* (2000) and several articles in scientific journals and anthologies.

Mala KHULLAR, Ph.D. is a freelance consultant and has also worked on an ongoing basis with the Asian Center for Women's Studies, Ewha Womans University, Seoul on several research and other projects since 1996. She is co-editor of the *Asian Journal of Women's Studies* and has been involved in research, publication and collaborative projects on education, development and gender studies. She has undertaken consultancy work for Asian Center for Women's Studies at Ewha Womans Univeristy, Seoul; UNICEF; the Asian Development Bank; Aga Khan Foundation; Global Agri-Business, New Delhi; and the Centre for Women's Development Studies, New Delhi. Previously she has worked with the Aga Khan Foundation, New Delhi; Bernard van Leer Foundation, the Hague; the Centre for Women's Development Studies, New Delhi; and University of Delhi. Her current research interests are in the fields of gender studies, education and development.

LEE Mikyoung, Ph.D. is the Director of Korea Association of Sexual Violence Relief Centers. She received her Ph.D. at Ewha Womans University with a thesis titled "The Rights of Sexual Violence Victims Viewed through the Lens of Secondary Victimization." She has served as a specially appointed Professor of Ewha Institute for Leadership Development at Ewha Womans University, a member of the Special Act on Sexual Violence Enactment Committee, a committee member of the Crime Victim's Protection Fund at the Ministry of Justice.

Kyungja JUNG, Ph.D. teaches in Social Inquiry at the University of Technology Sydney in Australia. Her academic interests are experientially grounded in and inspired by her involvement in women's activism in Australia and Korea. Drawing on feminist theory(s) of intersectionality of gender and sexuality her research has been interested in mapping the gendered nature of social processes from cross-cultural and interdisciplinary approaches. Her research has been published in academic journals including *Hecate*, *Pacific Review*, *Asian Survey*, *Asian Journal of Women's Studies* and *International Review of Korean Studies* and has book chapters in *Women's Movements: Flourishing or in Abeyance* and *The Work of Policy: An International Survey*. She has also published a co-authored book *Sex Trafficking Or Shadow Tourism?: The Lives of Foreign Sex Workers in Australia* (2009 with Jang, H, Dalton, B and Wilson, R.). Her book *Practicing Feminism in South Korea: The Women's Movement against Sexual Violence* (London: Routledge) was published in 2014.

Yonson AHN, Ph.D. is a Professor and Director of Korean Studies, Frankfurt University in Germany. Before Frankfurt she taught at Leipzig University in Germany and Ewha Womans University and Changwon National University in Korea. She was a visiting scholar at University of Tokyo and Waseda University in Japan. She completed her Ph.D. degree in Gender Studies at University of Warwick in Britain in 2000. She has been conducting research on Korean "comfort women" and Japanese soldiers during WWII and on historical controversies in East Asia, and currently transnationalism, migration and Korean diasporas.

ROH Jieun, Ph.D. is a senior research coordinator of the Asian Center for Women's Studies at Ewha Womans University, Seoul, Korea. She earned her Ph.D. in Women's Studies from Ewha Womans University in 2016. Her research interests are on glocal politics of sexual and reproductive rights in the context of Korea/Asia, gender politics of menstruation, and Asian feminism theory. She has been involved in various international academic networking, research and publication projects as a coordinator/project manager, such as Asian Association of Women's Studies, 9th International Interdisciplinary Congress on Women, Korea-ASEAN Cooperation Project and Ewha Global Empowerment Program. Her publication include "1970–90's Menstrual Products Advertisement and Gender in Korea" (2014), co-authored paper "Searching for Alternative 'Development' Paradigms" (2013), and co-authored books, *My Feminism Recipe* (2015), *First Period Party* (2002) published in Korean.

Asian Feminisms and Transnational Activism

Edited by CHANG Pilwha, LEE Myoung Sun and ROH Jieun

First published May 30, 2017
by Ewha Womans University Press
52, Ewhayeodae-gil, Seodaemun-gu, Seoul, Korea 03760
Tel.: 82-2-3277-2965, 362-6076 / Fax.: 82-2-312-4312
E-mail: press@ewha.ac.kr
Homepage: www.ewhapress.com

ISBN 979-11-5890-224-7 94330
979-11-85909-13-4(set)
Price: 28,000 won